CENSUS OF INDIA 1891

CENSUS OF INDIA, 1891

VOLUME XXII

REPORT ON THE CENSUS
OF THE DISTRICTS
OF
AJMERE-MERWARA

B. EGERTON

GYAN

Published by

Gyan Publishing House
5, Ansari Road
Daryaganj, New Delhi-110002
Phone: 011-47034999, 9811692060
E-mail: books@gyanbooks.com

Distribution Network
gyanbooks.com
India, USA, Canada, UK, Australia

ISBN: 978-81-212-7129-5 (Set) 28 Vols. In 49 Bindings

ISBN: 978-81-212-6905-6 (PB) Vol. XXII

First Published, 1893

2nd Impression 2024

Printed at: Gyan Press, Delhi.

CENSUS OF INDIA 1891

CENSUS OF INDIA, 1891.

REPORT

ON THE

CENSUS OF THE DISTRICTS OF AJMERE-MERWARA,

TAKEN ON

The 26th February 1891.

BY

B. EGERTON,
DISTRICT SUPERINTENDENT, POLICE, AJMERE-MERWARA.

CALCUTTA:
OFFICE OF THE SUPERINTENDENT, GOVERNMENT PRINTING, INDIA.
1893.

ERRATUM.

Page 37—

In para. beginning with the words "The total cost," etc., *for* "enumerators," *read* "enumeration."

CHAPTER I.

GENERAL DESCRIPTION. DENSITY—RURAL AND URBAN POPULATION.

Ajmere and Merwara together comprise 2,710 miles of country surrounded and intersected by Feudatory States. Merwara is formed of the main range of the Aravalli hills, the highest point being 3,000 feet. The general lie of the country is 1,500 feet above sea-level.

Ajmere is chiefly plain cultivated by Jats, Gujars, and some mixed tribes; *three-fifths are owned by Rajput Istimrardars, who pay a quit rent to the State,* and the rest by Zemindars, Jagirdars, and Bhumias, the latter of whom hold the land in return for service. Nearly one-fourth of the population live in the towns of Ajmere, Nasirabad, and Kekri.

Merwara is cultivated and owned almost entirely by the Mer clans. Beawar is the only town, and about one-fifth of the population live there.

Irrigation is by tanks and wells dependent entirely on the rainfall for their supply. The average fall is 22·8 inches, but subject to great variation causing periodical droughts, which often necessitate the temporary migration of a portion of the population. The staple food of the people is bajra, jowar, maize, and barley. Generations of periodical scarcity have kept the physical condition of the people below the standard of more favoured provinces.

In the two districts there are four towns and 741 villages: of the latter, three, namely Pushkar, Pisangan, Deoli, partake of a semi-urban character. The average area of towns is 10·1 square miles, and of inhabited villages 4·9 square miles in Ajmere and 1·9 square miles in Merwara. The number of towns and villages per square mile is 0·27.

The total population censused on the night of the 26th February and the number of occupied houses returned was as under:—

	Occupied houses.	Total population.	Males.	Females.
Ajmere	79,638	422,359	223,547	198,812
Merwara	22,016	119,999	64,778	55,221
Total .	101,654	542,358	288,325	254,033

The density and house-room of the population, as it now stands, will be seen from the following table:—

District.	Area, square miles.	No. of towns and villages	No. of occupied houses.	Total population, both sexes.	Houses per square mile.	Persons per village and town.	Persons per square mile.	Persons per house.
Ajmere . .	2,069·8	416	79,638	422,359	38·4	1,015	204	5·30
Merwara .	640·8	329	22,016	119,999	34·3	364	187·2	5·45
Total .	2,710·6	745	101,654	542,358	37·5	728	200	5·33

	Persons per village.	Square mile density.	Persons per house.
Ajmere	728	200	5·33
Jeypore	410	184	7·28
Jodhpore	536	67·3	5·02
Mewar	272	144·8	4·60
Tonk	281	140·6	4·52
Kishengarh	437	143·6	6·57

The density of the population has increased by 30 persons to the square mile in Ajmere and 29 to the square mile in Merwara since 1881. In the North-West Provinces the density is 442 and in the Punjab 187. A comparison with the contiguous Feudatory States is given in the marginal table.

The number of persons per house depends on the definition of house adopted. Owing to the number of enclosures with only one entrance, occupied by a number of distinct and separate families, the house, in the case of such enclosures, was taken to be the set of rooms occupied by each family, if four or more distinct families lived in the enclosure. The result of this has been a fall in the average number of persons per house as compared with 1881, when the figure was 7·18. In Bombay the figure is 5·5 and in the North-West Provinces 5·7, and there is no reason to think that Ajmere is more crowded as to its house-room than other districts.

The population returned in towns and villages will be found in Table I. Dwellers in towns number more than one-fifth of the whole population, and if the semi-urban population of Pushkar, Pisangan, Deoli, is added, they amount to one-fourth of the population.

The square mile density and house-room of urban and rural areas is as follows:—

		Area in square miles.	Occupied houses.	Population.	Persons per square mile.	Persons per house.
Ajmere City and Suburbs		27	14,949	68,843	2549·7	4·60
Nasirabad		8·58	4,980	21,710	2554·1	4·35
Kekri		3·07	1,353	7,100	2366·6	5·0
Ajmere	**Total Urban**	**38·65**	**21,282**	**97,653**	**2529·8**	**4·58**
	Total Rural	**2031·15**	**58,356**	**324,706**	**159·8**	**5·56**
Merwara	**Beawar City**	**1·75**	**4,505**	**20,978**	**11987·7**	**4·65**
	Total Rural	**639·11**	**17,511**	**99,021**	**154·9**	**5·65**
	Total Urban	**40·41**	**25,787**	**118,631**	**2936·6**	**4·60**
	Total Rural	**2670·27**	**75,867**	**423,727**	**158·7**	**5·58**

The population of Beawar is contained almost entirely within the city walls, and there is little or no suburb. Hence the high average of persons to the square mile. House-room is practically the same in Ajmere and Beawar.

Comparison between the Urban and Rural population will be found under each of the different chapters. The principal towns are noted below:—

Ajmere Town.—The population of Ajmere is 68,843 located as shown in the marginal table. The increase since 1881 has been 20,108, or 41·2 per cent., namely 36·3 per cent. of males and 44·2 per cent. of females. Hindus number 36,729, Mahomedans 26,433, and Jains 2,770. The disciples of the Arya Samaj number 1,097. Mahomedans have increased 41 per cent. since last Census, and Hindus (including Jains

	Houses.	Total.	Males.	Females.
Ajmere—Inside walls	8,737	41,416	21,794	19,622
„ Outside walls	3,112	11,585	6,555	5,030
„ Suburbs	2,334	13,746	8,300	5,446
„ Cantonment	766	1,814	1,096	718
Railway passengers	...	282	240	42

and Sikhs) by 39 per cent. The strength of some of the principal castes is given in the margin. There are 7,935 boys and 7,547 girls under 10 years of age. Out of every 1,000 persons 459 are females, 53 per cent. of the population is married, and 11 per cent. widowed; of females 29 per cent. are unmarried and 17 per cent. widowed. The total population employed in, or dependent on employees of, the Railway in Ajmere is 10,050, of whom 5,810 are males and 4,240 females. The Railway therefore employs 14 per cent. of the total population. There are 100 blind, 5 lepers and 15 lunatics in Ajmere

Caste.	Males.	Females.	Caste.	Males.	Females.
Rajput	1,038	602	European	290	199
Brahman	2,970	2,281	Eurasian	313	249
Oswal	688	602	Native Christian	259	187
Agarwal	1,659	1,405	Kumhar	265	260
Mahesri	406	353	Chamar	1,136	1,051
Saraogi	735	631	Balai	329	300
Kayasth	815	605	Mali	1,394	1,307
Sonar	485	434	Raigar	447	480

Beawar.—The population of Beawar, the chief and only town in the Merwara District, is 20,978, having increased by 5,149 since 1881, or 32·5 per cent. Males have increased by 29·2 per cent. and females by 36·6 per cent. Hindus number 14,551, or 68 per cent. of the population; Jains 2,484, and Mahomedans 3,641; children under 10 form 23 per cent. of the people, there being 2,473 boys and 2,465 girls. Out of every 1,000 persons 450 are females, the preponderance of males being due to the number of commercial men who reside in Beawar for business only and have their houses elsewhere; 53 per cent. of the population are married and 11 per cent. widowed; 29 per cent. of females and 40 per cent. of males are single. The principal castes in point of numbers are as shown in the marginal table. There are no lepers, and only 6 lunatics in Beawar and 55 persons are blind.

Caste.	Males.	Females.	Caste.	Males.	Females.
Rajput	197	123	Mer tribes	52	33
Brahmans	914	616	Native Christian	116	94
Oswal	1,161	924	Chamar	226	263
Agarwal	894	736	Balai	380	398
Mahesri	286	171	Mahomedans	1,987	1,654
Saraogi	179	154			

Beawar is growing into the chief market of import and export in Western Rajputana. Rail-carried exports amounted in 1889 to close on 20,000 tons, and the imports to about the same. The principal export is pressed cotton. Beawar as a town dates only from about 1835.

Nasirabad.—The population enumerated amounted to 21,710, distributed between the military and civil portion of the town as in the margin. The British regiment usually stationed in the cantonment was in course of relief and was not enumerated in Nasirabad. The civil population has increased by 6 per cent. only since 1881, there having been an exodus of the coolie classes to Ajmere and other places where labour was more in demand. The fact that females exceed the number of males would go to show that the migration was only temporary and that the women and children remained behind. Children bear a proportion of 27 per cent. to the population. Hindus number 15,195 in the whole cantonment and Mahomedans 5,472.

	Total.	Males.	Females.
Nasirabad Civil	19,624	9,793	9,831
" Cantonment	2,086	1,492	594

Kekri.—The population of Kekri is 7,100, the increase since 1881 being 16 per cent. This small town is increasing as a market and the small annual Tejaji Fair is becoming a recognised commercial as well as religious institution. Occupied houses were returned at 1,353 against 750 in 1881.

Deoli.—This cantonment has not been included among Towns, though it partakes more of an urban than rural character. It consists of the cantonment, the head quarters of the Deoli Irregular Force, the Sadar Bazar, and the Agency Bazar, of which the population is as under—

	TOTAL.	Males.	Females.
Deoli Cantonment	1,822	1,256	566
" Sadar Bazar	1,735	922	813
" Agency Bazar	1,727	1,023	704

CHAPTER II.

MOVEMENT OF THE POPULATION.

The population returned at each of the enumerations that have taken place in Ajmere-Merwara is given in the margin. The Census of 1872 was considered inaccurate, and the results were not abstracted. It was however estimated independently of the Census that 25 per cent. of the people had died or migrated during the famine of 1868-70, and the depopulation of that period is still traceable in the unduly small proportion of men and women between the ages of 20-30 at the present or between 10 and 20 at the last Census. The opening of the Railway in 1879 and the fact of Ajmere being made its head-quarters led to a great influx from outside in 1876-81, which has continued to a lesser degree during the last 10 years. The settlers of 1879 have brought their families to live with them or have married, and had children born to them, and the increase in the population of Ajmere and Beawar is even greater than it was in 1881. This applies only to those two towns however, and the general increase throughout rural areas (with the exception of Southern Merwara) is attributable to the general filling up of the districts after 20 years of comparative freedom from scarcity following the severe famine of 1868. In the south of Merwara, and in a lesser degree in the north, scarcity had led to the migration of a certain portion of the population before the recent Census. The number was estimated at 1,000 families.

Census.	Population.	Variation.
1865	426,268	
1872	316,590	—109,678
1876	396,331	+ 79,741
1881	460,722	+64,391
1891	542,358	+81,636

According to the mortuary returns the number to be accounted for by immigration would be nearly 60,000. Birth registration is however faulty and cannot be relied on for statistics of this character. Thus, the present population under 10 is 124,300; births were 117,900, and deaths of children under 10 years 48,600 during the decade; so that the probable addition to the population by birth according to the returns would be 69,300. This would leave some 55,000 children under 10 to be accounted for by immigration, a proportion of the total increase which is incompatible with the figures of increase in other ages.

Comparison with Mortuary Returns.	Total.	Males.	Females.
Population in 1881	460,722	248,844	211,878
Births, 1881-1891	117,932	64,431	53,501
Total	578,654	313,275	265,379
Deaths, 1881-1891	95,778	53,216	42,562
Total	482,876	260,059	222,817
Population, 1891	542,358	288,325	254,033
Balance	59,482	28,266	31,216

The greatest increase has been of children between the ages of 5 and 14, for whom immigration except to join their parents or husbands is an impossibility. No other age period shows anything approaching the increase of the two periods shown in the margin. From this and from the fact that the proportion of persons born

	5—9		10—14	
	Males.	Females.	Males.	Females.
1881	31,686	27,120	21,747	15,236
1891	40,168	36,024	32,594	24,922
Variation	8,482	8,904	10,847	9,686
Per cent.	26·7	32·8	49·8	63·5

in the districts has increased from 74 to 80 per cent., it is inferable that one cause of the increase is due to natural production. In towns the increase is primarily due to the immigration previous to 1881.

The total number of persons born outside the districts is returned at 108,000, or some 5,000 less than in 1881. Of these some 75,000 were born in Rajputana. Over 50,000 born in Ajmere have been censused in the different Rajputana States. It is the practice among some castes to marry or give their daughters in marriage in the surrounding States, so that these figures do not denote any special influx or departure.

	Visitors.		
	Total.	Males.	Females.
Ajmere Town	3,056	1,948	1,108
Nasirabad	865	554	311
Kekri	638	429	209
Beawar	1,805	1,356	449
Ajmere Rural	18,101	10,924	7,177
Merwara Rural	5,542	3,193	2,349
Total	30,007	18,404	11,603

The time of Census was exceptionally free from marriages or fairs which take the people away from their houses. The total number of visitors returned on the night* of the Census was only 30,000, of whom details are given in the margin.

Increase or decrease since the Census of 1881 is shown below:—

		Population.			Increase.			Per cent.		
		Total.	Males.	Females.	Total.	Males.	Females.	Total.	Males.	Females.
Ajmere	1881	359,288	192,669	166,619	63,071	30,878	32,193	17·5	16·0	19·3
	1891	422,359	223,547	198,812						
Merwara	1881	101,434	56,175	45,259	18,565	8,603	9,962	17·7	15·3	22·0
	1891	119,999	64,778	55,221						
Total	1881	460,722	248,844	211,878	81,636	39,481	42,155	17·7	15·8	19·8
	1891	542,358	288,325	254,033						

The increase in the different towns was as follows:—

		Population.			Increase.			Per cent.		
		Total.	Males.	Females.	Total.	Males.	Females.	Total.	Males.	Females.
Ajmere	1881	48,735	27,347	21,388	20,108	10,638	9,470	41·2	36·3	44·2
	1891	68,843	37,985	30,858						
Nasirabad	1881	21,320	11,462	9,858	390	—177	567	1·8	—1·5	5·7
	1891	21,710	11,285	10,425						
Kekri	1881	6,119	3,081	3,038	981	669	312	15·1	21·7	10·2
	1891	7,100	3,750	3,350						
Beawar	1881	15,829	8,859	6,970	5,149	2,587	2,562	32·5	29·2	36·6
	1891	20,978	11,446	9,532						
Total	1881	92,003	50,749	41,254	26,628	13,717	12,911	28·8	27·0	31·2
	1891	188,631	64,466	54,165						

The figures for rural population compared with 1881 are given below :—

		RURAL POPULATION.								
		POPULATION.			INCREASE.			PER CENT.		
		TOTAL.	Males.	Females.	TOTAL.	Males.	Females.	TOTAL.	Males.	Females.
Ajmere	1881	283,114	150,779	132,335	41,592	19,748	21,844	14·6	13·0	16·5
	1891	324,706	170,527	154,179						
Merwara	1881	85,605	47,316	38,289	13,416	6,016	7,400	15·6	12·7	19·3
	1891	99,021	53,332	45,689						
TOTAL	1881	368,719	198,095	170,624	55,008	25,764	29,244	14·9	13·0	17·1
	1891	423,727	223,859	199,868						

It is remarkable that in Ajmere the Khalsa rural population has increased to double the extent of Istimrari estates. This has, however, to be modified to the extent of 3 per cent. because Deoli Cantonment was included in Istimrari totals in 1881, but even then the difference is marked, namely 17 per cent. in Khalsa and 13 per cent. in Istimrari villages. Sáwar and Kekri show the smallest percentage of increase of Istimrari areas; Bhinai has increased 16 per cent, and Masuda nearly 20 per cent.

Ajmere Rural.

	1881.	1891.	Increase.	Per cent.
Khalsa	118,814	142,884	24,070	20·2
Istimrari	164,300	181,822	17,522	10·6

The total of the different divisions of the district is given below :—

		TOTAL.	Males.	Females.
KHALSA—AJMERE.	Ramsar	14,902	7,658	7,244
	Gangwana	17,470	9,187	8,283
	Deranthu	13,608	7,297	6,311
	Srinagar	15,926	8,328	7,598
	Rajgarh	28,007	14,915	13,092
AJMERE—ISTIMRARI.	Bhinai	57,800	29,739	28,061
	Masudah	39,153	20,694	18,459
	Kharwa	10,683	5,675	5,008
	Pisangan	13,980	7,237	6,743
	Kekri	40,920	21,256	19,664
	Sawar	19,286	10,105	9,181

		TOTAL.	Males.	Females.
MERWARA	Beawar Tehsil	55,552	29,778	25,774
	Todgarh Tehsil	43,469	23,554	19,915

In Ajmere the Rámsar Pergunnah has increased most, namely 26 per cent., and in Merwara the Beáwar Tehsil increased 22 per cent., and the Todgarh Tehsil by one per cent. only owing to the temporary migration of a number of villagers.

Population by religion compared with 1881.

		Total Population.			Increase.			Percentage of increase.			Ajmere.			Increase.			Percentage of increase.			Merwara.			Increase.			Percentage of increase.		
		Total.	Males.	Females.	Total.	Males.	Females	Total.	Males.	Females.	Total.	Males.	Females.	Total.	Males.	Females.	Total.	Males.	Females.	Total.	Males.	Females.	Total.	Males.	Females.	Total.	Males.	Females.
Hindu and Vedic.	1881	376,029	202,226	173,803	...	...	...	...	...	...	294,056	157,632	136,424	...	...	...	...	...	...	81,973	44,594	37,379	...	...	...	...	...	...
	1891	437,988	230,877	207,111	61,959	28,651	33,308	16·4	14·1	19·1	342,679	180,348	162,331	48,623	22,716	25,907	16·5	14·4	18·9	95,309	50,529	44,780	13,336	5,935	7,401	16·2	13·3	19·7
Jain	1881	24,308	12,846	11,462	...	...	...	...	...	...	17,806	9,180	8,626	...	...	...	...	...	...	6,502	3,666	2,836	...	...	...	...	...	...
	1891	26,939	14,426	12,513	2,631	1,580	1,051	10·8	12·2	9·1	19,687	10,502	9,185	1,881	1,322	559	10·5	14·4	6·4	7,252	3,924	3,328	750	258	492	11·5	70·3	17·3
Sikh	1881	182	115	67	...	...	...	...	...	...	182	115	67	...	...	...	...	...	...	...	...	...	...	...	...	...	...	...
	1891	213	151	62	31	36	—5	17·03	31·3	—7·4	189	138	51	7	23	—16	3·8	20	—23·8	24	13	11	24	13	11	...	...	...
Musalman	1881	57,809	31,999	25,810	...	...	...	...	...	...	45,185	24,265	20,920	...	...	...	...	...	...	12,624	7,734	4,890	...	...	...	...	...	...
	1891	74,265	41,130	33,135	16,456	9,131	7,325	28·4	28·5	28·3	57,223	31,029	26,194	12,038	6,764	5,274	26·6	27·8	25·2	17,042	10,101	6,941	4,418	2,367	2,051	34·9	30·6	41·9
Christian	1881	2,225	1,551	674	...	...	...	...	...	...	1,897	1,377	520	...	...	...	...	...	...	328	174	154	...	...	...	...	...	...
	1891	2,683	1,567	1,116	458	16	442	20·5	1·03	65·5	2,323	1,368	955	426	—9	435	22·4	—·6	83·6	360	199	161	32	25	7	9·7	14·3	4·5
Others	1881	169	107	62	...	...	...	...	...	...	162	100	62	...	...	...	...	...	...	7	7	...	...	...	...	...	...	...
	1891	270	174	96	101	67	34	59·7	62·6	54·8	258	162	96	96	62	34	59·2	62	56·4	12	12	...	5	5	...	17·4	71·4	...
Total	1881	460,722	248,844	211,878	...	...	...	...	...	...	359,288	192,669	166,619	...	...	...	...	...	...	101,434	56,175	45,259	...	...	...	...	...	...
	1891	542,358	288,325	254,033	81,636	39,481	42,155	17·7	15·8	19·8	422,359	223,547	198,812	63,071	30,878	32,193	17·5	16·02	19·3	119,999	64,778	55,221	18,565	8,603	9,962	18·3	15·3	22·01

CHAPTER III.

RELIGION.

The religions enumerated were the same as in 1881, except that the Vedic belief has asserted itself sufficiently to claim separate classification. The followers of it numbered 1,121, namely, 645 men and 476 women, chiefly residents of Ajmere, where the head-quarters of the Arya Somaj are. Its members inclined to recording their mother-tongue as Aryan, and their birthplace as "Arya Varta," which though possibly correct is scarcely definite enough for Census purposes.

The figures for each religion with the variation since 1881 is given on the opposite page. Hindus make up 80·7 per cent. of the whole population, Mahomedans 13·7, and Jains 4·9. Native Christians number 1,209, having increased by 51 per cent., since 1881. Parsis number 196, Sikhs 199, and Jews 71.

The figures for the various sects of Christians will be found in Table A. Of the Mahomedan sects, Sunnis number 99 per cent. of the population. Wahabis were only returned in three instances.

The Aboriginal Bhils return themselves as Hindus, and they have no doubt become partially Hinduised.

Of the Mer population, 20 per cent. are Mahomedan and 80 per cent. Hindu. In 1881 Mahomedans numbered 23 per cent., but it would be unsafe to deduct from this that Hinduism has made greater strides amongst the Mers than Islamism, for some of the Mahomedan villages were affected by scarcity at the time of Census, and it is possible that there was a greater proportion of Mahomedan absentees than Hindu. The difference between Hindu and Mahomedan Mer is but ill-defined, and neither sect is deeply imbued with religious doctrine.

In neither Rural Ajmere or Merwara have the priestly classes increased in a greater ratio than the rest of the population, but in towns the increase is exceptional.

CHAPTER IV.

AGE AND SEX.

AGE.

The ages of the population will be found in Imperial Table VII, from which the proportional table on the opposite page has been compiled. The figures are fairly in accord with those of Bombay or the North-West Provinces. The chief differences appear to be that Ajmere has (*a*) an excessive proportion of children, especially females, and (*b*) an unduly low proportion in the period 20—29. This latter is traceable to the effects of the famine of 1868-70, when there was great mortality among children.

Percentage to population.

	0—9		0—19	
	Males.	Females.	Males.	Females
Ajmere . . .	27·3	29·2	47·1	46·9
Bombay . . .	26·5	27·5	47·5	46·0
North-West Provinces	25·5	26·1	46·2	43·5

Though Ajmere rejoices in an excessive proportion of children, yet the proportion of population under 20 does not differ materially from that of Bombay or the North-West Provinces, and it is therefore inferable that the mortality of infants is higher here than in Bombay. This is borne out by the mortuary returns, according to which the death-rate of children under 10 is about 30 per mille, but in Bombay it is under 20 (1881).

Proportion in 10,000 of each sex.

	Under 1.		1 Year.		2 Years.		3 Years.		4 Years	
	Males.	Females.	Males.	Females.	Males.	Females.	Males.	Females.	Males.	Females.
Ajmere .	344	395	170	182	251	280	284	328	294	318
Bombay .	265	279	199	218	233	260	243	279	281	296
North-West Provinces	261	280	216	236	189	218	263	299	283	294

The table given in the margin would go to show that abnormal mortality occurs amongst children in their first year; the fall in the ratio of "under one year" and that of one year being so much more abrupt than in other Provinces. Some allowance may be made for inaccuracy in these two age-periods, as all children under one year were to be recorded in the schedules as "infants," and there may have been a tendency to apply this term to babies of over 12 months. The mortuary returns show that 18 per cent. of males and 19 per cent. of females die before attaining one year, but in this case also allowance must be made for inaccuracy in the registration of births. One deduction can safely be made from the above table, namely, that Ajmere has a very high average of births to population.

There is a higher proportion of males of the period 5—9 than in that of 1 to 4. This appears due partly to the fact that there were actually 4,366 less births registered from 1886 to 1891 than in the period 1881—1885, partly also to immigration.

Percentage of children under 10 to population.

	Males.	Females.
Urban population	22·0	25·7
Rural Ajmere	28·1	29·2
Rural Merwara	31·0	33·2
Total Ajmere-Merwara .	27·3	29·2
Ajmere-Merwara, 1881 . .	27·0	28·4
Bombay, 1881 . . .	26·5	27·5
North-West Provinces . .	25·5	26.1

Taking children generally, that is boys and girls under 10 years, the proportion is higher than in 1881; it is higher in rural than in urban areas; it is much higher in rural Merwara than in rural Ajmere, and this was also the case in 1881, and is possibly due to greater vitality in their early years of children born of fully matured parents, as the Mers and Merats are when they marry. Ajmere town with its large floating population returns the lowest proportion of children.

Ratio per 10,000 persons of each Age-period.

District.		0–4.		5–9.		10–14.		15–19.		20–24.		25–29.		30–39.		40–49.		50–59.		60 and over.	
		Males.	Females.	Males.	Females.	Males.	Females.	Males.	Females.	Males.	Females.	Males.	Females.	Males.	Females.	Males.	Females.	Males.	Females.	Males.	Females.
Ajmere	1881	1,400	1,511	1,254	1,245	864	711	880	821	1,035	1,068	1,018	974	1,575	1,500	975	1,032	625	662	369	472
	1891	1,329	1,477	1,347	1,368	1,098	953	852	796	764	831	888	862	1,551	1,468	1,124	1,069	613	636	430	546
Variation		−71	−34	+93	+123	+234	+242	−28	−25	−271	−237	−130	−112	−24	−32	+149	+37	−12	−26	+61	+74
Merwara	1881	1,535	1,751	1,336	1,408	907	748	885	815	944	985	951	931	1,490	1,455	902	891	610	576	436	436
	1891	1,391	1,597	1,550	1,595	1,239	1,078	804	764	686	769	850	788	1,405	1,372	997	967	600	542	474	523
Variation		−144	−154	+214	+187	+332	+330	−81	−51	−258	−216	−101	−143	−85	−83	+95	+76	−10	−34	+38	+87
Total	1881	1,430	1,563	1,273	1,279	873	723	882	820	1,015	1,051	1,003	965	1,556	1,491	958	1,001	622	642	384	464
	1891	1,343	1,503	1,393	1,418	1,130	981	841	780	746	818	879	846	1,518	1,447	1,095	1,047	610	615	440	541
Variation		−87	−60	+120	+139	+257	+258	−41	−40	−269	−233	−124	−119	−38	−44	+137	+46	−12	−27	+56	+77
Bombay	1881	1,221	1,332	1,438	1,418	1,275	1,077	816	781	828	917	974	961	1,543	1,463	934	917	588	645	383	489
North-Western Provinces		1,212	1,327	1,339	1,288	1,262	1,011	804	726	869	937	952	954	1,467	1,459	1,008	1,031	629	671	458	596

Proportion of Females to 1,000 males at each Age-period.

	Under 1 year.	1 year.	2 years.	3 years.	4 years.	Total 0—4.	5—9.	10—14.	15—19.	20—24.	25—29.	30—34.	35—39.	40—44.	45—49.	50—54.	55—59.	60 and over.	All ages.
Ajmere	1,012	924	990	1,032	952	988	903	772	818	968	863	858	814	913	706	966	772	1,130	889
Merwara	1,010	995	968	967	955	978	877	741	809	954	790	869	766	918	630	867	500	940	852
Total .	1,012	942	984	1,016	953	986	896	762	816	965	847	860	804	914	690	945	705	1,084	881

Urban and Rural Population by Age.

	Total Population.		Under 1 Year.		1 Year.		2 Years.		3 Years.		4 Years.		Total 0—4.	
	Males.	Females.	Males.	Females.	Males.	Females.	Males.	Females.	Males.	Females.	Males.	Females.	Males.	Females.
Ajmere Town .	37,985	30,858	1,288	1,281	492	477	751	825	797	897	849	727	4,177	4,207
Nasirabad .	11,285	10,425	458	484	109	153	258	276	274	319	338	321	1,437	1,553
Kekri . .	3,750	3,350	130	130	50	53	71	72	85	89	109	84	445	428
Beawar . .	11,446	9,532	395	403	216	199	244	258	247	269	236	239	1,338	1,368
Total Urban .	64,466	54,165	2,271	2,298	867	882	1,324	1,431	1,403	1,574	1,532	1,371	7,397	7,556
Rural Ajmere .	170,527	154,179	5,937	6,016	3,081	2,769	4,425	4,277	5,024	5,076	5,193	5,047	23,660	23,185
Rural Merwara .	53,332	45,689	1,720	1,734	972	984	1,481	1,412	1,759	1,672	1,741	1,651	7,673	7,453
Total Rural .	223,859	199,868	7,657	7,750	4,053	3,753	5,906	5,689	6,783	6,748	6,934	6,698	31,333	30,638

	5—9.		10—14.		15—19.		20—29.		30—39.		40—49.		50—59.		60 and over.	
	Males.	Females.	Males.	Females.	Males.	Females.	Males.	Females.	Males.	Females.	Males.	Females.	Males.	Females.	Males.	Females.
Ajmere Town .	3,758	3,340	3,298	2,445	3,344	2,667	7,899	6,455	6,860	4,659	4,596	3,244	2,401	2,049	1,652	1,792
Nasirabad .	1,452	1,492	1,153	916	877	878	2,357	1,880	1,676	1,376	1,151	1,058	627	628	555	644
Kekri . .	491	478	387	278	275	259	629	581	659	508	420	382	260	235	184	201
Beawar . .	1,135	1,097	1,068	784	882	839	2,392	1,891	2,043	1,397	1,390	1,041	708	575	490	540
Total Urban .	6,836	6,407	5,906	4,423	5,378	4,643	13,277	10,807	11,238	7,940	7,557	5,725	3,996	3,487	2,881	3,177
Rural Ajmere .	24,426	21,903	19,726	15,326	14,563	11,793	26,056	24,765	25,483	22,652	18,965	16,585	10,422	9,734	7,226	8,236
Rural Merwara .	8,906	7,714	6,962	5,173	4,330	3,381	7,569	6,711	7,060	6,184	5,071	4,303	3,179	2,421	2,582	2,349
Total Rural .	33,332	29,617	26,688	20,499	18,893	15,174	33,625	31,476	32,543	28,836	24,036	20,888	13,601	12,155	9,808	10,585

The proportion of children to population in the principal castes is given in the marginal table. Mahomedan Mers figure highest, because their women on marriage to Hindus mostly assume the Hindu religion, while Hindus marrying Mahomedan Mers often adhere to their Hindu faith in name. This has been clearly established by reference to the schedules themselves and accounts for much statistical discrepancy between the two sects of Mers at former Census. The proportion of boy children among Mahomedan Mers is 32·2, but that of females is 45·5. Of the other castes, the proportion of children gets smaller in an inverse ratio to the social position of the castes.

Percentage of children under 10 to total caste population.

Caste.	Per cent.	Caste.	Per cent.
Mahomedan Mers	37·3	Gujar	29·9
Bhils	33·4	Kumhar	29·0
Raigars	33·0	Jat	28·5
Chamars	32·5	Mahomedan races	26·9
Native Christian	32·5	Minas	24·7
Mehter	31·5	Brahmans	22·7
Hindu Mers	31·4	Jain Mahajans	22·5
Eurasians	30·6	Hindu "	21·3
Balai	30·0	Rajputs	20·7

The table given in the margin shows that in each religion female children are proportionately more numerous than males, but that after nine years the reverse is the case. The proportion of Mahomedan female children is abnormally high, and the decrease in the proportion after four years, abrupt, arguing high mortality. The proportions are however exaggerated, because Merat Mahomedan girls return themselves as Hindus on their marriage as is explained above. Taking the Jain figures as about normal, they being less affected by immigration than either of the others, then Hindus and Mahomedans are more prolific of children, the latter more especially of female children, but both Hindu and Mahomedan life suffers more after 14 years of age than Jain. Taking 20 to 40 as the prime of life, Jains show a proportion of 33 per cent. of males and 32 of females between those ages, Hindus 31 per cent. of males and females, and Mahomedans 31 per cent. of males and 30 per cent. of females. Hindus and Mahomedans have a higher proportion of the extreme old-aged than Jains.

Proportion to 10,000 of each religion and sex.

	Hindus.		Jains.		Mahomedans.	
	Males.	Females.	Males.	Females.	Males.	Females.
0—4	1,354	1,492	1,144	1,275	1,349	1,642
5—9	1,418	1,418	1,143	1,241	1,356	1,475
10—14	1,141	976	1,100	972	1,097	1,008
15—19	837	773	943	877	834	791
20—29	1,593	1,652	1,762	1,733	1,708	1,696
30—39	1,524	1,461	1,616	1,511	1,437	1,336
40—49	1,096	1,053	1,248	1,209	1,049	966
50—59	600	621	661	685	641	566
60 and over	433	550	377	493	511	519

The average age of the population of all ages is higher than in Bombay, but the average age of the population under 20 is lower owing to the greater mortality of children.

Mean age.

	All ages.	Under 20.	20 and over.	40 and over.
Ajmere	24.84	8·3	39·4	53·4
Bombay (1881)	24·5	9·0	38·2	52·7
England	26·4	9·3	40·1	54·9

The comparison given in the margin shows how greatly the average age has increased since 1881. In towns this is partly due to the immigration of adults, but in rural areas (more especially in Merwara) this is only the case to a very limited degree, and freedom from famine and sickness, and the general recovery of the population from the effects of the famine of 1868, must be taken into account.

Mean age.

	1881.		1891.	
	Males.	Females.	Males.	Females.
Ajmere Urban	23·54	23·05	26·52	26·10
Merwara Urban	23·86	23·03	26·69	25·86
Ajmere Rural	21·97	22·34	24·50	24·90
Merwara Rural	21·56	20·74	23·51	23·28

To take stock of the ages of the population it is necessary to compare each age-period with the preceding period of 1881. This gives the result shown in the margin, namely, great increase from outside between the ages 20—29, especially of females. The whole of this increase was, however, in the urban population. The rural population shows a decrease in this age-period as compared with 10—19 of 1881.

Age-period, 1891.	Males.		Females.	
	Difference to preceding period, 1881.	Per cent.	Difference to preceding period, 1891.	Per cent.
10—19	—10,421	—15·4	—15,497	—25·7
20—29	+ 3,207	+ 7·3	+ 9,662	+ 29·6
30—39	— 6,445	—12·8	— 5,953	—13·9
40—49	— 7,129	—18·4	— 4,980	—15·7
50—59	— 6,265	—26·2	— 5,588	—26·3
60 and over	— 2,794	—18·0	+ 139	+ 1·0

SEX.

The variations in the strength of each sex since 1881 is exactly the converse of the variations observed at last Census. The figures are given in the margin. Females have increased in a much higher ratio than men, the causes of which have been already touched on.

Percentage of increase in population.

	1876—81.		1881—91.	
	Males.	Females.	Males.	Females.
Ajmere	17·12	14·59	16·02	19·3
Merwara	17·64	17·06	15·3	22·0
Total	**17·23**	**15·11**	**15·9**	**19·8**

Out of every 1,000 males enumerated 532 were males and 468 females, the highest proportion yet recorded in Ajmere. The proportion in Bombay and the North-West Provinces (taken from the preliminary totals) was 482 females and in the Punjab 461. The Ajmere figure is much reduced by the small proportion of women in town where there is a considerable male floating population. The proportion of women in rural Merwara in 1881 was 447, while at this Census it is 461, the higher proportion being probably due to better enumeration. Some of the male population was absent owing to scarcity at the time of the Census, but there was an actual increase in the number of women of 22 per cent., which is not otherwise accounted for.

Females in every 1,000 persons.

	1876.	1881.	1891.
Ajmere	468	463	470
Merwara	447	446	460
Total	**464**	**460**	**468**

Females in 1,000 of population.

Urban population	456
Rural Ajmere	474
Rural Merwara	461

In comparing the proportion of female to male population by religions, Mer tribes should be excluded from both Hindus and Musulmans. In the marginal table Jains are included for the sake of comparison with former years. Excluding the Mer tribes, the proportion of Mahomedan women to males, namely, 460, is less than in 1876, but there has been a great influx of Mahomedan males in search of labour, and at the time of the Census the Urs Fair was just about to begin and the male population was abnormally high in consequence.

Females in every 1,000 of each religion.

	1865.	1876.	1881.	1891.	Excluding Mers, 1891
Hindus	452	464	462	472	471
Mahomedans	454	468	446	446	460

As in other Provinces the proportion of females varies greatly with different castes, the lowest proportion being generally found amongst the castes of highest social rank. The only explanation that can be offered for this is that in castes in which marriage is easy and remarriage of widows the custom, and in which the woman earns a portion of the family income, she is hardier and better cared for in youth and age than among social orders not subject to these conditions. The proportion of women in the principal castes is shown in the marginal table. As regards Minas, the tribe is not numerically strong, and a number of males come from the surrounding native territory for work or service in the Mina Regiment at Deoli.

Population of females to 1,000 of each caste.

Caste.		Caste.	
Chamar	497	Jain Mahajan	464
Raigar	495	Gujar	463
Kumhar	486	Hindu Mahajan	466
Bhil	484	Brahman	461
Balai	482	Mahomedan	460
Mali	480	Rajput	430
Jat	478	Mina	412
Hindu Mer	474	Mahomedan Mers	388

Some remarks are called for on the proportion of females to males at the different age-periods. The birth registers for the last 10 years show that male births exceed female by 20 per cent., while 18 per cent. of males and 19 per cent. of females die before attaining one year. Males should therefore exceed females in the first year by about 23 per cent., but the Census returns do not show this. Perhaps in a country where a common form of mild abuse is to call a man " a father of daughters, " registraton of female births can hardly be expected to be as punctual as that of males. The discrepancy between the Census returns and Birth Register is much greater in the case of females than males as will be seen from the following figures :—

	Males.	Females.
Population aged 0—4 from Census returns	38,730	*38,194*
Births registered during last 5 years	31,498	*25,534*
Difference	7,232	*12,660*

If the ratio of females to males as registered were correct, then 15 per cent. less males than females attain the age of 5, but the Census returns would show that the mortality of females was about 3 per cent. higher than males up to that age. From 5 to 10 male life gains about 9 per cent. on female, and between 10 and 14 (the period of early marriage) male life gains another 13 per cent. on female, after which period female life holds its own, and more female individuals attain extreme old age than men.

The average age of males is 24·78 and of females 23·73.

CHAPTER V.

CIVIL CONDITION.

Table VIII gives the civil condition of the population generally, and supplementary Table E gives similar information for each caste. Some of the many deductions that can be made from these tables are given below.

Out of every 1,000 males enumerated 484 are single, 466 married, and 50 widowed. The figures in 1881 were 500, 449, and 50 respectively, so that the proportion of married men has increased by 2 per cent. Some idea of how these proportions compare with other parts of India can be formed from the table given in the margin. Elsewhere married men preponderate, here the greater proportion are single. This seems to be due to the low proportion of married men amongst the Mer clans, which taken together number one-sixth of the total population. The proportion of married women does not differ materially from that of the other provinces given.

Proportion per 1,000 of each sex by condition.

		Single.		Married.		Widowed.	
		Males.	Females.	Males.	Females.	Males.	Females.
	Ajmere	484	336	466	509	50	155
1881	Bombay	459	303	489	514	52	183
1881	Central Provinces	464	344	493	508	43	148
1881	North-West Provinces	451	299	484	530	65	171

The figures for the urban and rural population are given below:—

			All Ages.		0—9		10—14		15—39		40 and over.	
			Males.	Females.	Males.	Females.	Males.	Females.	Males.	Females.	Males.	Females.
Ajmere.	Single	Urban	22,481	13,578	11,578	11,075	4,072	1,865	6,176	547	655	91
		Rural	81,595	49,643	46,254	41,039	15,540	7,586	17,402	916	2,399	102
	Married	Urban	27,358	23,619	168	410	751	1,754	17,357	17,183	9,082	4,272
		Rural	80,090	79,693	1,743	3,980	4,084	7,622	46,504	53,699	27,759	14,392
	Widowed	Urban	3,181	7,436	14	13	15	20	1,043	1,533	2,109	5,870
		Rural	8,842	24,843	89	69	102	118	2,196	4,595	6,455	20,061
Merwara.	Single	Urban	4,594	2,795	2,420	2,328	855	390	1,177	69	142	8
		Rural	30,848	19,223	16,438	14,794	6,511	3,856	7,360	547	539	26
	Married	Urban	6,115	5,111	48	134	209	390	3,921	3,694	1,937	893
		Rural	20,583	20,974	135	361	435	1,301	11,166	14,945	8,847	4,367
	Widowed	Urban	737	1,626	5	3	4	4	219	364	509	1,255
		Rural	1,901	5,492	6	12	16	16	433	784	1,446	4,680
Total.	Single	Urban	27,075	16,373	13,998	13,403	4,927	2,255	7,353	616	797	99
		Rural	112,443	68,866	62,692	55,833	22,051	11,442	24,762	1,463	2,938	128
	Married	Urban	33,473	28,730	216	544	960	2,144	21,278	20,877	11,019	5,165
		Rural	100,673	100,667	1,878	4,341	4,519	8,923	57,670	68,644	36,606	18,759
	Widowed	Urban	3,918	9,062	19	16	19	24	1,262	1,897	2,618	7,125
		Rural	10,743	30,335	95	81	118	134	2,629	5,379	7,901	24,741

and the proportions of each condition in the margin. In towns the proportion of children is smaller than in villages, and the marriage ratio is consequently higher. The ratio has increased 1·4 per cent. since 1881. In rural Ajmere the proportion of married have increased, and in Merwara married men have decreased by ·6 and females by 3 per cent. This is possibly accounted for by the fact that the proportion of the population under 15 has increased by about 4 per cent. since 1881. The proportion of widows is almost identical with 1881, Merwara still returning the lowest ratio accounted for by the fact that re-marriage is customary among widows of the Mer caste.

Proportion per 1,000 of each sex and condition.

		Single.		Married.		Widowed.	
		Males.	Females.	Males.	Females.	Males.	Females.
Ajmere	Urban	424	304	516	530	60	166
	Rural	479	323	470	517	51	160
Merwara	Urban	401	293	534	536	65	171
	Rural	578	420	386	460	36	120
Total	Urban	420	302	520	530	60	168
	Rural	502	344	450	504	48	152

A table is given on the following page showing the condition of the populations by religion. The figures for Parsis, Jews, and Sikhs are not given, these races being foreign to the districts and few in number. The highest ratio of married is among Hindus and the highest of widowed amongst Jains. Mahomedans number most spinsters compared to bachelors, namely, 626 per thousand. Hindus number 613 and Jains 545. Hindus include such a number of castes with varying marriage customs that a more accurate idea can be formed of their civil condition from a study of the caste return. The highest ratio of married is amongst the Jats, Gujars, Malis, Kumhars, Khatis, Bhils, and the leather-working castes of Chamar and Balai; all these castes marry early, the re-marriage of widows is allowable, and the obstacles to matrimony few. Saraogis, Mahesris, Rajputs, Oswals, and the Mer clans show the lowest ratio of married, and, except the Mers, the highest ratio of widowed. Wives exceed husbands in number amongst Chamars, Balais, and Raigars, many of whose men emigrate for work, and amongst the Bhils and Mers the more or less aboriginal tribes. The pro-

Conjugal condition of principal Castes.

	Married per 1,000.		Number of wives per 1,000 husbands.	Number of unmarried females to 1,000 unmarried males.	Number of widows to 1,000 wives.	Number of wives under 10 per 1,000 wives.	Number of wives under 15 per 1,000 wives.	Number of husbands under 15 per 1,000 husbands.
	Males.	Females.						
Jat	523	560	993	598	288	92	205	137
Gujar	488	554	978	578	251	81	189	112
Mali	523	533	954	658	306	45	138	59
Bhil	485	520	1,056	717	198	45	143	63
Khati	546	566	918	607	282	57	171	81
Kumhar	537	552	973	633	245	56	166	77
Chamar	529	520	1,016	762	246	42	140	65
Balai	496	536	1,006	674	242	49	143	64
Raigar	470	486	1,016	813	237	16	104	45
Kayasth	515	548	862	548	310	20	116	45
Brahman	492	507	884	517	451	27	125	46
Agarwala	493	508	902	566	411	7	94	35
Mahesri	432	476	956	523	484	7	82	27
Saraogi	459	495	973	517	468	2	83	22
Oswal	400	439	938	570	503	5	66	19
Sonar	493	540	950	524	355	35	122	47
Mahomedans	468	506	923	620	290	28	100	38
Rajputs	418	477	860	385	535	13	71	20
Mer tribes	369	447	1,029	613	263	7	56	13

portion of husbands and wives under the ages of 10 and 15 have slightly increased since 1881, but not in a ratio equal to the increased proportion of population under those ages. The average age of marriage in Ajmere is later than in the provinces mentioned in the foregoing table. For instance, in Bombay, where the proportion of young and middle-aged is very similar to Ajmere, 795 in every 1,000 bachelors are under 15 years of age, here only 743 are. In Bombay 173 out of every 1,000 wives are under 15, here only 123. This betokens a general average of later marriage here than in Bombay. In towns the proportion of wives under 15 is 93 per 1,000, in rural Ajmere 145, and in rural Merwara only 79.

Percentage to total married.

Sex.	Males.		Females.	
Age.	0—9	0—15	0—9	0—15
1881 . . .	·91	3·20	2·44	8·83
1891 . . .	1·56	5·65	3·88	12·33

Amongst Hindus 13 per cent. of the wives are under 15, amongst Mahomedans 9 per cent., among Jains 7 per cent., and Christians 2. Jats and Gujars marry as infants, Kumhars Khatis, Hindu Mahajans, and Kayasths marry generally between 10 and 14, and Rajputs and Jains after that. The Mer tribes seldom marry before 14 or 15. Their poverty offers an obstacle to matrimony, and they are under no religious obligations on the subject.

Polygamy is permissible amongst all castes, but is not common.

Of late years a movement has been set on foot to induce later marriage among the Mahajan caste, Kayasths, etc., as has been done among Rajputs.

Proportion per 1,000 of each sex and condition.

	Single.								Married.								Widowed.							
	0—14		15—24		25—39		40 and over.		0—14		15—24		25—39		40 and over.		0—14		15—24		25—39		40 and over.	
	Males.	Females.	Males.	Females.	Males.	Females.	Males.	Females.	Males.	Females.	Males.	Females.	Males.	Females.	Males.	Females.	Males.	Females.	Males.	Females.	Males.	Females	Males.	Females.
Ajmere-Merwara	743	973	156	20	75	5	26	2	56	123	175	294	414	398	355	185	17	7	46	24	220	161	717	808
Bombay . . (1881)	795	958	145	25	47	11	13	6	56	173	192	296	442	377	310	154	28	20	76	55	273	245	623	680
Central Provinces „	830	961	121	29	39	7	10	3	59	133	177	286	421	405	343	176	15	9	65	32	264	172	656	786
North-West Provinces „	773	970	141	21	62	6	24	3	67	134	202	270	406	390	325	186	18	8	94	40	264	194	624	758

Proportion of 1,000 of each sex by condition and religion and age.

	All Ages.						Males.											
	Single.		Married.		Widowed.		0—9			10—14			15—39			40 and over.		
	Males.	Females.	Males.	Females.	Males.	Females.	Single.	Married.	Widowed.	Single.	Married.	Widowed.	Single.	Married.	Widowed.	Single.	Married.	Widowed.
Hindus	478	327	472	518	50	155	562	18	9	194	45	10	220	587	268	24	350	713
Mahomedans	502	387	448	478	50	135	530	9	4	196	25	5	250	578	275	24	388	716
Jains	512	322	417	456	71	222	444	2	1	197	22	2	293	640	221	66	336	775
Christians	637	531	331	414	32	55	390	...	...	121	4	20	472	659	286	17	337	694

	Females.											
	0—9			10—14			15—39			40 and over.		
	Single.	Married.	Widowed.	Single.	Married.	Widowed.	Single.	Married.	Widowed.	Single.	Married.	Widowed.
Hindus	824	42	3	155	89	4	19	685	177	2	184	816
Mahomedans	773	27	2	174	69	7	47	710	183	6	194	808
Jains	772	5	2	202	70	1	21	754	278	3	171	719
Christians	670	2	...	204	4	...	125	872	803	1	122	197

CHAPTER VI.

INFIRMITIES.

The four infirmities about which particulars have been obtained at the Census are unsoundness of mind, congenital deafness, total blindness, and corrosive leprosy. There would appear to be some uncertainty about the statistics of these infirmities, for in 1881 the results of the enumeration showed an unaccountable increase on the figures for 1876, and the present record shows as remarkable a decrease on those of 1881. Possibly both enumerations were inaccurate in opposite extremes. At the recent Census enumerators acquired the impression that only those blind from birth or insane from birth should be entered, and though special instructions on this point were issued, omissions probably occurred. Compared with the figures of 1881 for other provinces the proportion of afflicted returned is below the average in about the same degree as it was above the average at the former Census. The actual figures are given below:—

Number afflicted in 10,000 of population.

	Total afflicted per 10,000.		Unsound Mind.		Deaf-Mute.		Blind.		Lepers.	
	Males.	Females.	Males.	Females.	Males.	Females.	Males.	Females.	Males.	Females.
Ajmere, 1891	25	24	2	1	4	2	18	20	1	...
Ajmere, 1881	51	60	7	4	8	5	35	51	1	...
Bombay, 1881	42	35	4	2	7	5	21	25	10	3
Central Provinces, 1881	42	42	3	2	8	6	22	30	9	4
North-Western Provinces, 1881	43	40	2	1	8	5	27	32	6	2

	Total.		Unsound Mind.		Deaf-Mutes.		Blind.		Lepers.	
	Males.	Females.	Males.	Females.	Males.	Females.	Males.	Females.	Males.	Females.
Ajmere . 1881 .	1,025	1,246	130	69	156	112	725	1,060	14	5
Ajmere . 1891 .	527	483	46	21	78	47	393	409	10	6
Difference .	—498	—763	—84	—48	—78	—65	—332	—651	—4	+1
Merwara . 1881 .	252	225	41	21	44	17	158	186	9	1
Merwara . 1891 .	193	139	18	2	35	15	128	121	10	1
Difference .	—59	—86	—23	—19	—9	—2	—30	—65	+1	...
Total 1881 .	1,277	1,471	171	90	200	129	883	1,246	23	6
Total 1891 .	720	622	64	23	113	62	523	530	20	7
Difference .	—557	—849	—107	—67	—87	—67	—360	—716	—3	+1

The proportion of afflicted is greater in Merwara than in Ajmere, except in the case of female insanes and lepers, and in this respect also the present return differs from that of 1881. This is, however, in accordance with the Census of 1876. Except that the population are poorer and more ill-fed than in Ajmere, there is no apparent cause for Merwara returning a higher per centage of afflicted.

Number afflicted in 100,000 of population.

	Total afflicted per 100,000		Unsound mind.		Deaf-mutes.		Blind.		Lepers.	
	Males.	Females.	Males.	Females.	Males.	Females.	Males.	Females.	Males.	Females.
Ajmere .	235	242	25	10	34	24	176	205	4	3
Merwara .	298	252	28	8	54	37	197	219	15	2

Judging from the proportion of afflicted at each period, the number of infants born infirm is decreasing, especially in the case of the deaf and dumb. With such a very minute number however as are returned it is unsafe to try and make general deductions.

Number afflicted in 100,000 of each age-period.

	All ages.		0—9		10—19		20—29		30—39		40—49		50—59		60 and over.	
	Males.	Females.	Males.	Females.	Males.	Females.	Males.	Females.	Males.	Females.	Males.	Females.	Males.	Females.	Males.	Females.
Unsound mind	22	9	10	2	16	4	30	5	36	13	28	22	34	19	16	29
Deaf-mutes	39	24	20	12	40	16	40	26	50	29	54	37	57	38	47	87
Blind	181	208	51	52	95	109	115	92	148	160	243	270	500	600	1,143	1.293
Lepers	7	2	0	0	2	2	2	...	11	3	12	7	17	13	47	7

A table showing the proportion of afflicted in some of the principal castes is given in the margin. Native Christians show by far the highest proportion of blind due to the charitable adoption of infants so afflicted, while Sadhus show a very high proportion of all four infirmities, the infirmity being probably the cause of their becoming Sadhus. Of the other castes, Khatiks show an apparently large proportion of lepers, but the actual number affected is only 3. If the figures are at all correct, Ajmere-Merwara would appear to be satisfactorily free from leprosy.

Proportion afflicted per 100,000 of each caste.

Caste.	Unsound mind.	Deaf-mutes.	Blind.	Lepers.
Rajput	36	36	158	6
Gujar	10	26	177	...
Jat	11	38	198	...
Mali	36	61	73	6
Mer clans	15	38	131	10
Brahman	11	48	357	15
Sadhu	50	133	852	16
Mahajan	9	41	298	4
Kumhar	35	29	209	...
Teli	21	63	420	...
Chamar	29	40	190	...
Khatik	...	...	253	84
Balai	6	28	326	...
Native Christian	...	...	1,240	...
Musalman	23	13	106	2

CHAPTER VII.

EDUCATION.

The educational column of the schedule comprised details of the learning, the literate and the illiterate, as also of the language known by the literate. The value of the record, as regards those who are learning, has been nullified by students, regardless of instructions, returning themselves as literate. The total number of males enumerated as learning was only 6,179, while from the annual returns of the Education Department we know that over 8,000 boys are being educated at the various Government schools and private institutions. On the other hand, over 2,000 boys under 15 have been returned as literate, who are in all probability still in the hands of the schoolmaster, and no doubt a fair proportion of the 7,618 "literates" between 15 and 24 are under instruction also.

The general average of those learning or educated in Ajmere-Merwara is high, which is natural when the figures include a large proportion of urban population and of the trading classes. The proportion of the illiterate in this and other Provinces is given in the margin.

Illiterate per 1,000.

	Males.	Females.
Ajmere	867	992
Bombay, 1881	888	993
Central Provinces	953	998
North-West Provinces	940	998

The figures for the urban and rural population are as under:—

		Learning.		Literate.		Illiterate.	
		Males.	Females.	Males.	Females.	Males.	Females.
Ajmere	Urban	2,752	344	11,151	817	39,117	43,472
	Rural	2,125	67	15,371	570	153,031	153,542
Merwara	Urban	479	43	3,014	109	7,953	9,380
	Rural	823	16	2,578	44	49,931	45,629
Total	Urban	3,231	387	14,165	926	47,070	52,852
	Rural	2,948	83	17,949	614	202,962	199,171

Beawar, with its trading community, contains the smallest percentage of illiterate males, while rural Merwara, inhabited almost exclusively by agricultural and menial classes, returns the greatest proportion of illiterates, both male and female.

Illiterate per 1,000.

		1891.	
		Males.	Females.
Ajmere	Urban	737	973
	Rural	897	995
Merwara	Urban	694	984
	Rural	935	998
Total	Urban	730	975
	Rural	906	996

Compared with 1881 and 1876 education seems to be spreading slowly, but surely, and female education to have made an appreciable advance. The rapid increase in the number of the instructed between 1876 and 1881 was due to the sudden influx of educated persons which the opening of the railway gave rise to, and was not likely to be repeated during the last decade.

	1876.		1881.		1891.	
	Learning and Literate.	Per cent.	Learning and Literate.	Per cent.	Learning and Literate.	Per cent.
Males .	19,228	9·05	30,183	12·12	38,293	13·28
Females .	377	0·20	1,208	0·57	2,010	0·79

The table given in the margin, from which children under 5 have been omitted as being incapable of learning, shows that education has spread most amongst Christians, Jains, and Musalmans. Amongst "Others" are included Sikhs, Parsis, and Jews. The proportion of Mahomedan boys and girls under 15, who are seeking or have acquired some education, is much higher than that of Hindus, while Jains naturally far distance either. It will be observable, however, that the proportion of educated Jain women, though higher than Hindu or Mahomedan, is meagre in the extreme.

Number of Learning and Literate per 1,000 (excluding children under 5)

	5 and upwards, 1881.		5 and upwards, 1891.		5—14		15—24		25 and over.	
	Males.	Females.	Males.	Females.	Males.	Females.	Males.	Females.	Males.	Females.
All religions	141	*6*	154	*9*	97	*9*	188	*11*	172	*9*
Hindu .	101	*3*	113	*5*	66	*3*	143	*7*	129	*5*
Musalman .	95	*4*	117	*6*	90	*8*	132	*8*	125	*5*
Jain . .	763	*12*	791	*15*	590	*10*	854	*10*	860	*19*
Christian	885	*808*	912	*817*	895	*903*	915	*789*	989	*765*
Others .	644	*163*	684	*398*	763	*454*	581	*287*	714	*410*

Of the languages known by the literate details have only been abstracted of those who know English. They amount to 2,521 males and 321 females, out of whom only 2,058 males and 52 females belong to non-English speaking races. The proportion of Natives who have been returned as knowing English is 0·71 per cent. of males and 0·02 of females. The following are the principal castes numbering English scholars among them:—

Rajput .	76 males.	Mahomedan .	306 males.
Brahman .	449 ,,	Native Christian .	267 ,,
Kayasth .	211 ,,	Parsi . .	58 ,,
Mahajan .	503 ,,	Sonar . .	20 ,,

In supplementary Table C is shown the number of literate in each caste. A table showing the proportion of literate in some of the principal classes is given marginally. The leather-workers are the least educated of all, but the agricultural classes run them close. Of these latter the Gujars are the most ignorant, with 0·9 per cent. of literate males, the Mer tribes next with 1·5 per cent., and then the Jats with 1·9 per cent.

Percentage of Literate.

No.	Class.	Males.	Females.	No.	Class.	Males.	Females.
1	Military and Dominant.	11·9	4·8	22	Tailors . .	9·5	0·3
2	Agricultural .	1·7	·0	23	Dyers . .	7·5	0·0
5	Priests . .	33·6	1·4	28	Potters . .	2·0	·0
6	Devotees .	12·6	1·0	35	Fishermen, Cooks, etc. .	4·0	·1
9	Writers .	56·1	4·8	36	Distillers .	10·1	·0
14	Traders .	60·8	·7	38	Leather workers.	1·3	·0
17	Goldsmiths .	22·2	·4	48	Non-Indian races . .	9·8	·5
19	Blacksmiths .	7·6	·0	50	Europeans .	66·1	67·8
20	Carpenters .	4·0	·0	51	Eurasians .	36·8	27·5
21	Coppersmiths	23·1	·0	52	Native Christians . .	71·1	40·2

Of the Mahajan class the proportions are as under :—

Percentage of Literate.

	Males.	Females.
Saraogi	64·2	0·9
Oswals	61·7	0·8
Agarwal	62·4	0·5
Mahesri	56·0	0·4

CHAPTER VIII.

LANGUAGES.

The languages returned at the Census are shown in Imperial Table X. The prevailing language of Ajmere-Merwara is Hindi, the Marwari dialect of it being spoken in Ajmere and the Merwara dialect in Merwara. Ajmeri, though returned by a large number of persons, is not a well-defined distinct dialect. The percentage of population returning the vernaculars of the Province or of other countries is shown in the marginal table. Hindustani has not been included as a vernacular of the Province, though it is so among Mahomedans. In Ajmere 76 per cent. of the population return the language of the District, namely Marwari and Ajmeri, and 12 per cent. other dialects of Rajputana.

	Total	Ajmere.	Merwara.
Vernaculars of Rajputana .	90·58	88·7	97·15
Ditto of India .	9·09	10·9	2·83
Ditto of Asia .	·03	·04	·00
Ditto of Europe .	·30	·36	·02

In Merwara 71 per cent., or nearly the whole rural population, speak Merwari.

The purely Indian vernaculars returned with their locality is shown below :—

Vernaculars of India.

Family.	Group.	Language.	Dialect.	Locality, etc.
Aryan .	India .	Hindi .	Marwari . .	Rajputana generally.
			Ajmeri . .	Ajmere dialect of Marwari.
			Merwari . .	Merwara Ditto.
			Meywari . .	Meywar Ditto.
			Dundhari . .	Jeypore Ditto.
			Haraoti . .	Dialect of South-West Rajputana.
			Mewati . .	Dialect of Northern Rajputana.
			Hindi (unspecified).	Common to all Rajputana.
			Hindustani . .	Common to Mahomedans.
			Purbi . . .	North-West Provinces and Oudh.
			Malwi . . .	Central India.
		Marathi .	Marathi . .	Western India.
			Dakani . .	Ditto.
		Gujrati .	Gujrati . .	Cutch, Central Provinces, etc.
		Bengali .	Bengali . .	Eastern Bengal.
		Uria .	Uria . . .	Orissa and Central Provinces.
		Panjabi .	Panjabi . .	Panjab
		Kashmiri .	Kashmiri . .	Kashmir.
		Sindhi .	Sindhi . .	Sind.
Dravidian.	Southern	Tamil .	Tamil . .	Madras.
		Telagu .	Têlagu .	
			Madrasi .	

In all 98 per cent. of the people enumerated speak Hindi.

The following dialects returned in the schedules have been included in the main dialects to which they belong :—Kishengarhi, Haryani, Sekhawati, Maharastri, Brij-bhasha, Alwari, Bharatpuri, Lashkari, Bundelkhandi, Nāgărchal, Pahari, Karnatăki, Nāgărwāli, Rewari, Jhallawari, Guwalior, Khāndes, Nagri, Narnoli, Khairarí, Rathi, Perdesi, Kachi, Peshawri, Allahabadi, Godwari, Mathura.

CHAPTER IX.

BIRTH-PLACE.

Birth-place has been abstracted from the schedules by districts and states if born in Rajputana, and by the province or country if born elsewhere. Classified according to the method adopted by the Census Commissioner the figures are as under :—

	TOTAL.	Per cent.	Ajmere.	Per cent.	Merwara.	Per cent.
Born in district where enumerated	433,664	80·0	3,31,009	78·3	93,170	77·6
Born in district or state contiguous to former	74,954	13·8	60,188	14·2	21,725	18·1
Born in distant parts of Rajputana	6,553	1·2	6,182	1·4	2,897	2·4
Born in other parts of India	26,643	4·9	24,456	5·7	2,187	1·8
Asiatic foreigners	109	·02	102	·02	7	·0
European and other foreigners	435	·08	422	·1	13	·01

The proportion of indigenous population is low. In 1881 *few* districts in other provinces showed less than 84 per cent. of indigenous population. The causes for this seem to be, *1st*, the prevalent custom of extraneous marriage; *2ndly*, the periodical migrations of the people owing to scarcity, and *3rdly*, the large number of outsiders in the towns of Ajmere and Beawar. The figures for the male and female population are given in the margin, and show how large a proportion of the female element belong to contiguous states. Similarly, the number of females enumerated in other states of Rajputana who were born in Ajmere is nearly double that of males.

	Males.	Per cent.	Females.	Per cent.
Born in Ajmere-Merwara	236,621	82·0	1,97,043	77·5
Born in contiguous States	30,906	10·7	44,048	17·3
Born in other parts of Rajputana	3,801	1·3	2,752	1·0

In 1881 the percentage of indigenous population was 74·5, namely 77·8 of males and 70·7 of females. Compare this with the figures now returned, and it shows that the proportion of those born in the districts has increased 4·2 in the case of males and 6·8 in the case of females. This is partially due to the time of Census not being the marriage season, as it was in 1881.

Ajmere and Merwara were included in Rajputana, and not abstracted separately in several provinces, but the following are the figures received of persons born in Ajmere :—

	TOTAL.	Males.	Females.
Assam	4,877	3,943	934
North-West Provinces	1,088	584	504
Bombay	1,971	1,306	665
Rajputana	49,963	18,261	31,702
Punjab	659	363	296
Central India	2,757	1,660	1,097

CHAPTER X.

CASTE AND RACE.

An exhaustive description of the castes composing the population of Ajmere-Merwara was given in the Census Report for 1881, and it only remains to bring the information up to date. Marriage and education in relation to caste have been added to the subjects for enquiry during the recent Census, as also the sub-divisions of each caste. These latter amount to over three thousand recorded sub-divisions, but in many cases they represent mere family distinctions, and in some are obviously incorrect.

In Imperial Table XVI castes have been grouped according to their hereditary occupation or by nationality; the six main classes and the proportion that each bears to the population was as under:—

A—Agricultural	40 per cent.
B—Professional	10 "
C—Commercial	9 "
D—Artisan and Menial . . .	29 "
E—Vagrant and Minor Artisan . .	1 "
F—Races and Nationalities . .	11 "

Percentage to total population.

	TOTAL.	Ajmere.	Merwara.
Rajput . . .	3·0	3·6	0·8
Jat . . .	6·0	8·2	1·4
Gujar . . .	7·0	8·5	1·5
Mer tribes . .	15·6	5·5	51·1
Mali . . .	3·0	3·4	1·6
Brahman and Devotees . .	7·0	8·0	3·4
Mahajan . .	8·5	8·5	8·4
Kumhar . .	3·0	3·2	2·4
Chamar . .	3·2	3·9	0·7
Balai . . .	5·9	5·3	7·0
Raigar . . .	3·8	4·1	3·0
Mahomedan races .	10·8	12·8	4·2
Others . . .	22·5	25·8	14·5

The principal castes and their proportion to the whole population is shown in the table in the margin. After the Mahomedan race Jats, Gujars, Brahmans, and Mahajans are the predominating castes in Ajmere. In Merwara, Mers, Mahajans, and Balais make up 70 per cent. of the people.

The Rajput aristocracy number 3 per cent. of the population, the actual increase since 1881 being 9 per cent. The 12 principal clans given in the margin give their names to sub-divisions of almost every menial and artisan caste returned. By the Walter Krit Hitkarna Sabha Convention of 1886 the Rajputs of Rajputana are prohibited from marrying before the age of 16 as boys and 14 as girls. The 16 males and 46 females under 10 returned as married belong mostly to the imported Rajputs of the North-West Provinces and Oudh.

Rajput Clans.

		TOTAL.	Males.	Females.
SOLAR RACE.	Rahtor . .	7,354	4,782	2,572
	Sisodia . .	1,164	484	680
	Kachwaha . .	2,638	1,114	1,524
	Bar Gujar . .	51	29	22
LUNAR RACE.	Jadubansi . .	32	26	6
	Tanwār . .	258	152	106
	Bhātti . . .	711	381	330
	Chohan . . .	1.375	716	659
	Panwar . . .	275	305	222
	Solankhi . .	411	214	197
	Gaur . . .	756	455	301
	Parihar . . .	163	95	68
	Others . . .	942	580	362
	TOTAL .	16,382	9,333	7,049

Jats excel all other castes in husbandry; they occupy villages in all the Ajmere Pergunnahs, but there are only 7 villages of them in Merwara. The number of sub-divisions recorded is 296; these "gots," or sub-castes, are very local, but at the same time well defined; intermarriage in the same sub-caste is not allowed, except in the case of widow re-marriage. Infant marriage is the custom.

Gujars exceed the Jats in numbers, and their sub-castes are nearly as numerous. They also marry as infants, constant feuds and quarrels being the result.

The **Mer** tribes number 23,525 in Ajmere and 61,348 in Merwara, having increased by 13 per cent. since 1881; but as 1,000 families are estimated to have emigrated previous to the Census owing to scarcity, they must have increased to a greater extent than this. The origin of these tribes and their descent from Mina ancestors was fully discussed in the report of 1881. For purposes of comparison all the tribes have been treated as one, for, though there are Mers and Rawats, Chitas and Merats, Hindus and Musalmans, they were all originally one, and at the present day differ so little in habit, religion, social custom, or occupation that they can but be treated as one tribe. In 1876 Mr. White described the separate nationality of the Mers as on the wane, and in 1881 Pundit Bhag Ram predicted the early Brahmanism or Islamism of the whole of Merwara. Efforts in this direction have, however, fallen very flat, and, notwithstanding meetings and agreements and the general acceptance of the theory of religious reform, the Mer retains a strong objection to putting Brahminical theories into practice. He draws the line at out-casting his erring brethren who may eat cow or swine, as the case may be. In Ajmere the Merats and Chitas show some signs of Islamism, but, generally speaking, Hindu and Musalman eat and drink, smoke and marry together with as little restriction as heretofore. Hindu Mers have increased since 1881 by 15 per cent., and Musalman Mers by only ·4 per cent., but this is owing to a larger number of Merat absentees, and not to any religious changes. The numbers returned of each clan was as under:—

		Ajmere.		Merwara.	
		Males.	Females.	Males.	Females.
Mer	Hindu	9,258	8,891	5,477	6,841
	Musalman	...	...	14	18
Chita	Hindu	143	50	102	75
	Musalman	402	236	297	263
Merat	Hindu	249	84	4,692	3,997
	Musalman	1,324	855	6,629	4,057
Rawat	Hindu	1,195	730	8,798	9,598
	Musalman	...	...	32	43
Barar Rawat	Hindus	62	46	7,180	3,265

Rawat is a title of nobility, and is adopted by various clans or individuals of a clan, and the number shown in the above return includes Chitas, Merats, and Mers. The Barar Mers have always been called Rawats. Barars and Chitas were originally Chohan Minas, and Merats are really Chitas, descended from Mera, the common ancestor of the Gorat and Kātāt Merats. The other clans of separate stock appear to be the Powars, Mothis, Gehlots. The former include Delat, Kallat, Dodhing, Boya, Khiyat, Pokharya.

The Mer clans marry later in life than any other caste; widow re-marriage is customary; they have little education; they are all lovers of home, and are an indolent, good-humoured, impecunious race.

Malis number 14,414 in Ajmere and 1,959 in Merwara. They return 60 sub-castes, which are distinct from the main sub-divisions of Phularia, or flower-growers, and Kheter and Bhoi, or cultivators.

Minas number 4,593 in Ajmere, and are found chiefly in the Sāwăr and Kekri pergunnas. In Merwara there are 19 men and 36 females. They return 27 sub-castes, of which the principal are Parihar and Motis. The tribe return a lower proportion of females to males than any other. Fifty-five per cent. of their males are unmarried, 34 per cent being adults.

Bhils have returned themselves as Hindus, and there is no doubt they are becoming Hinduised, worshiping Ramdeo and other gods in the place of the "Darti mata," or mother-earth.

Brahmans number 24,415 in Ajmere, but only 2,206 in Merwara, and there 1,530 of them are in the town of Beawar. The distribution in urban and rural population is as under:—

		Total.	Males.	Females.
Ajmere	Urban	6,870	3,865	3,005
	Rural	17,545	9,167	8,378
Merwara	Urban	1,530	914	616
	Rural	676	396	280

Rural Merwara supplies only 676 Brahmans against 787 in 1881, and most of these are cultivators. Brahmans as a whole have increased 22 per cent., 41 per cent. in Beawar, 43 per cent. in Ajmere town, and 13 per cent. in rural Ajmere They return 47 sub-castes, of which the numerical strength of the principal is as under:—

	Ajmere.			Merwara.		
	Total.	Males.	Females.	Total.	Males.	Females.
Gorh	1,751	1,285	466	760	472	288
Gujargorh	4,548	2,514	2,034	146	91	55
Prohit	184	93	91	3	1	2
Vedic	15	9	6	7	3	4
Sewak	110	49	61	16	8	8
Nanwana	38	21	17	1	1	...
Pārāser	870	502	368	18	9	9
Sikhwal	1,577	834	743	229	129	100
Sanadh	838	551	287	142	70	27
Daima	4,132	2,349	1,783	161	101	60
Pokarna	340	225	115	48	26	22
Kanojia	442	363	79	46	32	14
Tuvari	9	8	1	14	7	7
Srimali	182	93	89	37	26	11
Gujrati	361	199	162	9	5	4
Chobey	75	67	8	88	61	27
Sarsut	927	596	331	35	22	13
Parik	2,553	1,390	1,163	50	32	18
Adgorh	663	369	294	31	16	15
Punchdrawer	6	6	...	14	4	10
Khăndelwal	934	479	455	44	21	23
Māhārāster	88	88	...	...	...	...
Dikshet	1	1	...	...	...	...
Gerweria	42	30	12	...	...	...
[illegible]ar	6	4	2	39	36	3
[illegible]	...	...	...	22	11	11
[illegible]	9	4	5	...	...	...
[illegible]	3	2	1	...	...	...
West Pr[illegible]	42	34	8	13	6	7
[illegible]s (unspecified)	3,669	867	2,802	233	120	113
Ajm[illegible] Total	24,415	13,032	11,383	2,206	1,310	896

Shami is an incorrect caste appellation, but has been returned in 158 cases.

Jattis, or Jain priests, have been returned in some instances as Sadhus and some as Jattis. They number in all—

	TOTAL.	Males.	Females.
Ajmere	117	64	53
Merwara	24	19	5

Kayasths have increased from 1,658 in 1881 to 2,916, the railway being the chief cause of this influx of the writer caste. Here, as elsewhere, this caste are striving for social promotion, and Ajmere is announced as the meeting-place of the next Kayasth conference.

Mahajans number 46,117, having increased by 13·7 per cent. since 1881, or less than the general average of increase. They are distributed as under :—

		TOTAL.	Males.	Females.
AJMERE	Urban	11,341	6,061	5,280
	Rural	24,776	13,199	11,577
MERWARA	Urban	4,992	2,811	2,18
	Rural	5,008	2,703	2,305

The leaders of the castes are the Seths of Ajmere, and their caste fellows and clients are found in every village. The strength of each caste division is shown below :—

	AJMERE.			MERWARA.		
	TOTAL.	Males.	Females.	TOTAL.	Males.	Females.
Mahesri	7,140	3,774	3,366	505	318	187
Khandelwal	387	217	170	191	123	68
Mahore	29	23	6	1	1	...
Bijabárgi	695	326	369	103	53	50
Jeswal	80	51	29	...	...	...
Khátri	1,115	601	514	213	125	88
Palliwal	346	195	551	22	17	5
Dhunser	41	26	15	5	2	3
Agerwal	8,417	4,502	3,915	1,673	922	751
Niterwal	31	18	13	...	...	...
Bhandari	-	4	4	...	...	...
Oswal	12,557	6,750	5,807	6,817	3,693	3,124
Saraogi	5,078	2,666	2,412	348	186	162
Mahajan (unspecified)	193	107	86	122	74	48
TOTAL	36,117	19,260	16,857	10,000	5,514	4,486

Of the four main divisions Saraogis are all Jains of the Digambri sects; they have increased since 1881 by 26 per cent.; they number a greater proportion of literate of both sexes among them than other Mahajans, and they are skilful traders.

Oswals are Jains of the Swetambri sect, only 22 having been returned as Hindus; they have increased only 6 per cent. since last Census.

Mahesris are all Hindus, and they also have increased by 6 per cent. only.

Agarwals number 962 Jains and 4,462 Hindus; they have increased by nearly 20 per cent., considerable numbers from the North-West Provinces and Oudh having come to Ajmere.

Some Dhunsars have returned themselves as Mahajans, and some as Brahmans; they are all engaged in trade or professional occupations, and do not officiate in any way as priests.

Khattris have returned themselves as Mahajans; they number only 726.

Sonars return 3,244, of whom 750 live in Merwara. There are two main divisions of the caste, Bahmaniya and Medh, and the 28 other sub-castes returned are included in these.

Kumhars number 16,732, and are divided into the Khetars, or cultivators, and the Materas, or potters.

Darogha or **Chākur** is numerically the strongest of the servant castes; they are descendants of illegitimate Rajputs, and distinguish themselves by the name of the Rajput clan they belonged to, though such distinctions have ramified into mere family names, such as Bakshiramot and Bhowanidasot.

The leather-working castes make up 14 per cent. of the population. **Khatiks, Chamar, Balai, Raigar** have increased in a marvellous ratio since the opening of the railway and the consequent demand for labour. These four castes have increased by no less than 22,600, or 44 per cent. since 1876, and by 20 per cent. since 1881.

The number of **Sansis** and **Kanjars** enumerated was 670, but there must be some 2,000 Sansis moving about the borders of the district. They are settled in only one village, namely Galti, where there are two or three families. Baories number 161, of whom 47 males and 46 females are more or less adults, that is to say, over 15 years of age.

Mahomedans generally, with the exception of Mers, have been all included in non-Indian Asiatic races. Deswalis, Mewatis, and Kaim Khanis are, however, purely Indian, though returning themselves as Mogal, Pathans, etc. The former, *viz.* Deswalis, number 4,010, divided between Sheikhs, Syads, Mogal, and Pathans, according to the fancy of the individual. There has been a large influx of Mahomedans to Ajmere in recent years; since 1881 they have increased by 35 per cent.

European British subjects number 729 against 872 in 1881, the decrease being due to the absence of the British regiment from Nasirabad, which was in course of relief. Foreigners number 109. The number of Europeans and Foreigners enumerated within Military limits was as under:—

	TOTAL.	Males.	Females.
Nasirabad Cantonment	246	201	45
Ajmere Cantonment	4	4	...
Deoli Cantonment	13	9	4

The number of Foreigners was as under:—

	TOTAL.	Males.	Females.
French	3	1	2
Italian	1	...	1
German	8	5	3
Spanish	1	...	1
Swiss	1	...	1
Danish	1	...	1
Portuguese	78	51	27
American	3	2	1
African	2	5	7
Foreigner	1	1	...
TOTAL	109	65	44

Eurasians number 616 in Ajmere and 20 in Merwara. In 1881 only 196 Eurasians were returned.

Native Christians have increased from 799 to 1,209; there are 885 in Ajmere and 324 in Merwara.

CHAPTER XI.

OCCUPATION.

Table XVII shows the occupations of the people, and in the case of non-workers the occupation from which their living is derived. The table shows three age-periods, namely 0—4, 5—14, and 15 and over. For the purposes of this table persons of the latter period can be considered as adults, though no doubt in some occupations boys and girls are contributing to the work and earnings of the family before that age. The total number of adult males is 176,833 and of females 154,893. By excluding the whole population over 60, the following estimate of non-workers is arrived at. Religious mendicants have not been included in this list, as this term is applied to many who are more or less employed

	Total.			Town.			Country.		
	Total.	Males.	Females.	Total.	Males.	Females.	Total.	Males.	Females.
Under 15	210,632	111,492	*99,140*	38,525	20,139	*18,386*	172,107	91,353	*80,754*
Over 60	26,451	12,689	*13,762*	6,058	2,881	*3,177*	20,393	9,808	*10,585*
Independent of work	7,960	5,168	*2,792*	3,012	1,908	*1,104*	4,948	3,260	*1,688*
Dependent on others	45,281	...	*45,281*	21,033	...	*21,033*	24,248	...	*24,248*
Total	290,324	129,349	160,975	68,628	24,928	43,700	221,696	104,421	117,275
PER CENT.	53·5	44·8	*63·3*	57·5	38·6	*80·6*	52·3	46·6	*58·6*

in priestly duties. Their labour, however, must be considered unproductive, and if they are included, the percentage of non-workers is 54·6 per cent. of the population; or, in other words, 45·4 per cent. are engaged in more or less productive pursuits, a low proportion compared with other provinces, accounted for by a high ratio of children and aged.

The smaller proportion of children in towns results in an increased ratio of male workers, namely 61·4 per cent., but in towns only 19·4 per cent. of the women do any work. In villages 53·4 per cent. of the men and 41·4 of women work for their living.

The classification of occupations adopted for abstraction with the figures for each class and for adults is shown below—

		TOTAL.						TOWN.						COUNTRY.					
		TOTAL.		MALES.		FEMALES.		TOTAL.		MALES.		FEMALES.		TOTAL.		MALES.		FEMALES.	
		Total.	Adults.	Total.	Adults.	Total.	Adults.	Total.	Adults.	Total.	Adults.	Total.	Adults.	Total.	Adults.	Total.	Adults.	Total.	Adults.
A	Government	14,883	10,406	9,931	7,322	4,952	3,084	7,982	5,707	5,440	4,126	2,542	1,581	6,901	4,699	4,491	3,196	2,410	1,503
B	Pasture and Agriculture	269,114	156,158	142,302	82,235	126,812	73,923	7,760	4,988	4,251	2,807	3,509	2,181	263,354	151,170	138,051	79,428	123,303	71,742
C	Personal Service	34,536	22,831	18,676	12,536	15,860	10,295	19,572	13,285	10,434	7,188	9,138	6,097	14,964	9,546	8,242	5,348	6,722	4,198
D	Preparation and supply of material	97,027	60,822	51,411	32,348	45,616	28,474	42,018	27,839	22,295	14,804	19,723	13,035	55,009	32,983	29,116	17,544	25,893	15,439
E	Commerce, Transport, Storage	40,061	26,464	21,558	14,583	18,503	11,881	18,227	12,530	9,318	6,647	8,909	5,883	21,834	13,934	12,240	7,936	9,594	5,998
F	Professions	19,878	12,748	10,297	6,661	9,581	6,087	5,704	4,003	3,054	2,175	2,650	1,828	14,174	8,745	7,243	4,486	6,931	4,259
G	Indefinite and independent	66,859	42,297	34,150	21,148	32,709	21,149	17,368	11,754	9,674	6,580	7,694	5,174	49,491	30,543	24,476	14,568	25,015	15,975
	TOTAL	542,358	331,726	288,325	176,833	254,033	154,893	118,631	80,106	64,466	44,327	54,165	35,779	423,727	251,620	223,859	132,506	199,868	119,124

PERCENTAGE OF POPULATION IN EACH CLASS	Total.			Town.	Country.
	Total.	Males.	Females	Total.	Total.
A	2.7	3.5	1.8	6.7	1.6
B	49.6	49.4	50.0	6.5	61.6
C	6.5	6.5	6.2	16.5	3.5
D	17.9	17.8	18.0	35.4	13.0
E	7.4	7.5	7.3	15.4	5.2
F	3.7	3.5	3.8	4.8	3.4
G	12.2	11.8	12.9	14.6	11.7

This table gives the percentages shown in the margin, from which it will be seen that nearly 50 per cent. of the population are dependent on agriculture for their livelihood; or if the figures for those combining agriculture with other pursuits be included, the proportion is nearly 53 per cent.

The system under which occupations were tabulated in 1881 does not admit of accurate comparison with the present returns, which show the number dependent on each occupation, and not the number actually employed in it. In the agricultural class the definition of occupant and tenant differed in 1881 from that now adopted. The proportion of agriculturists according to their connection with the land is shown in the margin. There was a tendency on the part of some tenants to return themselves as proprietors, but the number finally returned erroneously is probably very small. The agricultural population of each division of the districts is given below, excluding Herdsmen and Stock-breeders:—

Non-cultivating occupants	3.6
Cultivating occupants	37.4
Tenants and sharers, non-cultivating	9.7
ditto cultivating	40.6
Farm labourers	8.7

	Total Agriculture.						Occupants and Tenants.		Farm Laborers, Gardeners, etc.		Combining Agriculture and other occupations.	
	Both sexes.		Males.		Females.							
	Total.	Adults.	Total.	Adults.	Total.	Adults.	Males.	Females.	Males.	Females.	Males.	Females.
Bhinai	35,388	20,164	18,332	10,506	17,056	9,658	14,782	13,848	130	36	3,420	3,172
Masudah	24,131	13,219	13,012	6,800	11,119	6,419	12,797	11,086	178	...	37	33
Khurwa	6,357	3,579	3,378	1,929	2,979	1,650	3,270	2,927	50	8	58	44
Risangan	6,584	4,024	3,216	1,946	3,368	2,078	2,915	2,640	280	728	21	...
Kekri	22,235	13,270	12,110	7,253	10,125	6,017	11,382	9,902	222	223	506	...
Sawer	11,429	6,782	5,954	3,501	5,475	3,281	5,339	4,708	220	220	395	547
Total Istimrar	106,124	61,038	56,002	31,935	50,122	29,103	50,485	45,111	1,080	1,215	4,437	3,796
Jageer	25,239	15,245	12,943	7,791	12,296	7,454	12,789	11,988	124	298	30	10
Khalsa	58,026	34,893	30,937	18,457	27,089	16,436	30,142	26,743	316	207	472	139
Towns	6,531	4,291	3,507	2,386	3,024	1,905	2,142	2,259	513	113	852	652
Total Ajmere	195,920	115,467	103,389	60,569	92,531	54,898	95,558	86,101	2,033	1,833	5,798	4,597
Merwara Rural	82,721	45,574	44,218	24,329	38,503	21,245	33,397	23,510	6,387	12,400	4,434	2,593
Do. Towns	1,755	1,112	1,106	724	649	388	804	443	62	23	240	183
Total Merwara	84,476	46,686	45,324	25,053	39,152	21,633	34,201	23,953	6,449	12,423	4,674	2,776
Grand Total	280,396	162,153	148,713	85,622	131,683	76,531	129,759	110,054	8,482	14,256	10,472	7,373

The number returned as combining other occupations with agriculture is 17,845. The number of both sexes returned in 1881 who combined agriculture with their ordinary profession was 8,791. The number of the money-lending class owning or working land is returned as follows :—

	TOTAL.	Males.	Females.
Money-lenders	1,301	638	663
Merchants	76	48	28
Shop-keepers	1,483	736	747
TOTAL	2,860	1,422	1,438

Of these 35 per cent. cultivate themselves and 65 per cent. are non-cultivating.

Of other occupations the Railway supports 10,649 persons in all, not counting coolies and unskilled labour. Adult male employés number 4,444. The number employed in 1881 was 2,016.

Cotton industries provide for 24,184, including 7,264 adult males and 8,213 females. New presses at Kekri, Beáwar and elsewhere have given considerable impetus to this industry.

Printers, gold and silver smiths, potters, merchants and leather workers all show an increase of adult males since 1881, while the number employed in education, literature, law or in musical professions have also increased.

The number of general labourers has risen from 19,054 to 33,682 adults, the greater proportion being women; and the number of ordinary beggars has decreased by 760 adults.

CHAPTER XII.

ADMINISTRATION.

Census operations practically began in August 1890, when indents for schedules were despatched, officers appointed to make preliminary arrangements and instructions issued to them.

The numbering of the houses began in villages on 10th September and later in towns. The preparation of the villages and ward lists showing the name of the occupant of every house, and of the preliminary register A showing the locality of the houses, etc., numbered, went on at the same time as the numbering. All numbering was completed by 15th October, by which date also most of the Charge Superintendents had submitted proposals for the division of their charges into circles and blocks. There being no record of the circles and blocks adopted in 1881, this work was done afresh. By 15th November circles and blocks were finally confirmed and supervisors, and most of the enumerators appointed, and their instruction went on up till the preliminary Census, which began on the 15th January.

The preliminary arrangements were carried out in Khalsa areas by Tehsildars and in Istimrari villages by the Istimrardar supervised by the Deputy Magistrate, Kekri, and the Revenue Extra Assistant Commissioner. In towns the preliminary arrangements were carried out by the Municipalities or Cantonment Committees.

The number of circles and blocks was as follows :—

	Circle.	Blocks.	Average houses per block.	Average population per block.
Ajmere City and Suburbs	52	411	36·3	167·5
Nasirabad Civil	11	123	33·5	159·5
„ Military	4	6	161·5	347·6
Kekri	5	46	29·4	156·5
Deoli	8	31	51·4	170·5
Ajmere Tehsil	113	1,034	23·2	133·8
Bhinai	46	281	36·1	205·6
Masuda	11	246	27·7	159·1
Kharwa	6	56	34·8	190·7
Pisangan	9	80	39·1	174·7
Kekri	42	219	32·8	186·8
Sawar	12	104	33·6	185·4
TOTAL AJMERE	319	2,637	30·2	160·1
Beawar Town	16	126	35·7	166·4
Beawar Tehsil	40	397	22·3	139·9
Todgarh Tehsil	40	328	26·3	132·5
TOTAL MERWARA	96	851	25·8	141·0
TOTAL	415	3,488	29·1	155·4

Besides the above, 267 special enumerators for roads, travellers, etc., were appointed, and the encampments of wandering tribes were enumerated through the Police. A fixed number of dwellings were appointed to each enumerator, and the village lands outside the village dwellings were apportioned territorially. On the night of the Census tickets were issued to all travellers, or persons about to travel, to prevent them being enumerated twice.

The following is a synopsis of the classes from which supervisors and enumerators were drawn:—

	Official.									Non-official.						
	Railway.	Revenue and Judicial.	Police.	Education.	Military.	Patwari.	Medical.	Others.	Total.	Bankers and traders.	Landholders.	Petition-writers.	Servants of Istimrardars.	Religious.	Others.	Total.
Supervisors .	15	35	11	43	7	166	...	...	277	7	5	4	83	...	39	138
Enumerators .	20	41	9	38	33	25	...	1	167	2,374	101	38	6	1	801	3,321

Census officers were appointed under the Act by the Commissioner. No prosecutions under the Act took place.

The non-official Census officers were mostly volunteers and did their work cheerfully and in most instances with intelligence.

The schedules were bound up in books of 50, 30 and 12 pages each, and spare schedules were sewn in to the covers by supervisors if needed; if two books were used for 1 block they were sewn together.

The number of books issued was as under—

	Hindi Books.	Urdu Books.	English Books.	Spare Schedules.	Household Schedules, English.
Ajmere	3,504	399	83	3,479	79
Merwara	1,020	68	...	1,568	15
Total .	4,524	467	83	5,047	94

or in all 198,412 schedules, of which 5,628 were returned unused. The average number of entries per schedule issued was therefore 2·8 persons.

The morning after the Census enumerators and supervisors filled in the preliminary total abstracts and forwarded them to head-quarters. The totals of these abstracts were found very generally correct, but owing to the non-receipt of some railway abstracts, the preliminary total for the districts differed from the final total by 468 persons.

The total cost of the Census enumerators was as follows:—

	R	a.	p.	R	a.	p.
I.—District Charges—						
Light ink, etc.	339	10	3			
Remuneration of Census officials . .	120	0	0			
Special travelling allowances . .	17	1	10			
Freight of schedules form, station, etc. .	13	12	10			
Total District Charges .				520	8	11
II.—Printing, etc.—						
Paper for schedules	378	13	11			
Printing and binding	357	8	5			
Despatching from Press . . .	78	11	7			
Total Printing ..				815	1	11
III.—Superintendence—						
Office establishment	95	12	3			
Contingencies	45	8	0			
Total Superintendence .				141	4	3
Total Cost Enumeration R				1,476	15	1

(Note.—Rupees 153-5-9 shown in accounts submitted to Comptroller were on account of schedules supplied to the Rajputana-Malwa Railway and are omitted from above cost of the Ajmere-Merwara Census.)

The Census of the Rajputana-Malwa Railway and the British Cantonments in Rajputana and Central India having been abstracted in the Ajmere office, a special staff was engaged, but superintendence, correspondence, etc., was done by the Ajmere staff, and a rateable deduction has therefore been made from the total cost of establishment under these heads calculated on the number abstracted.

A similar deduction has been made in the printing charges. This gives the following cost of abstraction :—

	R a. p.	R a. p.
Tabulation and Abstraction—		
Office furniture	72 0 0	
Office establishment	2,258 0 0	
Travelling allowance to and from office	41 0 c	
Freight of schedules	27 0 0	
Petty stationery and contingencies	130 0 0	
TOTAL OFFICE ESTABLISHMENT		2,528 0 0
Printing—		
Paper	359 0 0	
Printing, etc.	168 0 0	
Freight	389 0 0	
TOTAL PRINTING		916 0 0
Superintendence—		
Personal charges	802 0 0	
Contingencies	36 0 0	
TOTAL SUPERINTENDENCE		838 0 0
GRAND TOTAL		4,282 0 0

NOTE.—The total expenditure in the Ajmere office was R9,134-4-7, of which R3,298-5-10 is debited to Railways and cantonments, R594-4-4 of this being expenditure on enumeration, R2,523-10-2 on abstraction and R180-7-4 on superintendence.

The cost of printing this report is not included in the above.

The total cost of the Census was therefore—

(*a*) Enumeration	1,476 15 1
(*b*) Abstraction and compilation	3,444 0 0
(*c*) Superintendence	838 0 0
TOTAL	5,758 15 1

The total cost per 1,000 persons enumerated was R10-9-10. In 1881 the cost was for enumeration R1,519-0-0 and abstraction 1,112-9-11, no specially paid establishment having been employed.

The average number of abstractors and tabulators employed on the Hindi work was as follows :—

	Room Inspectors.	Abstractors, etc.
April	5	100
May	5	82
June	5	45
July	5	62
August	5	20

In addition to the above one Assistant Superintendent, two Branch Superintendents two record-keepers, and one correspondence and account clerk were employed.

The brunt of the work fell on the educational establishment and patwaris, who were employed, first of all, as supervisors and subsequently as abstractors, inspectors and tabulators. Deputy Inspector of Schools, Munshi Thakur Dass, was Assistant Superintendent, and conducted the Hindi portion of the work to its conclusion, in a most creditable manner.

Suggestions for future guidance.—The Nagri and Urdu editions of the schedule, forms and registers, in use in the North-West Provinces will probably be found suitable for Ajmere-Merwara, and a special translation or a special set of forms is unnecessary. The schedules should be bound in books of two sizes only, namely of 60 pages and 30 pages—that is, if the practice of entering one house only on each page is adhered to. The issue of two books to one enumerator gives rise to confusion. Abstraction should be done by a paid staff instead of by Patwaris and School Pandits. The interference with the Revenue and Educational work which ensues from their being brought into Ajmere for 3 or 4 months is not compensated for by the small expense saved. In the long run it would be more economical to employ a special staff.

TABLE I.—Area, Houses and Population.

DISTRICT.	Area in Square Miles.	NUMBER OF		OCCUPIED HOUSES.			POPULATION.								
							TOTAL.			MALES.			FEMALES.		
		TOWNS.	VILLAGES.	TOTAL.	TOWNS.	VILLAGES.	Total.	Towns.	Villages.	Total.	Towns.	Villages.	Total.	Towns.	Villages.
1	2	3	4	5	6	7	8	9	10	11	12	13	14	15	16
AJMERE	2,069·816	3	413	79,638	21,282	58,356	422,359	97,653	324,706	223,547	53,020	170,527	198,812	44,633	154,179
MERWARA	640·864	1	328	22,016	4,505	17,511	119,999	20,978	99,021	64,778	11,446	53,332	55,221	9,532	45,689
Total	2,710·680	4	741	101,654	25,787	75,867	542,358	118,631	423,727	288,325	64,466	223,859	254,033	54,165	199,868

TABLE II.—Variation in the enumerated Population since last Census.

DISTRICT OR STATE.	TOTAL.			MALES.			FEMALES.		
	1891.	1881.	Variation.	1891.	1881.	Variation.	1891.	1881.	Variation.
1	2	3	4	5	6	7	8	9	10
AJMERE	422,359	359,288	+ 63,071	223,547	192,669	+ 30,878	198,812	166,619	+ 32,193
MERWARA	119,999	101,434	+ 18,565	64,778	56,175	+ 8,603	55,221	45,259	+ 9,962
Total	542,358	460,722	+ 81,636	288,325	248,844	+ 39,481	254,033	211,878	+42,155

TABLE III.—Towns and Villages Classified by Population.

DISTRICT OR STATE.	Total number of Towns and Villages.	Total Population.	1—199.		200—499.		500—999.		1,000—1,999.		2,000—2,999.		3,000—4,999.		5,000—9,999.		10,000—14,999.		15,000—19,999.		20,000—49,999.		50,000 and over.	
			No.	Population.	No.	Population.	No.	Population.	No.	Population.	No.	Population.	No.	Population.	No.	Population.	No.	Population.	No.	Population.	No.	Population.	No.	Population.
1	2	3	4	5	6	7	8	9	10	11	12	13	14	15	16	17	18	19	20	21	22	23	24	25
Ajmere	416	422,359	69	8,986	139	45,296	116	81,574	59	81,153	15	38,167	10	38,670	6	37,960	...	...	...	...	1	21,710	1	68,843
Merwara	329	119,999	179	17,478	101	29,646	29	19,517	14	18,673	4	10,570	1	3,137	...	...	...	...	...	...	1	20,978	...	...
Total	745	542,358	248	26,464	240	74,942	145	101,091	73	99,826	19	48,737	11	41,807	6	37,960	...	...	...	...	2	42,688	1	68,843

TABLE IV.—Towns according to Population, compared with the preceding Census.

TOWN.	DISTRICT OR STATE.	Municipality, Suburbs or Cantonment.	TOTAL POPULATION.			MALES.			FEMALES.			NOTES (CHANGE IN AREAS, ETC.)
			1891.	1881.	Variation.	1891.	1881.	Variation.	1891.	1881.	Variation.	
1	2	3	4	5	6	7	8	9	10	11	12	13
Ajmere	Ajmere	Municipality	68,843	48,735	20,108	37,985	27,347	10,638	30,858	21,388	9,470	
Nasirabad	Ajmere	Cantonment	21,710	21,320	390	11,285	11,462	177	10,425	9,858	567	
Kekri	Ajmere	Municipality	7,100	6,119	981	3,750	3,081	669	3,350	3,038	312	
Beawar	Merwara	Ditto	20,978	15,829	5,149	11,446	8,859	2,587	9,532	6,970	2,562	
Total	...	...	118,631	92,003	26,628	64,466	50,749	13,717	54,165	41,254	12,911	

TABLE V.—Towns arranged territorially, with Population by Religion.

District.	Town.	Total Population. Total.	Total Population. Males.	Total Population. Females.	Hindu. Total.	Hindu. Males.	Hindu. Females.	Arya. Total.	Arya. Males.	Arya. Females.	Musalman. Total.	Musalman. Males.	Musalman. Females.	Christian. Total.	Christian. Males.	Christian. Females.	Jain. Total.	Jain. Males.	Jain. Females.	Sikh. Total.	Sikh. Males.	Sikh. Females.	Parsi. Total.	Parsi. Males.	Parsi. Females.	Jew. Total.	Jew. Males.	Jew. Females.	Unspecified. Total.	Unspecified. Males.	Unspecified. Females.
1	2	3	4	5	6	7	8	9	10	11	12	13	14	15	16	17	18	19	20	21	22	23	24	25	26	27	28	29	30	31	32
Ajmere	Ajmere	68,843	37,985	30,858	36,729	20,522	16,207	1,097	627	470	26,433	14,259	12,174	1,497	862	635	2,770	1,4[illegible]6	1,274	159	114	45	147	98	49	11	7	4	...	...	...
	Nasirabad	21,710	11,285	10,425	15,195	7,884	7,311	3	3	...	5,472	2,777	2,695	564	357	207	367	1[illegible]8	169	16	16	...	33	19	14	60	31	29	...	...	...
	Kekri	7,100	3,750	3,350	5,809	3,046	2,763	...	...	...	900	477	423	4	2	2	381	219	162	...	...	...	6	6	...	...	...	...	...	...	...
Merwara	Beawar	20,978	11,446	9,532	14,551	7,914	6,637	21	15	6	3,641	1,987	1,654	246	134	112	2,484	1,372	1,112	24	13	11	10	10	...	...	...	...	1	1	...
Total	...	118,631	64,466	54,165	72,284	39,366	32,918	1,121	645	476	36,446	19,500	16,946	2,311	1,355	956	6,002	3,285	2,717	199	143	56	196	133	63	71	38	33	1	1	...

TABLE VI.—Religion.

District.	Total Population. Total.	Total Population. Males.	Total Population. Females.	Hindus. Total.	Hindus. Males.	Hindus. Females.	Arya. Total.	Arya. Males.	Arya. Females.	Musalman. Total.	Musalman. Males.	Musalman. Females.	Christian. Total.	Christian. Males.	Christian. Females.	Jain. Total.	Jain. Males.	Jain. Females.	Sikh. Total.	Sikh. Males.	Sikh. Females.	Parsi. Total.	Parsi. Males.	Parsi. Females.	Jew. Total.	Jew. Males.	Jew. Females.	Unspecified. Total.	Unspecified. Males.	Unspecified. Females.
1	2	3	4	5	6	7	8	9	10	11	12	13	14	15	16	17	18	19	20	21	22	23	24	25	26	27	28	29	30	31
Ajmere	422,359	223,547	198,812	341,543	179,701	161,842	1,136	647	489	57,223	31,029	26,194	2,323	1,368	955	19,687	10,502	9,185	189	138	51	187	124	63	71	38	33	...	...	...
Merwara	119,999	64,778	55,221	95,288	50,514	44,774	21	15	6	17,042	10,101	6,941	360	199	161	7,252	3,924	3,328	24	13	11	11	11	...	...	...	...	1	[illegible]	...
Total	542,358	288,325	254,033	436,831	230,215	206,616	1,157	662	495	74,265	41,130	33,135	2,683	1,567	1,116	26,939	14,426	12,513	213	151	62	198	135	63	71	38	33	1	1	...

TABLE VII.—Ages by Religion.—Part A.—TOTAL POPULATION.

DISTRICT.	TOTAL POPULATION.			AGE PERIODS.															
				Under 1 Year.		1 Year.		2 Years.		3 Years.		4 Years.		Total 0–4		5–9		10–14	
	Total.	Males.	Females.	Males.	Females.	Males.	Females.	Males.	Females.	Males.	Females.	Males.	Females.	Males.	Females.	Males.	Females.	Males.	Females.
1	2	3	4	5	6	7	8	9	10	11	12	13	14	15	16	17	18	19	20
Ajmere	422,359	223,547	198,812	7,813	7,911	3,732	3,452	5,505	5,450	6,180	6,381	6,489	6,179	29,719	29,373	30,127	27,213	24,564	18,965
Merwara	119,999	64,778	55,221	2,115	2,137	1,188	1,183	1,725	1,670	2,006	1,941	1,977	1,890	9,011	8,821	10,041	8,811	8,030	5,957
Total .	542,358	288,325	254,033	9,928	10,048	4,920	4,635	7,230	7,120	8,186	8,322	8,466	8,069	38,730	38,194	40,168	36,024	32,594	24,922

DISTRICT.	AGE PERIODS.																			
	15–19		20–24		25–29		30–34		35–39		40–44		45–49		50–54		55–59		60 and over.	
	Males.	Females.	Males.	Females.	Males.	Females.	Males.	Females.	Males.	Females.	Males.	Females.	Males.	Females.	Males.	Females.	Males.	Females.	Males.	Females.
	21	22	23	24	25	26	27	28	29	30	31	32	33	34	35	36	37	38	39	40
Ajmere	19,059	15,597	17,081	16,535	19,860	17,146	21,800	18,705	12,878	10,490	16,968	15,503	8,164	5,766	10,588	10,233	3,122	2,413	9,617	10,873
Merwara	5,212	4,220	4,449	4,247	5,512	4,355	5,874	5,107	3,229	2,474	4,406	4,049	2,055	1,295	2,861	2,482	1,026	514	3,072	2,889
Total .	24,271	19,817	21,530	20,782	25,372	21,501	27,674	23,812	16,107	12,964	21,374	19,552	10,219	7,061	13,449	12,715	4,148	2,927	12,689	13,762

TABLE VII.—Ages by Religion.—Part B.—HINDUS AND ARYAS.

DISTRICT.	TOTAL POPULATION.			AGE PERIODS.															
				UNDER 1 YEAR.		1 YEAR.		2 YEARS.		3 YEARS.		4 YEARS.		TOTAL 0—4		5—9		10—14	
	TOTAL.	Males.	Females.	Males.	Females.	Males.	Females.	Males.	Females.	Males.	Females.	Males.	Females.	Males.	Females.	Males.	Females.	Males.	Females.
1	2	3	4	5	6	7	8	9	10	11	12	13	14	15	16	17	18	19	20
AJMERE	342,679	180,348	162,331	6,317	6,416	3,037	2,832	4,482	4,415	5,124	5,281	5,311	5,090	24,271	21,034	24,858	22,325	20,043	15,457
MERWARA . . .	95,309	50,529	44,780	1,652	1,635	928	912	1,325	1,324	1,558	1,536	1,543	1,474	7,006	6,881	7,885	7,044	6,301	4,764
Total .	437,988	230,877	207,111	7,969	8,051	3,965	3,744	5,807	5,739	6,682	6,817	6,854	6,564	31,277	30,915	32,743	29,369	26,344	20,221

DISTRICT.	AGE PERIODS.																			
	15—19		20—24		25—29		30—34		35—39		40—44		45—49		50—54		55—59		60 AND OVER.	
	Males.	Females.	Males.	Females.	Males.	Females.	Males.	Females.	Males.	Females.	Males.	Females.	Males.	Females.	Males.	Females.	Males.	Females.	Males.	Females.
	21	22	23	24	25	26	27	28	29	30	31	32	33	34	35	36	37	38	39	40
AJMERE	15,329	12,598	13,326	13,274	15,795	13,965	17,672	15,359	10,362	8,625	13,816	12,689	6,471	4,673	8,388	8,412	2,417	1,979	7,600	8,941
MERWARA . . .	3,991	3,419	3,364	3,470	4,326	3,517	4,689	4,254	2,480	2,021	3,537	3,425	1,485	1,034	2,283	2,084	775	404	2,407	2,463
Total .	19,320	16,017	16,690	16,744	20,121	17,482	22,361	19,613	12,842	10,646	17,353	16,114	7,956	5,707	10,671	10,496	3,192	2,383	10,007	11,404

TABLE VII.—Ages by Religion.—Part C.—MUSSALMANS.

DISTRICT.	TOTAL POPULATION.			AGE PERIODS.															
				UNDER 1 YEAR.		1 YEAR.		2 YEARS.		3 YEARS.		4 YEARS.		TOTAL. 0–4		5–9		10–14	
	TOTAL.	Males.	Females.	Males.	Females.	Males.	Females.	Males.	Females.	Males.	Females.	Males.	Females.	Males.	Females.	Males.	Females.	Males.	Females.
1	2	3	4	5	6	7	8	9	10	11	12	13	14	15	16	17	18	19	20
AJMERE	57,223	31,029	26,194	1,116	1,096	496	423	736	770	796	847	864	818	4,008	3,954	3,908	3,558	3,217	2,510
MERWARA	17,042	10,101	6,941	338	362	199	201	309	273	343	318	352	334	1,541	1,488	1,672	1,332	1,296	832
Total .	**74,265**	**41,130**	**33,135**	**1,454**	**1,458**	**695**	**624**	**1,045**	**1,043**	**1,139**	**1,165**	**1,216**	**1,152**	**5,549**	**5,442**	**5,580**	**4,890**	**4,518**	**3,342**

DISTRICT.	AGE PERIODS.																			
	15–19		20–24		25–29		30–34		35–39		40–44		45–49		50–54		55–59		60 AND OVER.	
	Males.	Females.	Males.	Females.	Males.	Females.	Males.	Females.	Males.	Females.	Males.	Females	Males.	Females.	Males.	Females.	Males.	Females.	Males.	Females.
	21	22	23	24	25	26	27	28	29	30	31	32	33	34	35	36	37	38	39	40
AJMERE	2,595	2,140	2,638	2,370	2,879	2 232	3,005	2 460	1,658	1,213	2,318	2,039	1,068	649	1,654	1,311	472	265	1,609	1,493
MERWARA	839	483	699	475	810	531	799	512	452	242	575	375	355	141	414	234	156	66	493	230
Total .	**3,434**	**2,623**	**3,337**	**2,845**	**3,689**	**2,763**	**3,804**	**2,972**	**2,110**	**1,455**	**2,893**	**2,414**	**1,423**	**790**	**2,068**	**1,545**	**628**	**331**	**2,102**	**1,723**

TABLE VII.—Ages by Religion.—Part D.—JAINS.

DISTRICT.	TOTAL POPULATION.			AGE PERIODS.																
				UNDER 1 YEAR.		1 YEAR.		2 YEARS.		3 YEARS.		4 YEARS.		TOTAL 0–4		5–9		10–14	
	TOTAL.	Males.	Females.	Males.	Females.	Males.	Females.	Males.	Females.	Males.	Females.	Males.	Females.	Males.	Females.	Males.	Females.	Males.	Females.
1	2	3	4	5	6	7	8	9	10	11	12	13	14	15	16	17	18	19	20
AJMERE	19,687	10,502	9,185	328	345	175	165	241	227	212	208	266	228	1,222	1,173	1,209	1,152	1,174	875
MERWARA	7,252	3,924	3,328	119	133	53	66	84	64	96	84	77	76	429	423	441	401	414	342
Total .	26,939	14,426	12,513	447	478	228	231	325	291	308	292	343	304	1,651	1,596	1,650	1,553	1,588	1,217

DISTRICT.	AGE PERIODS.																			
	15–19		20–24		25–29		30–34		35–39		40–44		45–49		50–54		55–59		60 AND OVER.	
	Males.	Females.	Males.	Females.	Males.	Females.	Males.	Females.	Males.	Females.	Males.	Females.	Males.	Females.	Males.	Females.	Males.	Females.	Males.	Females.
	21	22	23	24	25	26	27	28	29	30	31	32	33	34	35	36	37	38	39	40
AJMERE	990	789	876	765	953	832	949	786	745	585	752	726	554	423	493	493	209	162	376	424
MERWARA	371	309	367	284	348	289	353	317	285	203	284	246	210	118	160	161	93	42	169	193
Total .	1,361	1,098	1,243	1,049	1,301	1,121	1,302	1,103	1,030	788	1,036	972	764	541	653	654	302	204	545	617

TABLE VII.—Ages by Religion.—Part E.—CHRISTIANS.

DISTRICT.	TOTAL POPULATION.			AGE PERIODS.															
				UNDER 1 YEAR.		1 YEAR.		2 YEARS.		3 YEARS.		4 YEARS.		TOTAL 0—4.		5—9.		10—14.	
	TOTAL.	Males.	Females.	Males.	Females.	Males.	Females.	Males.	Females.	Males.	Females.	Males.	Females.	Males.	Females.	Males.	Females.	Males.	Females.
1	2	3	4	5	6	7	8	9	10	11	12	13	14	15	16	17	18	19	20
AJMERE . . .	2,323	1,368	955	47	50	21	27	39	33	42	37	41	37	190	184	125	155	107	105
MERWARA . . .	360	199	161	6	7	8	4	7	8	8	3	5	5	34	27	41	32	16	18
Total .	**2,683**	**1,567**	**1,116**	**53**	**57**	**29**	**31**	**46**	**41**	**50**	**40**	**46**	**42**	**224**	**211**	**166**	**187**	**123**	**123**

DISTRICT.	AGE PERIODS.																			
	15—19.		20—24.		25—29.		30—34.		35—39.		40—44.		45—49.		50—54.		55—59.		60 AND OVER.	
	Males.	Females.	Males.	Females.	Males.	Females.	Males.	Females.	Males.	Females.	Males.	Females.	Males.	Females.	Males.	Females.	Males.	Females.	Males.	Females.
	21	22	23	24	25	26	27	28	29	30	31	32	33	34	35	36	37	38	39	40
AJMERE . . .	116	61	194	108	199	104	139	87	93	54	61	42	55	19	41	14	19	7	29	15
MERWARA . . .	9	9	11	17	24	18	32	24	11	7	10	3	3	1	4	2	1	2	3	1
Total .	**125**	**70**	**205**	**125**	**223**	**122**	**171**	**111**	**104**	**61**	**71**	**45**	**58**	**20**	**45**	**16**	**20**	**9**	**32**	**16**

TABLE VII.—Ages by Religion.—Part F.—SIKHS.

DISTRICT.	TOTAL POPULATION.			AGE PERIODS.															
				UNDER 1 YEAR.		1 YEAR.		2 YEARS.		3 YEARS.		4 YEARS.		TOTAL 0—4.		5—9		10—14.	
	Total.	Males.	Females.	Males.	Females.	Males.	Females.	Males.	Females.	Males.	Females.	Males.	Females.	Males.	Females.	Males.	Females.	Males.	Females.
1	2	3	4	5	6	7	8	9	10	11	12	13	14	15	16	17	18	19	20
AJMERE . . .	189	138	51	2	1	...	1	2	3	1	3	1	3	6	11	5	6	10	4
MERWARA . . .	24	13	11	...	...	...	...	...	1	1	...	...	1	1	2	2	2	3	1
Total .	213	151	62	2	1	...	1	2	4	2	3	1	4	7	13	7	8	13	5

DISTRICT.	AGE PERIODS.																			
	15—19		20—24		25—29		30—34		35—39		40—44		45—49		50—54		55—59		60 AND OVER.	
	Males.	Females.	Males.	Females.	Males.	Females.	Males.	Females.	Males.	Females.	Males.	Females.	Males.	Females.	Males.	Females.	Females.	Females.	Males.	Females.
	21	22	23	24	25	26	27	28	29	30	31	32	33	34	35	36	37	38	39	40
AJMERE . . .	19	6	32	6	17	5	18	5	5	2	8	4	7	1	8	1	2	...	1	...
MERWARA . . .	1	...	...	1	3	...	...	...	1	1	...	...	1	1	...	1	1	...	...	2
Total .	20	6	32	7	20	5	18	5	6	3	8	4	8	2	8	2	3	...	1	2

TABLE VII.—Ages by Religion.—Part G.—PARSIS.

DISTRICT.	TOTAL POPULATION.			AGE PERIODS.															
				UNDER 1 YEAR.		1 YEAR.		2 YEARS.		3 YEARS.		4 YEARS.		TOTAL 0—4		5—9		10—14	
	TOTAL.	Males.	Females.	Males.	Females.	Males.	Females.	Males.	Females.	Males.	Females.	Males.	Females.	Males.	Females.	Males.	Females.	Males.	Females.
1	2	3	4	5	6	7	8	9	10	11	12	13	14	15	16	17	18	19	20
AJMERE . . .	187	124	63	1	1	1	...	3	2	4	4	4	2	13	9	14	12	9	9
MERWARA . . .	11	11	...	...	...	...	...	...	...	...	...	...	...	...	...	...	...	...	...
Total .	198	135	63	1	1	1	...	3	2	4	4	4	2	13	9	14	12	9	9

DISTRICT.	AGE PERIODS.																			
	15—19		20—24		25—29		30—34		35—39		40—44		45—49		50—54		55—59		60 AND OVER.	
	Males.	Females.	Males.	Females.	Males.	Females.	Males.	Females.	Males.	Females.	Males.	Females.	Males.	Females.	Males.	Females.	Males.	Females.	Males.	Females.
	21	22	23	24	25	26	27	28	29	30	31	32	33	34	35	36	37	38	39	40
AJMERE . . .	7	2	15	7	15	5	14	7	11	8	11	3	6	1	4	...	3	...	2	...
MERWARA . . .	1	...	8	...	1	...	...	...	...	...	...	...	1	...	...	...	...	...	...	...
Total .	8	2	23	7	16	5	14	7	11	8	11	3	7	1	4	...	3	...	2	...

TABLE VII.—Ages by Religion.—Part H.—JEWS.

DISTRICT.	TOTAL POPULATION.			AGE PERIODS.															
				UNDER 1 YEAR.		1 YEAR.		2 YEARS.		3 YEARS.		4 YEARS.		TOTAL 0–4		5–9		10–14	
	TOTAL.	Males.	Females.	Males.	Females.	Males.	Females.	Males.	Females.	Males.	Females.	Males.	Females.	Males.	Females.	Males.	Females.	Males.	Females.
1	2	3	4	5	6	7	8	9	10	11	12	13	14	15	16	17	18	19	20
AJMERE . . .	71	38	33	2	2	2	4	2	...	1	1	2	1	9	8	8	5	4	5
MERWARA . . .	...	...	...	...	...	...	...	...	...	...	...	...	...	...	...	...	...	...	...
Total .	71	38	33	2	2	2	4	2	...	1	1	2	1	9	8	8	5	4	5

DISTRICT.	AGE PERIODS.																			
	15–19		20–24		25–29		30–34		35–39		40–44		45–49		50–54		55–59		60 AND OVER.	
	Males.	Females.	Males.	Females.	Males.	Females.	Males.	Females.	Males.	Females.	Males.	Females.	Males.	Females.	Males.	Females.	Males.	Females.	Males.	Females.
	21	22	23	24	25	26	27	28	29	30	31	32	33	34	35	36	37	38	39	40
AJMERE . . .	3	1	...	5	2	3	3	1	4	3	2	...	3	...	...	2	...	...	...	...
MERWARA . . .	...	...	...	...	...	...	...	...	...	...	...	...	...	...	...	...	...	...	...	...
Total .	3	1	...	5	2	3	3	1	4	3	2	...	3	...	...	2	...	...	...	...

TABLE VIII.—Civil Condition by Religion and Age.—Part A.—TOTAL POPULATION.

DISTRICT.	TOTAL.			AGE PERIODS.																										
				0—4		5—9		10—14		15—19		20—24		25—29		30—34		35—39		40—44		45—49		50—54		55—59		60 AND OVER.	
	Total.	Males.	Females.	Males.	Females.	Males.	Females.	Males.	Females.	Males.	Females.	Males.	Females.	Males.	Females.	Males.	Females.	Males.	Females.	Males.	Females.	Males.	Females.	Males.	Females.	Males.	Females.	Males.	Females.	Males.	Females.
1	2	3	4	5	6	7	8	9	10	11	12	13	14	15	16	17	18	19	20	21	22	23	24	25	26	27	28	29	30
(1) UNMARRIED.																													
AJMERE . .	167,297	104,076	63,221	29,460	28,663	28,372	23,451	19,612	9,451	10,303	950	5,532	191	3,829	148	2,667	111	1,247	63	1,267	88	564	34	572	35	157	5	494	31
MERWARA .	57,460	35,442	22,018	8,980	8,746	9,878	8,376	7,366	4,246	3,818	476	2,063	49	1,542	38	861	38	253	15	291	16	89	3	127	8	43	2	131	5
Total .	224,757	139,518	85,239	38,440	37,409	38,250	31,827	26,978	13,697	14,121	1,426	7,595	240	5,371	186	3,528	149	1,500	78	1,558	104	653	37	699	43	200	7	625	36
(2) MARRIED.																													
AJMERE . .	210,760	107,448	103,312	238	696	1,673	3,694	4,835	9,376	8,559	14,392	11,173	15,780	15,307	15,967	18,059	16,268	10,763	8,475	14,062	9,806	6,528	3,087	8,043	3,723	2,263	730	5,945	1,318
MERWARA .	52,783	26,698	26,085	30	73	153	422	644	1,691	1,356	3,699	2,318	4,112	3,825	4,146	4,801	4,611	2,787	2,071	3,756	2,847	1,788	789	2,339	1,072	805	169	2,096	383
Total .	263,543	134,146	129,397	268	769	1,826	4,116	5,479	11,067	9,915	18,091	13,491	19,892	19,132	20,113	22,860	20,879	13,550	10,546	17,818	12,653	8,316	3,876	10,382	4,795	3,068	899	8,041	1,701
(3) WIDOWED.																													
AJMERE . .	44,302	12,023	32,279	21	14	82	68	117	138	197	255	376	564	724	1,031	1,074	2,326	868	1,952	1,639	5,609	1,072	2,645	1,973	6,475	702	1,678	3,178	9,524
MERWARA .	9,756	2,638	7,118	1	2	10	13	20	20	38	45	68	86	145	171	212	458	189	388	359	1,186	178	503	395	1,402	178	343	845	2,501
Total .	54,058	14,661	39,397	22	16	92	81	137	158	235	300	444	650	869	1,202	1,286	2,784	1,057	2,340	1,998	6,795	1,250	3,146	2,368	7,877	880	2,021	4,023	12,025

TABLE VIII.—Civil Condition by Religion and Age.—Part B.—HINDUS AND ARYAS.

(1) UNMARRIED.

DISTRICT.	TOTAL.			AGE PERIOD. 0—4		5—9		10—14		15—19		20—24	
	Total.	Males.	Females.	Males.	Females.	Males.	Females.	Males.	Females.	Males.	Females.	Males.	Females.
1	2	3	4	5	6	7	8	9	10	11	12	13	14
Ajmere . .	133,266	82,804	50,462	24,046	23,386	23,240	18,898	15,604	7,217	7,890	589	3,964	95
Merwara .	44,802	27,537	17,265	6,979	6,823	7,739	6,669	5,732	3,297	2,944	353	1,577	36
Total .	178,068	110,341	67,727	31,025	30,209	30,979	25,567	21,336	10,514	10,834	942	5,541	131

DISTRICT.	25—29		30—34		35—39		40—44		45—49		50—54		55—59		60 AND OVER.	
	Males.	Females.	Males.	Females.	Males.	Females.	Males.	Females.	Males.	Females.	Males.	Females.	Males.	Females.	Males.	Females.
1	15	16	17	18	19	20	21	22	23	24	25	26	27	28	29	30
Ajmere . .	2,775	77	2,068	58	950	39	956	45	416	20	416	23	112	2	367	13
Merwara .	1,224	31	692	25	189	8	209	12	54	2	85	5	26	1	87	3
Total .	3,999	108	2,760	83	1,139	47	1,165	57	470	22	501	28	138	3	454	16

(2) MARRIED.

DISTRICT.	Total.	Males.	Females.	0—4 Males.	0—4 Females.	5—9 Males.	5—9 Females.	10—14 Males.	10—14 Females.	15—19 Males.	15—19 Females.	20—24 Males.	20—24 Females.
Ajmere . .	173,533	87,988	85,545	206	638	1,543	3,370	4,332	8,132	7,276	11,819	9,070	12,747
Merwara .	42,771	20,993	21,778	26	56	137	365	552	1,449	1,019	3,033	1,737	3,375
Total .	216,304	108,981	107,323	232	694	1,680	3,735	4,884	9,581	8,295	14,852	10,807	16,122

DISTRICT.	25—29 Males.	25—29 Females.	30—34 Males.	30—34 Females.	35—39 Males.	35—39 Females.	40—44 Males.	40—44 Females.	45—49 Males.	45—49 Females.	50—54 Males.	50—54 Females.	55—59 Males.	55—59 Females.	60 and over Males.	60 and over Females.
Ajmere . .	12,435	13,075	14,753	13,448	8,720	7,019	11,557	8,065	5,180	2,531	6,448	3,043	1,771	613	4,688	1,450
Merwara .	2,992	3,384	3,827	3,883	2,143	1,732	3,040	2,464	1,306	637	1,910	926	627	138	1,677	336
Total .	15,427	16,459	18,580	17,331	10,863	8,751	14,597	10,529	6,495	3,168	8,358	3,969	2,398	751	6,365	1,381

(3) WIDOWED.

DISTRICT.	Total.	Males.	Females.	0—4 Males.	0—4 Females.	5—9 Males.	5—9 Females.	10—14 Males.	10—14 Females.	15—19 Males.	15—19 Females.	20—24 Males.	20—24 Females.
Ajmere . .	35,880	9,556	26,324	19	10	75	57	107	108	163	190	292	432
Merwara .	7,736	1,999	5,737	1	2	9	10	17	18	28	33	50	59
Total .	43,616	11,555	32,061	20	12	84	67	124	126	191	223	342	491

DISTRICT.	25—29 Males.	25—29 Females.	30—34 Males.	30—34 Females.	35—39 Males.	35—39 Females.	40—44 Males.	40—44 Females.	45—49 Males.	45—49 Females.	50—54 Males.	50—54 Females.	55—59 Males.	55—59 Females.	60 and over Males.	60 and over Females.
Ajmere . .	585	813	851	1,853	692	1,567	1,303	4,579	866	2,122	1,524	5,345	534	1,364	2,545	7,883
Merwara .	110	102	170	346	148	281	288	949	125	395	288	1,153	122	265	643	2,124
Total .	695	915	1,021	2,199	840	1,848	1,591	5,528	991	2,517	1,812	6,499	656	1,629	3,188	10,007

TABLE VIII.—Civil Condition by Religion and Age.—Part C.—MUSSALMANS.

DISTRICT.	TOTAL.			AGE PERIODS.																									
				0—4		5—9		10—14		15—19		20—24		25—29		30—34		35—39		40—44		45—49		50—54		55—59		60 AND OVER.	
	Total.	Males.	Females.	Males.	Females.	Males.	Females.	Males.	Females.	Males.	Females.	Males.	Females.	Males.	Females.	Males.	Females.	Males.	Females.	Males.	Females.	Males.	Females.	Males.	Females.	Males.	Females.	Males.	Females.
1	2	3	4	5	6	7	8	9	10	11	12	13	14	15	16	17	18	19	20	21	22	23	24	25	26	27	28	29	30
(1) UNMARRIED.																													
AJMERE	24,132	14,865	9,267	3,982	3,895	3,778	3,250	2,829	1,568	1,710	287	1,052	65	633	61	347	44	136	20	162	35	55	12	76	12	22	3	83	15
MERWARA	9,328	5,780	3,548	1,537	1,473	1,655	1,280	1,218	659	613	95	318	10	205	6	110	10	20	7	33	3	15	...	21	3	6	1	29	1
Total	33,460	20,645	12,815	5,519	5,368	5,433	4,530	4,047	2,227	2,323	382	1,370	75	838	67	457	54	156	27	195	38	70	12	97	15	28	4	112	16
(2) MARRIED.																													
AJMERE	27,521	14,469	13,052	25	56	123	300	379	917	858	1,819	1,514	2,220	2,138	2,045	2,493	2,141	1,419	998	1,943	1,338	893	367	1,265	541	362	77	1,057	233
MERWARA	6,771	3,990	2,781	4	15	16	52	77	171	220	384	370	458	582	504	664	470	415	199	508	266	326	103	342	106	127	21	339	32
Total	34,292	18,459	15,833	29	71	139	352	456	1,088	1,078	2,203	1,884	2,678	2,720	2,549	3,157	2,611	1,834	1,197	2,451	1,604	1,219	470	1,607	647	489	98	1,396	265
(3) WIDOWED.																													
AJMERE	5,570	1,695	3,875	1	3	7	8	9	25	27	34	72	85	108	126	165	275	103	195	213	666	120	270	313	758	88	185	469	1,245
MERWARA	943	331	612	...	...	1	...	1	2	6	4	11	7	23	21	25	32	17	36	34	106	14	38	51	125	23	44	125	197
Total	6,513	2,026	4,487	1	3	8	8	10	27	33	38	83	92	131	147	190	307	120	231	247	772	134	308	364	883	111	229	594	1,442

TABLE VIII.—Civil Condition by Religion and Age.—Part D.—JAINS.

DISTRICT.	TOTAL.			AGE PERIOD.																									
				0—4		5—9		10—14		15—16		20—24		25—29		30—34		35—39		40—44		45—49		50—54		55—59		60 AND OVER.	
	Total.	Males.	Females.	Males.	Females.	Males.	Females.	Males.	Females.	Males.	Females.	Males.	Females.	Males.	Females.	Males.	Females.	Males.	Females.	Males.	Females.	Males.	Females.	Males.	Females.	Males.	Females.	Males.	Females.
1	2	3	4	5	6	7	8	9	10	11	12	13	14	15	16	17	18	19	20	21	22	23	24	25	26	27	28	29	30
(1) UNMARRIED.																													
Ajmere	8,320	5,408	2,912	1,214	1,170	1,202	1,126	1,056	545	575	44	332	7	289	4	213	1	154	3	144	8	86	2	78	...	21	...	44	2
Merwara	3,104	1,985	1,119	429	422	441	393	397	272	251	24	156	3	101	1	54	1	42	...	49	1	20	1	19	...	11	...	15	1
Total	11,424	7,393	4,031	1,643	1,592	1,643	1,519	1,453	817	826	68	488	10	390	5	267	2	196	3	193	9	106	3	97	...	32	...	59	3
(2) MARRIED.																													
Ajmere	8,625	4,375	4,250	7	2	7	23	118	325	408	714	532	711	635	739	683	591	527	396	496	367	389	176	289	132	108	38	176	36
Merwara	3,084	1,636	1,448	...	1	...	5	15	70	116	277	205	261	235	240	283	237	219	132	198	115	151	47	86	40	50	9	78	14
Total	11,709	6,011	5,698	7	3	7	28	133	395	524	991	737	972	870	979	966	828	746	528	694	482	540	223	375	172	158	47	254	50
(3) WIDOWED.																													
Ajmere	2,742	719	2,023	1	1	...	3	...	5	7	31	12	47	29	89	53	194	64	186	112	351	79	245	126	361	80	124	156	386
Merwara	1,064	303	761	...	...	...	3	2	...	4	8	6	20	12	48	16	79	24	71	37	130	39	70	55	121	32	33	76	178
Total	3,806	1,022	2,784	1	1	...	6	2	5	11	39	18	67	41	137	69	273	88	257	149	481	118	315	181	482	112	157	232	564

TABLE VIII.—Civil Condition by Religion and Age—Part (E).—CHRISTIANS.

DISTRICT.	Total.			Age Periods.																									
				0—4		5—9		10—14		15—19		20—24		25—29		30—34		35—39		40—44		45—49		50—54		55—59		60 and over.	
	Total.	Males.	Females.	Males.	Females.	Males.	Females.	Males.	Females.	Males.	Females.	Males.	Females.	Males.	Females.	Males.	Females.	Males.	Females.	Males.	Females.	Males.	Females.	Males.	Females.	Males.	Females.	Males.	Females.
1	2	3	4	5	6	7	8	9	10	11	12	13	14	15	16	17	18	19	20	21	22	23	24	25	26	27	28	29	30
(1) UNMARRIED.																													
Ajmere	1,384	872	512	190	184	125	155	104	104	109	29	170	24	118	6	35	8	6	1	5	...	7	...	2	...	1	...	...	1
Merwara	208	127	81	34	26	41	32	16	17	9	4	8	...	11	...	4	2	2	...	...	...	...	...	2	...	...	...	...	...
Total	1,592	999	598	224	210	166	187	120	121	118	33	178	24	129	6	39	10	8	1	5	...	7	...	4	...	1	...	...	1
(2) MARRIED.																													
Ajmere	839	451	388	...	...	...	...	2	1	7	32	24	84	79	95	101	75	80	49	46	29	41	11	30	6	18	2	23	4
Merwara	142	68	74	...	1	...	...	...	1	...	5	2	17	13	18	27	21	9	7	10	2	3	1	1	...	1	1	2	...
Total	981	519	462	...	1	...	...	2	2	7	37	26	101	92	113	128	96	89	56	56	31	44	12	31	6	19	3	25	4
(3) WIDOWED.																													
Ajmere	100	45	55	...	...	...	...	1	...	...	...	...	...	2	3	3	4	7	4	10	13	7	8	9	8	...	5	6	10
Merwara	10	4	6	...	...	...	...	...	...	...	...	1	...	...	...	1	1	...	...	...	1	...	...	1	2	...	1	1	1
Total	110	49	61	...	...	...	...	1	...	...	...	1	...	2	3	4	5	7	4	10	14	7	8	10	10	...	6	7	11

TABLE VIII.—Civil Condition by Religion and Age.—Part (F).—SIKHS.

DISTRICT.	TOTAL.			AGE PERIODS. 0—4		5—9		10—14		15—19		20—24		25—29		30—34		35—39		40—44		45—49		50—54		55—59		60 AND OVER.	
	Total.	Males.	Females.	Males.	Females.	Males.	Females.	Males.	Females.	Males.	Females.	Males.	Females.	Males.	Females.	Males.	Females.	Males.	Females.	Males.	Females.	Males.	Females.	Males.	Females.	Males.	Females.	Males.	Females.
1	2	3	4	5	6	7	8	9	10	11	12	13	14	15	16	17	18	19	20	21	22	23	24	25	26	27	28	29	30
(1) UNMARRIED.																													
Ajmere . .	67	47	20	6	11	5	5	7	4	12	...	8	...	8	...	1	...	...	...	...	...	...	...	...	...	...	...	...	...
Merwara . .	13	8	5	1	2	2	2	3	1	1	...	...	...	1	...	...	...	...	...	...	...	...	...	...	...	...	...	...	...
Total .	80	55	25	7	13	7	7	10	5	13	...	8	...	9	...	1	...	...	...	...	...	...	...	...	...	...	...	...	...
(2) MARRIED.																													
Ajmere . .	118	88	30	...	...	...	1	3	...	7	6	24	6	9	5	15	5	5	2	8	4	7	1	8	...	2	...	...	...
Merwara . .	8	4	4	...	...	...	...	...	...	...	...	...	1	2	...	...	...	1	1	...	...	1	1	...	...	...	...	...	1
Total .	126	92	34	...	...	...	1	3	...	7	6	24	7	11	5	15	5	6	3	8	4	8	2	8	...	2	...	...	1
(3) WIDOWED.																													
Ajmere . .	4	3	1	...	...	...	...	...	...	...	...	...	...	...	...	2	...	...	...	...	...	...	...	...	1	...	...	1	...
Merwara . .	3	1	2	...	...	...	...	...	...	...	...	...	...	...	...	...	...	...	...	...	...	...	...	...	1	1	...	...	1
Total .	7	4	3	...	...	...	...	...	...	...	...	...	...	...	...	2	...	...	...	...	...	...	...	...	2	1	...	1	1

TABLE VIII.—Civil Condition by Religion and Age.—Part (G).—PARSIS.

DISTRICT.	TOTAL.			AGE PERIOD.																									
				0—4		5—9		10—14		15—19		20—24		25—29		30—34		35—39		40—44		45—49		50—54		55—59		60 AND OVER.	
	Total.	Males.	Females.	Males.	Females.	Males.	Females.	Males.	Females.	Males.	Females.	Males.	Females.	Males.	Females.	Males.	Females.	Males.	Females.	Males.	Females.	Males.	Females.	Males.	Females.	Males.	Females.	Males.	Females.
1	2	3	4	5	6	7	8	9	10	11	12	13	14	15	16	17	18	19	20	21	22	23	24	25	26	27	28	29	30
(1).—UNMARRIED.																													
Ajmere . .	86	56	30	13	9	14	12	8	8	4	1	6	...	6	...	3	...	1	...	...	...	...	...	...	...	1	...	...	...
Merwara . .	4	4	...	...	...	...	...	...	...	...	...	4	...	...	...	...	...	...	...	...	...	...	...	...	...	...	...	...	...
Total .	90	60	30	13	9	14	12	8	8	4	1	10	...	6	...	3	...	1	...	...	...	...	...	...	...	1	...	...	...
(2).—MARRIED.																													
Ajmere . .	96	63	33	...	...	...	...	1	1	3	1	9	7	9	5	11	7	8	8	10	3	6	1	3	...	2	...	1	...
Merwara . .	7	7	...	...	...	...	...	...	...	1	...	4	...	1	...	...	...	...	...	...	...	1	...	...	...	...	...	...	...
Total .	103	70	33	...	...	...	...	1	1	4	1	13	7	10	5	11	7	8	8	10	3	7	1	3	...	2	...	1	...
(3).—WIDOWED.																													
Ajmere . .	5	5	...	...	...	...	...	...	...	...	...	...	...	...	...	...	...	2	...	1	...	...	...	1	...	...	...	1	...
Merwara . .	...	...	...	...	...	...	...	...	...	...	...	...	...	...	...	...	...	...	...	...	...	...	...	...	...	...	...	...	...
Total .	5	5	...	...	...	...	...	...	...	...	...	...	...	...	...	...	...	2	...	1	...	...	...	1	...	...	...	1	...

TABLE VIII.—Civil Condition by Religion and Age.—Part (H).—JEWS.

DISTRICT.	TOTAL.			AGE PERIODS.																									
				0—4		5—9		10—14		15—19		20—24		25—29		30—34		35—39		40—44		45—49		50—54		55—59		60 AND OVER.	
	TOTAL.	Males.	Females.	Males.	Females.	Males.	Females.	Males.	Females.	Males.	Females.	Males.	Females.	Males.	Females.	Males.	Females.	Males.	Females.	Males.	Females.	Males.	Females.	Males.	Females.	Males.	Females.	Males.	Females.
1	2	3	4	5	6	7	8	9	10	11	12	13	14	15	16	17	18	19	20	21	22	23	24	25	26	27	28	29	30
(1) UNMARRIED.																													
AJMERE	42	24	18	9	8	8	5	4	5	3	...	...	...	...	...	...	...	...	...	...	...	...	...	...	...	...	...	...	...
MERWARA	...	...	...	...	...	...	...	...	...	...	...	...	...	...	...	...	...	...	...	...	...	...	...	...	...	...	...	...	...
Total	42	24	18	9	8	8	5	4	5	3	...	...	...	...	...	...	...	...	...	...	...	...	...	...	...	...	...	...	...
(2) MARRIED.																													
AJMERE	28	14	14	...	...	...	...	...	...	...	1	...	5	2	3	3	1	4	3	2	...	3	...	...	1	...	...	...	...
MERWARA	...	...	...	...	...	...	...	...	...	...	...	...	...	...	...	...	...	...	...	...	...	...	...	...	...	...	...	...	...
Total	28	14	14	...	...	...	...	...	...	...	1	...	5	2	3	3	1	4	3	2	...	3	...	...	1	...	...	...	...
(3) WIDOWED.																													
AJMERE	1	...	1	...	...	...	...	...	...	...	...	...	...	...	...	...	...	...	...	...	...	...	...	...	1	...	...	...	...
MERWARA	...	...	...	...	...	...	...	...	...	...	...	...	...	...	...	...	...	...	...	...	...	...	...	...	...	...	...	...	...
Total	1	...	1	...	...	...	...	...	...	...	...	...	...	...	...	...	...	...	...	...	...	...	...	...	1	...	...	...	...

TABLE IX.—Education by Religion and Age.—Part A.—TOTAL POPULATION.

DISTRICT.	TOTAL POPULATION.			TOTAL BY EDUCATION.						AGE PERIODS.																							
										0–14								15–24								25 and over.							
				Learning		Literate.		Illiterate.		Total.		Learning.		Literate.		Illiterate.		Total.		Learning.		Literate.		Illiterate.		Total.		Learning.		Literate.		Illiterate.	
	Total.	Males.	Females.	Males.	Females.	Males.	Females.	Males.	Females.	Males.	Females.	Males.	Females.	Males.	Females.	Males.	Females.	Males.	Females.	Males.	Females.	Males.	Females.	Males.	Females.	Males.	Females.	Males.	Females.	Males.	Females.	Males.	Females.
1	2	3	4	5	6	7	8	9	10	11	12	13	14	15	16	17	18	19	20	21	22	23	24	25	26	27	28	29	30	31	32	33	34
Ajmere	422,359	223,547	198,812	4,877	411	26,522	1,387	192,148	197,014	84,410	75,551	3,973	378	1,742	123	78,695	75,050	36,140	32,132	823	17	6,284	381	29,033	31,734	102,997	91,129	81	16	18,496	883	84,420	90,230
Merwara	119,999	64,778	55,221	1,302	59	5,592	153	57,884	55,009	27,082	23,589	1,069	49	270	10	25,743	23,530	9,661	8,467	203	4	1,334	45	8,124	8,418	28,035	23,165	30	6	3,988	98	24,017	23,061
Total	542,358	288,325	254,033	6,179	470	32,114	1,540	250,032	252,023	111,492	99,140	5,042	427	2,012	133	104,438	98,580	45,801	40,599	1,026	21	7,618	426	37,157	40,152	131,032	114,294	111	22	22,484	981	108,437	113,291

Part B.—HINDUS AND ARYAS.

DISTRICT.	2	3	4	5	6	7	8	9	10	11	12	13	14	15	16	17	18	19	20	21	22	23	24	25	26	27	28	29	30	31	32	33	34
Ajmere	342,679	180,348	162,331	2,986	123	16,312	696	161,050	161,512	69,172	61,816	2,338	102	977	54	65,857	61,660	28,655	25,872	590	9	3,825	198	24,240	25,665	82,521	74,643	58	12	11,510	444	70,953	74,187
Merwara	95,309	50,529	44,780	635	16	2,675	38	47,219	44,726	21,192	18,689	495	9	117	2	20,580	18,678	7,355	6,889	127	3	629	10	6,599	6,876	21,982	19,202	13	4	1,929	26	20,040	19,172
Total	437,988	230,877	207,111	3,621	139	18,987	734	208,269	206,238	90,364	80,505	2,833	111	1,094	56	86,437	80,338	36,010	32,761	717	12	4,454	208	30,839	32,541	104,503	93,845	71	16	13,439	470	90,993	93,359

Part C.—MUSSALMANS.

DISTRICT.	2	3	4	5	6	7	8	9	10	11	12	13	14	15	16	17	18	19	20	21	22	23	24	25	26	27	28	29	30	31	32	33	34
Ajmere	57,223	31,029	26,194	806	49	2,746	121	27,477	26,024	11,133	10,022	646	47	117	17	10,370	9,958	5,233	4,510	146	...	628	37	4,459	4,473	14,663	11,662	14	2	2,001	67	12,648	11,593
Merwara	17,042	10,101	6,941	170	3	431	5	9,500	6,933	4,509	3,652	131	2	12	...	4,366	3,650	1,538	958	35	1	87	5	1,416	952	4,054	2,331	4	..	332	...	3,718	2,331
Total	74,265	41,130	33,135	976	52	3,177	126	36,977	32,957	15,642	13,674	777	49	129	17	14,736	13,608	6,771	5,468	181	1	715	42	5,875	5,425	18,717	13,993	18	2	2,333	67	16,366	13,924

Part D.—JAINS.

DISTRICT.	2	3	4	5	6	7	8	9	10	11	12	13	14	15	16	17	18	19	20	21	22	23	24	25	26	27	28	29	30	31	32	33	34
Ajmere	19,687	10,502	9,185	841	11	6,436	120	3,225	9,054	3,605	3,200	774	9	600	14	2,231	3,177	1,866	1,554	60	1	1,534	16	272	1,537	5,031	4,431	7	1	4,302	90	722	4,340
Merwara	7,252	3,924	3,328	445	5	2,382	32	1,097	3,291	1,284	1,166	400	3	139	1	745	1,162	738	593	40	...	591	5	107	588	1,902	1,569	5	2	1,652	26	245	1,541
Total	26,939	14,426	12,513	1,286	16	8,818	152	4,322	12,345	4,889	4,366	1,174	12	739	15	2,976	4,339	2,604	2,147	100	1	2,125	21	379	2,125	6,933	6,000	12	3	5,954	116	967	5,881

TABLE IX.—Education by Religion and Age.—Part E.—CHRISTIANS.

DISTRICT.	Total Population: Total.	Total Population: Males.	Total Population: Females.	Total by Education: Learning: Males.	Learning: Females.	Literate: Males.	Literate: Females.	Illiterate: Males.	Illiterate: Females.	0–14 Total: Males.	0–14 Total: Females.	0–14 Learning: Males.	0–14 Learning: Females.	0–14 Literate: Males.	0–14 Literate: Females.	0–14 Illiterate: Males.	0–14 Illiterate: Females.	15–24 Total: Males.	15–24 Total: Females.	15–24 Learning: Males.	15–24 Learning: Females.	15–24 Literate: Males.	15–24 Literate: Females.	15–24 Illiterate: Males.	15–24 Illiterate: Females.	25 and over Total: Males.	25 and over Total: Females.	25 and over Learning: Males.	25 and over Learning: Females.	25 and over Literate: Males.	25 and over Literate: Females.	25 and over Illiterate: Males.	25 and over Illiterate: Females.
1	2	3	4	5	6	7	8	9	10	11	12	13	14	15	16	17	18	19	20	21	22	23	24	25	26	27	28	29	30	31	32	33	34
Part E.—CHRISTIANS.																																	
Ajmere	2,333	1,368	955	209	212	872	415	287	328	422	444	184	206	37	32	201	206	310	169	23	6	260	123	27	40	636	342	2	...	575	260	59	82
Merwara	360	199	161	52	35	93	78	54	48	91	77	43	35	2	7	46	35	20	26	1	...	18	25	1	1	88	58	8	...	73	46	7	12
Total	2,683	1,567	1,116	261	247	965	493	341	376	513	521	227	241	39	39	247	241	330	195	24	6	278	148	28	41	724	400	10	...	648	306	66	94
Part F.—SIKHS.																																	
Ajmere	189	138	51	6	...	50	5	82	46	21	21	5	...	...	1	16	20	51	12	1	...	15	1	35	11	66	18	...	...	35	3	31	15
Merwara	24	13	11	...	...	...	...	13	11	6	5	...	...	...	...	6	5	1	1	...	...	...	...	1	1	6	5	...	...	...	...	6	5
Total	213	151	62	6	...	50	5	95	57	27	26	5	...	...	1	22	25	52	13	1	...	15	1	36	12	72	23	...	...	35	3	37	20
Part G.—PARSIS.																																	
Ajmere	187	124	63	22	14	83	20	19	29	36	30	19	12	4	1	13	17	22	9	...	1	19	4	...	4	66	24	...	1	60	15	6	8
Merwara	11	11	...	..	...	11	...	..	...	...	...	...	..	...	...	...	...	9	...	...	...	9	...	...	...	2	...	...	...	2	...	...	...
Total	198	135	63	22	14	94	20	19	29	36	30	19	12	4	1	13	17	31	9	3	1	28	4	...	4	68	24	...	1	62	1 5	6	8
Part H.—JEWS.																																	
Ajmere	71	38	33	7	2	23	10	8	21	21	18	7	2	7	4	7	12	3	6	...	...	3	2	...	4	14	9	...	...	13	4	1	5
Merwara	...	...	...	...	...	...	...	...	...	...	...	...	...	...	...	...	...	...	...	...	...	...	...	...	...	...	...	...	...	...	...	...	...
Total	71	38	33	7	2	23	10	8	21	21	18	7	2	7	4	7	12	3	6	...	...	3	2	...	4	14	9	...	...	13	4	1	5

TABLE X.—Parent Tongue.

Group.	Language.	Total.			Ajmere.			Merwara.		
		Total.	Males.	Females.	Total.	Males.	Females.	Total.	Males.	Females.
1	2	3	4	5	6	7	8	9	10	11
A.—Vernaculars of India.	Ajmeri	113,168	60,226	52,942	111,534	59,539	51,995	1,634	687	947
	Merwari	87,298	47,518	39,780	,123	1,096	1,027	85,175	46,422	38,753
	Marwari	228,867	120,590	108,277	208,667	110,049	98,618	20,200	10,541	9,659
	Meywari	29,429	15,112	14,317	24,137	12,394	11,743	5,292	2,718	2,574
	Dundhari	27,309	12,570	14,739	23,636	10,577	13,059	3,673	1,993	1,680
	Mewati	1,631	915	716	1,474	848	626	157	67	90
	Haraoti	959	464	495	945	452	493	14	12	2
	Hindi	2,634	1,481	1,153	2,077	1,190	887	557	291	266
	Total Vernaculars of the Province	491,295	258,876	232,419	374,593	196,145	178,448	116,702	62,731	53,971
	Hindustani	41,334	23,553	17,781	38,924	22,065	16,859	2,410	1,488	92
	Purbi	2,783	1,648	1,135	2,253	1,335	918	530	313	217
	Madrassi	128	76	52	128	76	52	...	...	...
	Tamil	6	3	3	6	3	3	...	...	...
	Telagu	55	30	25	49	27	22	6	3	3
	Uria	1	1	...	...	...	...	1	1	...
	Marathi	1,365	856	509	1,345	841	504	20	15	5
	Malwi	335	169	166	277	132	145	58	37	1
	Bengali	352	214	138	341	206	135	11	8	3
	Gujrati	1,484	886	598	1,407	825	582	77	61	16
	Sindhi	7	5	2	6	5	1	1	...	1
	Panjabi	1,154	754	400	1,041	681	360	113	73	40
	Dakani	238	130	108	212	110	102	26	20	6
	Kashmiri	35	20	15	33	18	15	2	2	...
	Total A	540,572	287,221	253,351	420,615	222,469	198,146	119,957	64,752	55,205
B.—Vernaculars of Countries beyond India.	Nepali	12	11	1	11	10	1	1	1	...
	Pushtu	84	79	5	79	74	5	5	5	...
	Persian	88	87	1	84	83	1	4	4	...
	Arabic	10	10	...	9	9	...	1	1	...
	Biluchi	2	2	...	2	2	...	...	...	...
	Chinese	5	5	...	5	5	...	...	...	...
	Hebrew	11	7	4	11	7	4	...	...	...
	Total B	212	201	11	201	190	11	11	11	...
C.—European Languages.	English	1,429	804	625	1,399	790	609	30	14	16
	French	2	...	2	2	...	2	...	...	...
	German	2	1	1	1	...	1	1	1	...
	Portuguese	139	98	41	139	98	41	...	...	...
	Italian	1	...	1	1	...	1	...	...	...
	Danish	1	...	1	1	...	1	...	...	...
	Total C	1,574	903	671	1,543	888	655	31	15	16
	Total	542,358	288,325	254,033	422,359	223,547	198,812	119,999	64,778	55,221

TABLE XI.—Birth-place.

Group.	District, State, Country or Province of Birth.	TOTAL. Total.	TOTAL. Males.	TOTAL. Females.	DISTRICT. Ajmere. Total.	DISTRICT. Ajmere. Males.	DISTRICT. Ajmere. Females.	DISTRICT. Merwara. Total.	DISTRICT. Merwara. Males.	DISTRICT. Merwara. Females.
1	2	3	4	5	6	7	8	9	10	11
A.—Districts and States within the Province.	Ajmere	338,047	183,596	154,451	331,009	180,029	150,980	7,038	3,567	3,471
	Merwara	95,617	53,025	42,592	2,447	1,448	999	93,170	51,577	41,593
	Kishenghur	7,556	2,695	4,861	7,422	2,646	4,776	134	49	85
	Jaipur	24,730	10,488	14,242	22,428	9,312	13,116	2,302	1,176	1,126
	Marwar	25,344	12,553	12,791	17,785	7,508	10,277	7,559	5,045	2,514
	Meywar	16,912	5,010	11,902	9,784	3,180	6,604	7,128	1,830	5,298
	Tonk	412	160	252	322	145	177	90	15	75
	Alwar	1,618	998	620	1,392	852	540	226	146	80
	Bikanir	145	104	41	117	96	21	28	8	20
	Bharatpur	1,892	1,148	744	1,860	1,125	735	32	23	9
	Sirohi	27	14	13	25	14	11	2	...	2
	Dolpur	36	18	18	19	11	8	17	7	10
	Karauli	43	26	17	24	15	9	19	11	8
	Kotah	2,087	1,228	859	2,054	1,208	846	33	20	13
	Bundi	478	105	373	475	102	373	3	3	...
	Jhallawar	42	21	21	32	20	12	10	1	9
	Jasalmir	1	...	1	1	...	1	...	...	...
	Partabgarh	14	12	2	14	12	2	...	...	...
	Rajputana	170	127	43	169	126	43	1	1	...
	Total A.	515,171	271,328	243,843	397,379	207,849	189,530	117,792	63,479	54,313
B.—Provinces and States of India beyond the Province.	North-West Provinces.	16,483	10,274	6,209	16,206	10,067	6,139	277	207	70
	Oude	1,204	817	387	1,099	746	353	105	71	34
	Punjab	2,540	1,725	815	1,774	1,243	531	766	482	284
	Bengal	979	477	502	478	275	203	501	202	299
	Bombay	1,332	876	456	1,313	859	454	19	17	2
	Gujrat	720	446	274	648	397	251	72	49	23
	Central India	1,940	1,069	871	1,714	957	757	226	112	114
	Madras	105	59	46	105	59	46	...	...	...
	Deccan	915	581	334	793	499	294	122	82	40
	Central Provinces	208	120	88	208	120	88	...	...	...
	Burma	4	2	2	3	2	1	1	...	1
	India (unspecified)	213	134	79	115	73	42	98	61	37
	Total B.	26,643	16,580	10,063	24,456	15,297	9,159	2,187	1,283	904
C.—Countries in Asia beyond India.	Nepal	12	10	2	11	9	2	1	1	...
	Ceylon	3	1	2	3	1	2	...	...	...
	Afghanistan	74	68	6	73	67	6	1	1	...
	Beluchistan	4	4	...	4	4	...	...	...	...
	Turkestan	5	4	1	1	...	1	4	4	...
	China	2	1	1	2	1	1	...	...	...
	Persia	1	...	1	1	...	1	...	...	...
	Arabia	8	8	...	7	7	...	1	1	...
	Total C.	109	96	13	102	89	13	7	7	...
D.—Countries in Europe.	England and Wales	320	248	72	315	244	71	5	4	1
	Scotland	41	28	13	36	25	11	5	3	2
	Ireland	40	27	13	40	27	13	...	...	...
	France	10	5	5	10	5	5	...	...	...
	Germany	4	2	2	3	1	2	1	1	...
	Denmark	2	1	1	2	1	1	...	...	...
	Switzerland	1	...	1	1	...	1	...	...	...
	Spain	1	...	1	1	...	1	...	...	...
	Portugal	2	...	2	2	...	2	...	...	...
	Italy	1	1	...	1	1	...	...	...	...
	Iceland	1	...	1	1	...	1	...	...	...
	Turkey	1	1	...	...	...	...	1	1	...
	Total D.	424	313	111	412	304	108	12	9	3
E.	Africa	5	5	...	5	5	...	...	...	...
F.	America	5	3	2	4	3	1	1	...	1
G.	Australia	1	...	1	1	...	1	...	...	...
	Total	542,358	288,325	254,033	422,359	223,547	198,812	119,999	64,778	55,221

TABLE XII.—Persons of Unsound Mind by Age.

DISTRICT.	TOTAL AFFLICTED.			DISTRIBUTION BY AGE.									
				0—4		5—9		10—14		15—19		20—24	
	Total.	Males.	Females.	Males.	Females.	Males.	Females.	Males.	Females.	Males.	Females.	Males.	Females.
1	2	3	4	5	6	7	8	9	10	11	12	13	14
Ajmere	67	46	21	4	...	2	2	5	...	...	2	3	1
Merwara	20	18	2	...	...	2	...	4	...	...	...	1	1
Total	87	64	23	4	...	4	2	9	...	...	2	4	2

DISTRICT.	DISTRIBUTION BY AGE.															
	25—29		30—34		35—39		40—44		45—49		50—54		55—59		60 AND OVER.	
	Males.	Females.	Males.	Females.	Males.	Females.	Males.	Females.	Males.	Females.	Males.	Females.	Males.	Females.	Males.	Females.
	15	16	17	18	19	20	21	22	23	24	25	26	27	28	29	30
Ajmere	8	...	4	4	8	1	2	5	4	...	4	2	1	1	1	3
Merwara	2	...	2	...	2	...	3	1	...	...	1	...	...	...	1	...
Total	10	...	6	4	10	1	5	6	4	..	5	2	1	1	2	3

TABLE XIIA.—Persons of Unsound Mind by Caste, Tribe or Race.

CASTE, TRIBE OR RACE.	TOTAL.			DISTRIBUTION BY DISTRICTS.			
				Ajmere.		Merwara.	
	Total.	Males.	Females.	Males.	Females.	Males.	Females.
1	2	3	4	5	6	7	8
Mali	6	4	2	4	2	...	...
Khatri	2	2	...	1	...	1	...
Khati	1	1	...	1	...	...	...
Chamar	5	4	1	3	1	1	...
Kharol	1	1	...	1	...	...	...
Gujar	4	4	...	3	...	1	...
Mer	8	7	1	5	1	2	...
Rajput	6	4	2	4	1	...	1
Sadhu	3	3	...	3	...	...	...
Jat	4	4	...	3	...	1	...
Sonar	1	1	...	1	...	...	...
Brahmin	3	2	1	1	1	1	...
Mehter	1	1	...	1	...	...	...
Kumhar	6	2	4	2	4	...	...
Merat	5	5	...	...	...	5	...
Raibari	2	1	1	1	1	...	...
Nai	1	...	1	...	1	...	...
Jaiswar	1	...	1	...	1	...	...
Kasera	1	...	1	...	1	...	...
Balai	2	1	1	...	1	1	...
Bhil	2	...	2	...	2	...	...
Teli	1	...	1	...	1	...	...
Mahajan	4	4	...	1	...	3	...
Jogi	1	1	...	...	...	1	...
Mina	2	2	...	1	...	1	...
Musalman	14	10	4	10	3	...	1
Total	87	64	23	46	21	18	2

TABLE XIII.—Deaf-Mutes by Age.

DISTRICT.	TOTAL AFFLICTED.			DISTRIBUTION BY AGE.									
				0—4		5—9		10—14		15—19		20—24	
	Total.	Males.	Females.	Males.	Females.	Males.	Females.	Males.	Females.	Males.	Females.	Males.	Females.
1	2	3	4	5	6	7	8	9	10	11	12	13	14
Ajmere	125	78	47	5	1	5	4	9	4	4	3	5	2
Merwara	50	35	15	...	1	6	3	7	...	3	...	4	2
Total	**175**	**113**	**62**	**5**	**2**	**11**	**7**	**16**	**4**	**7**	**3**	**9**	**4**

DISTRICT.	DISTRIBUTION BY AGE.															
	25—29		30—34		35—39		40—44		45—49		50—54		55—59		60 and over.	
	Males.	Females.	Males.	Females.	Males.	Females.	Males.	Females.	Males.	Females.	Males.	Females.	Males.	Females.	Males.	Females.
	15	16	17	18	19	20	21	22	23	24	25	26	27	28	29	30
Ajmere	10	5	9	2	6	2	9	5	4	2	5	3	3	3	4	11
Merwara	...	2	4	1	3	2	3	3	1	...	...	...	2	...	2	1
Total	**10**	**7**	**13**	**3**	**9**	**4**	**12**	**8**	**5**	**2**	**5**	**3**	**5**	**3**	**6**	**12**

TABLE XIIIA.—Deaf-Mutes.

CASTE, TRIBE OR RACE.	TOTAL.			DISTRIBUTION BY DISTRICTS.			
				Ajmere.		Merwara.	
	Total.	Males.	Females.	Males.	Females.	Males.	Females.
1	2	3	4	5	6	7	8
Kayasth	1	1	...	1	...	...	...
Raigar	9	7	2	6	1	1	1
Chamár	7	3	4	3	4	...	...
Darzi	2	2	...	1	...	1	...
Teli	3	3	...	3	...	...	...
Lohár	1	...	1	...	1	...	...
Kháti	5	3	2	3	2	...	...
Mahájan	19	12	7	5	5	7	2
Jat	14	7	7	7	7	...	...
Mer	9	8	1	7	...	1	1
Raibari	2	...	2	...	2	...	...
Sadhu	8	7	1	7	1	...	...
Rajput	6	3	3	3	3	...	...
Brahman	13	10	3	9	2	1	1
Balái	9	6	3	5	3	1	...
Máli	10	2	8	2	8	...	...
Gujar	10	7	3	7	3	...	...
Mehter	2	2	...	1	...	1	...
Khárol	1	1	...	1	...	...	...
Nai	1	...	1	...	1	...	...
Mina	4	3	1	3	1	...	...
Kumahar	5	3	2	1	2	2	...
Merát	14	9	5	...	...	9	5
Ráwat	9	6	3	...	...	6	3
Bhil	1	1	...	...	...	1	...
Dhobi	1	1	...	...	...	1	...
Beldar	1	...	1	...	...	...	1
Musalmán	8	6	2	3	1	3	1
Total	**175**	**113**	**62**	**78**	**47**	**35**	**15**

TABLE XIV.—Blind by Age.

DISTRICT.	TOTAL AFFLICTED.			DISTRIBUTION BY AGE.									
				0—4		5—9		10—14		15—19		20—24	
	Total.	Males.	Females.	Males.	Females.	Males.	Females.	Males.	Females.	Males.	Females.	Males.	Females.
1	2	3	4	5	6	7	8	9	10	11	12	13	14
Ajmere	804	395	409	10	12	24	20	25	21	19	15	22	14
Merwara	249	128	121	2	2	4	5	4	6	6	7	4	2
Total	1,053	523	530	12	14	28	25	29	27	25	22	26	16

DISTRICT.	DISTRIBUTION BY AGE.															
	25—29		30—34		35—39		40—44		45—49		50—54		55—59		60 AND OVER.	
	Males.	Females.	Males.	Females.	Males.	Females.	Males.	Females.	Males.	Females.	Males.	Females.	Males.	Females.	Males.	Females.
	15	16	17	18	19	20	21	22	23	24	25	26	27	28	29	30
Ajmere	20	20	32	27	17	18	39	38	24	18	35	41	31	32	97	133
Merwara	8	3	11	6	5	8	12	12	2	4	18	16	4	5	48	45
Total	28	2	43	33	22	26	51	50	26	22	53	57	35	37	145	178

TABLE XIVA.—Blind by Caste, Tribe or Race.

CASTE, TRIBE OR RACE.	TOTAL.			DISTRIBUTION BY DISTRICTS.			
				Ajmere.		Merwara.	
	Total.	Males.	Females.	Males.	Females.	Males.	Females.
1	2	3	4	5	6	7	8
Nai	21	3	18	...	15	3	3
Mahájan	137	72	65	53	57	19	8
Gujar	67	28	39	27	39	1	—
Rajput	26	18	8	18	8	...	...
Khatik	9	9	...	9	...	...	...
Mer	111	44	67	8	24	36	43
Balai	104	67	37	54	29	13	8
Kháti	28	17	11	16	9	1	2
Raigar	61	25	36	20	27	5	9
Jat	72	29	43	28	40	1	3
Chipa	6	2	4	...	4	2	...
Brahman	95	47	48	42	43	5	5
Sonár	17	3	14	...	14	3	...
Kumhár	35	17	18	12	12	5	6
Sargara	3	3	...	3	...	...	...
Dhánka	6	6	...	6	...	...	...
Teli	20	8	12	7	10	1	2
Bhát	4	...	4	...	2	...	2
Mehter	10	8	2	7	...	1	2
Chamár	33	8	25	8	25	...	...
Mina	5	3	2	3	2	...	...
Máli	12	6	6	4	3	2	3
Naik	7	...	7	...	7	...	...
Sadhu	51	35	16	33	13	2	3
Raibari	3	...	3	...	3	...	...
Daroga	2	...	2	...	2	...	...
Khatri	1	...	1	...	...	...	1
Dhobi	2	...	2	...	...	...	2
Jogi	4	4	...	...	...	4	...
Mochi	2	1	1	...	...	1	1
Bhil	3	...	3	...	...	...	3
Gushain	1	...	1	...	...	...	1
Kalal	1	...	1	...	...	...	1
Tamboli	1	...	1	...	...	...	1
Kayesth	1	1	...	...	...	1	...
Musalman	63	36	27	27	21	9	6
Native Christian	15	15	...	10	...	5	...
Hindus, unspecified	14	8	6	...	...	8	6
Total	1,053	523	530	395	409	128	121

TABLE XV.—Lepers by Age.

DISTRICT.	TOTAL AFFLICTED.			DISTRIBUTION BY AGE.									
				0—4		5—9		10—14		15—19		20—24	
	Total.	Males.	Females.	Males.	Females.	Males.	Females.	Males.	Females.	Males.	Females.	Males.	Females.
1	2	3	4	5	6	7	8	9	10	11	12	13	14
Ajmere	16	*10*	6	...	...	...	...	*1*	...	...	1	...	...
Merwara	11	*10*	1	...	...	...	...	...	...	...	...	*1*	...
Total	**27**	**20**	**7**	...	...	...	...	**1**	...	...	**1**	**1**	...

DISTRICT.	DISTRIBUTION BY AGE.															
	25—29		30—34		35—39		40—44		45—49		50—54		55—59		60 AND OVER.	
	Males.	Females.	Males.	Females.	Males.	Females.	Males.	Females.	Males.	Females.	Males.	Females.	Males.	Females.	Males.	Females.
	15	16	17	18	19	20	21	22	23	24	25	26	27	28	29	30
Ajmere	...	...	*1*	1	*1*	...	*1*	...	*1*	1	*1*	1	...	1	*4*	1
Merwara	...	...	*1*	...	*2*	...	*1*	1	*1*	...	*1*	...	*1*	...	*2*	...
Total	...	...	**2**	**1**	**3**	...	**2**	**1**	**2**	**1**	**2**	**1**	**1**	**1**	**6**	**1**

TABLE XVA.—Lepers by Caste, Tribe or Race.

CASTE, TRIBE OR RACE.	TOTAL.			DISTRIBUTION BY DISTRICTS.			
				Ajmere.		Merwara.	
	Total.	Males.	Females.	Males.	Females.	Males.	Females.
1	2	3	4	5	6	7	8
Brahman	4	*4*	...	*4*	...	...	...
Rajput	1	*1*	...	*1*	...	...	...
Sadhu	1	*1*	...	*1*	...	...	...
Khatik	3	*2*	1	*2*	1	...	...
Kháti	1	*1*	...	1	...	...	...
Mer	4	*3*	1	...	1	*3*	...
Máli	1	...	1	...	1	...	...
Mahájan	2	*1*	1	...	1	*1*	...
Raigar	1	...	1	...	1	...	...
Chákar	1	...	1	...	1	...	...
Od	1	*1*	1	...	...	*1*	...
Merát	1	*1*	...	...	...	*1*	...
Ráwat	4	*3*	...	...	...	*3*	
Lohar	1	*1*	...	...	...	*1*	...
Musalmán	1	*1*	...	*1*	...	...	...
Total	**27**	**20**	**7**	**10**	**6**	**10**	

TABLE XVI.—Caste Return.

Class.	Group.	Caste, Tribe, etc.	Number of recorded sub-divisions, clans, etc.	Strength.			Religion.	Strength.
				Total.	Males.	Females.		
1	2	3	4	5	6	7	8	9
A.—Agricultural.	I.—Military and Dominant.	1. Rajput	27	16,382	9,333	7,049	Hindu	All.
		2. Mahratta	9	475	352	123	Do.	Do.
		3. Thákur	6	6	6	...	Do.	Do.
		4. Sikh	3	231	164	67	Sikh Hindu	213 18
		Total I 4	45	17,094	9,855	7,239		
	II.—Other Agricultural.	1. Ját	296	36,324	18,929	17,395	Hindu	All.
		2. Gujar	229	37,868	20,332	17,536	Do.	Do.
		3. Ahir	15	2,226	1,290	936	Do.	Do.
		4. Mer	108	30,499	14,749	15,750	Hindu Musalman	30,467 32
		5. Ráwat	20	30,919	17,237	13,682	Hindu Musalman	30,844 75
		6. Chita	6	1,568	944	624	Hindu Musalman	370 1,198
		7. Merát	8	21,887	12,894	8,993	Hindu Musalman	9,022 12,865
		8. Naik	39	2,771	1,415	1,356	Hindu	All.
		9. Thori	6	97	57	40	Do.	Do.
		10. Mina	27	4,648	2,731	1,917	Do.	Do.
		11. Máli	60	16,373	8,452	7,921	Do.	Do.
		12. Lodha	8	1,337	638	699	Do.	Do.
		13. Kachhi	1	61	41	20	Do.	Do.
		14. Kurmi	1	327	155	172	Do.	Do.
		15. Kalumbi	6	119	76	43	Do.	Do.
		16. Aheri	28	881	471	410	Do.	Do.
		17. Kunbi	1	123	84	39	Do.	Do.
		18. Ghosi	1	204	109	95	Do.	Do.
		19. Satia	1	61	23	38	Do.	Do.
		20. Purubia	2	14	8	6	Do.	Do.
		21. Morai	1	6	5	1	Do.	Do.
		22. Dhákur	9	210	119	91	Do.	Do.
		Total II 22	881	188,528	100,759	87,764		
	IV.—Forest and Hill Tribes.	1. Bhil	67	7,752	3,999	3,753	Hindu	All.
		2. Gometi	1	8	3	5	Do.	Do.
		Total IV 2	68	7,760	4,002	3,758		
B.—Professional.	V.—Priests	1. Brahman	47	26,621	14,342	12,279	Hindu	All.
		2. Shámi	35	158	92	66	Do.	Do.
		3. Acháraj	6	654	332	322	Do.	Do.
		4. Jatti	4	14	13	1	Jain	Do.
		5. Pundit	1	3	3	...	Do.	Do.
		Total V 5	93	27,450	14,782	12,668		
	VI.—Devotees	1. Sádhu	13	5,985	3,322	2,663	Hindu Jain	5,858 127
		2. Gusain	2	1,217	681	536	Hindu	All.
		3. Agori	1	18	12	6	Do.	Do.
		4. Jogi	3	2,774	1,487	1,287	Do.	Do.
		5. Vishnui	1	45	25	20	Do.	Do.
		6. Fakir	4	697	412	285	Musalman	Do.
		Total VI 6	24	10,736	5,939	4,797		
	VII.—Temple Servants.	1. Bhopa	7	23	15	8	Hindu	All.
		Total VII 1	7	23	15	8		
	VIII.—Genealogists	1. Jaga	3	1,139	663	476	Hindu	All.
		2. Barwa	25	257	117	140	Do.	Do.
		3. Bhát	28	1,121	572	549	Do.	Do.
		4. Rao	13	374	170	204	Do.	Do.
		5. Mirási	7	25	12	13	Hindu Musalman	3 22
		Total VIII 5	76	2,916	1,534	1,382		
	IX.—Writers	1. Káyasth	6	2,168	1,197	971	Hindu	All.
		Total IX 1	6	2,168	1,197	971		

TABLE XVI.—Caste Return.

Class.	Group.	Caste, Tribe, etc.	Number of recorded sub-divisions, clans, etc.	Strength. Total.	Strength. Males.	Strength. Females.	Religion.	Strength.
1	2	3	4	5	6	7	8	9
B.—PROFESSIONAL—contd.	X.—Astrologers	1. Garura	25	318	179	139	Hindu	All.
		2. Dákot	13	623	329	294	Do.	Do.
		3. Guru	5	379	215	164	Do.	Do.
		4. Jotshi	1	2	2	...	Do.	Do.
		Total X 4	**44**	**1,822**	**725**	**597**		
	XI.—Musicians and Ballad-reciters.	1. Kámar	7	75	42	33	Hindu	All.
		2. Kaláwat	1	4	4	...	Do.	Do.
		3. Jachak	12	85	43	42	Do.	Do.
		4. Damámi	2	4	3	1	Do.	Do.
		5. Dhánka	9	1,030	519	511	Do.	Do.
		6. Sargara	23	926	474	452	Do.	Do.
		7. Dholi	104	6,440	3,364	3,076	Hindu	6,419
							Musalman	21
		8. Garmanga	1	31	20	11	Hindu	26
							Musalman	5
		9. Bajansai	1	3	2	1	Hindu	All.
		10. Dhádhi	6	134	71	63	Do.	17
							Musalman	117
		11. Baret	3	6	4	2	Hindu	All.
		12. Cháran	20	499	276	223	Do.	Do.
		13. Nagárchi	1	7	3	4	Do.	Do.
		14. Halimanga	1	7	...	7	Do.	Do.
		15. Rawenia	1	9	5	4	Do.	Do.
		Total XI 15	**192**	**9,260**	**4,880**	**4,480**		
	XII.—Dancers and Singers.	1. Bhagat	1	33	14	19	Hindu	All.
		2. Pátar	2	15	...	15	Do.	Do.
		Total XII 2	**3**	**48**	**14**	**34**		
C.—COMMERCIAL	XIII.—Actors and Mimers.	1. Rána	1	2	...	2	Hindu	All.
		2. Bháud	19	117	60	57	Hindu	111
							Musalman	6
		3. Ráwal	7	92	41	51	Hindu	All.
		Total XIII 3	**27**	**211**	**101**	**110**		
	XIV.—Traders	1. Mahájan	13	46,117	24,774	21,343	Hindu	19,322
							Jain	26,795
		Total XIV 1	**13**	**46,117**	**24,774**	**21,343**		
	XVI.—Carriers	1. Banjára	8	102	84	18	Hindu	All.
		2. Raibári	53	2,255	1,216	1,039	Do.	Do.
		Total XVI 2	**61**	**2,357**	**1,300**	**1,057**		
	XVII.—Goldsmith	1 Sonár	30	3,994	2,137	1,857	Hindu	All.
		Total XVII 1	**30**	**3,994**	**2,137**	**1,857**		
D.—ARTISAN AND VILLAGE MENIAL	XVIII.—Barbers	1. Nai	48	7,511	3,912	3,599	Hindu	All.
		2. Barbers	12	284	142	142	Do.	Do.
		Total XVIII 2	**60**	**7,795**	**4,054**	**3,741**		
	XIX.—Blacksmith	1. Lohar	45	2,658	1,446	1,212	Hindu	2,606
							Musalman	52
		2. Sekligar	4	36	29	7	Hindu	All.
		3. Gadolia	1	17	9	8	Do.	Do.
		Total XIX 3	**50**	**2,711**	**1,484**	**1,227**		
	XX.—Carpenters	1. Kháti	78	8,075	4,279	3,796	Hindu	All.
		2. Gawária	7	521	251	270	Do.	Do.
		3. Dustri	1	9	5	4	Do.	Do.
		Total XX 3	**86**	**8,605**	**4,535**	**4,070**		

TABLE XVI.—Caste Return.

Class.	Group.	Caste, Tribe, etc.	Number of recorded sub-divisions, clans, etc.	Strength. Total.	Males.	Females.	Religion.	Strength.
1	2	3	4	5	6	7	8	9
D.—ARTISAN AND VILLAGE MENIAL—*contd.*	XXA.—Grain parchers and confectioners.	1. Bhanbhuja	6	107	*51*	56	Hindu	All.
		Total XXA 1	6	107	51	56		
	XXB.—Perfume, drug and betel-leaf sellers.	1. Tamboli	11	312	*166*	146	Hindu	All.
		Total XXB 1	11	312	166	146		
	XXI.—Brass and coppersmith.	1. Kaserá	4	113	*55*	58	Hindu	All.
		2. Tathera	9	165	*99*	66	Do.	Do.
		3. Bharawá	7	9	*6*	3	Do.	Do.
		Total XXI 3	20	287	160	127		
	XXII.—Tailors	1. Darzi	20	2 742	*1,475*	1,267	Hindu	All.
		2. Patwa	4	6	*3*	3	Do.	Do.
		Total XXII 2	24	2,748	1,478	1,270		
	XXIII.—Weavers, calenderers and dyers.	1. Chhipa	17	2,267	*1,152*	1,115	Hindu	All.
		2. Nilgar	3	5	*2*	3	Hindu Musalman	3 2
		3. Koli	19	4,724	*2,453*	2,271	Hindu	All.
		Total XXIII 3	39	6,996	3,607	3,389		
	XXIV.—Washermen	1 Dhobi	55	2,784	*1,395*	1,389	Hindu	All.
		Total XXIV 1	55	2,784	1,395	1,389		
	XXV.—Cotton cleaners.	1. Pinara	8	12	*7*	5	Hindu	All.
		Total XXV 1	8	12	7	5		
	XXVI.—Shepherd and wool weavers.	1. Játia	1	15	*5*	10	Hindu	All.
		2. Gádri	3	104	*71*	33	Do.	Do.
		Total XXVI 2	4	119	76	43		
	XXVII.—Oil pressers	1. Teli	88	4,762	*2,443*	2,319	Hindu Musalman	4,734 28
		Total XXVII 1	88	4,762	2,443	2,319		
	XXVIII.—Potters	1. Kumhar	23	16,732	*8,596*	8,136	Hindu Musalman	16,715 17
		Total XXVIII 1	23	16,732	8,596	8,136		
	XXIX.—Glass workers.	1. Lakhera	15	950	*478*	472	Hindu	All.
		2. Panigar	1	9	*5*	4	Do.	Do.
		Total XXIX 2	16	959	483	476		
	XXX.—Salt workers	1. Khárol	39	2,980	*1,505*	1,475	Hindu	All.
		2. Khári	3	205	*110*	95	Do.	Do.
		Total XXX 2	42	3,185	1,615	1,570		
	XXXV.—Fishermen boatmen, palki-bearers, cook, etc.	1. Kahár	32	3,277	*1,748*	1,529	Hindu	All.
		2. Kir	15	1,089	*552*	537	Do.	Do.
		3. Bari	6	198	*116*	82	Do.	Do.
		4. Darogah	87	10,691	*5,352*	5,339	Do.	Do.
		5. Bhoi	10	80	*49*	31	Do.	Do.
		6. Bhishty	1	3	*2*	1	Do.	Do.
		Total XXXV 6	151	15,338	7,819	7,519		

TABLE XVI.—Caste Return.

Class.	Group.	Caste, Tribe, etc.	Number of recorded sub-divisions, clans, etc.	Strength. Total.	Strength. Males.	Strength. Females.	Religion.	Strength.
1	2	3	4	5	6	7	8	9
D.—ARTISAN AND VILLAGE MENIAL—*concld.*	XXXVI.—Distillers and toddy drawers.	1. Kalál	39	1,687	*891*	796	Hindu . .	All.
		2. Pasi	1	26	*19*	7	Do. . .	Do.
		Total XXXVI 2 .	**40**	**1,713**	**910**	**803**		
	XXXVII.—Butchers	1. Kasai	1	36	*23*	13	Musalman . .	All.
		Total XXXVII 1 .	**1**	**36**	**23**	**13**		
	XXXVIII.—Leather workers.	1. Chupparband . .	1	36	*19*	17	Hindu . .	All.
		2. Jeswara . . .	1	75	*63*	12	Do. . .	Do.
		3. Khatik	45	3,541	*1,799*	1,742	Do. . .	Do.
		4. Chamár . . .	111	17,376	*8,733*	8,643	Do. . .	Do.
		5. Dábgar . . .	5	62	*35*	27	Do. . .	Do.
		6. Balai	99	31,909	*16,510*	15,399	Do. . .	Do.
		7. Mochi	23	1,239	*650*	589	Do. . .	Do.
		8. Raiger	146	21,053	*10,614*	10,439	Do. . .	Do.
		9. Bola	4	49	*26*	23	Do. . .	Do.
		10. Bhánbhi . . .	16	61	*37*	24	Do. . .	Do.
		11. Máhar	1	368	*207*	161	Do. . .	Do.
		12. Mong	1	32	*22*	10	Do. . .	Do.
		Total XXXVIII 12 .	**453**	**75,801**	**38,715**	**37,086**		
E.—VAGRANT, MINOR ARTISANS AND PERFORMERS, ETC.	XXXIX.—Scavengers.	1. Mehtar	58	5,917	*3,163*	2,754	{ Hindu . { Musalman .	5,909 8
		2. Sarbhangi . . .	1	4	*1*	3	Hindu . .	All.
		3. Bargi	1	8	*6*	2	Do. . .	Do.
		Total XXXIX 3 .	**60**	**5,929**	**3,170**	**2,759**		
	XLI.—Earth workers and stone dressers.	1. Odh	6	202	*119*	83	Hindu . .	All.
		2. Beldar	4	74	*36*	38	Do. . .	Do.
		3. Med	1	6	*3*	3	Do. . .	Do.
		Total XLI 3 .	**11**	**282**	**158**	**124**		
	XLIII.—Mat makers, cane splitters.	1. Gánchha . . .	9	55	*27*	28	Hindu . .	All.
		Total XLIII 1 .	**9**	**55**	**27**	**28**		
	XLIV.—Hunters, fowlers, etc.	1. Sánsi	6	135	*65*	70	Hindu . .	All.
		2. Kanjar	6	535	*242*	293	Do. . .	Do.
		Total XLIV 2 .	**12**	**670**	**307**	**363**		
	XLV.—Miscellaneous and disreputable livers	1. Janglia	2	6	*2*	4	Hindu . .	All.
		2. Baori	3	161	*86*	75	Do. . .	Do.
		3. Bágaria	0	423	*227*	196	Do. . .	Do.
		4. Kasbi	1	2	...	2	Do. . .	Do.
		Total XLV 4 .	**12**	**592**	**315**	**277**		
	XLVI.—Tumblers and acrobats.	1. Náth	20	579	*290*	289	Hindu . .	All.
		Total XLVI 1 .	**20**	**579**	**290**	**289**		
	XLVII.—Jugglers, snake charmers and animal exhibitors.	1. Kalbelia . . .	1	12	*9*	3	Hindu . .	All.
		Total XLVII 1 .	**1**	**12**	**9**	**3**		

TABLE XVI.—Caste Return.

Class.	Group.	Caste, Tribe, etc.	Number of recorded sub-divisions, clans, etc.	Strength. Total.	Males.	Females.	Religion.	Strength.
1	2	3	4	5	6	7	8	9
F.—Races and Nationalities.	XLVIII.—Non-Indian Asiatic races.	1. Sheikh	69	32,554	17,105	15,449	Musalman	All.
		2. Syad	41	5,754	3,185	2,569	Do.	Do.
		3. Pathan	73	14,602	7,934	6,668	Do.	Do.
		4. Mogal	20	1,676	937	739	Do.	Do.
		5. Mewati	6	11	8	3	Do.	Do.
		6. Musalman	...	4,486	2,705	1,781	Do.	Do.
		7. Belochi	1	1	1	...	Do.	Do.
		8. Parsi	8	198	135	63	Parsi	Do.
		9. Jew	1	71	38	33	Jew	Do.
		Total XLVIII 9	**219**	**59,353**	**32,048**	**27,305**		
	L.—Non-Asiatic races.	1. British	4	729	484	245	Christian	All.
		2. Foreign	10	109	65	44	Do.	Do.
		Total L 2	**14**	**838**	**549**	**289**		
	LI.—Eurasian	1. Eurasian	10	636	356	280	Christian	All.
		Total LI 1	**10**	**636**	**356**	**280**		
	LII.—Christian Converts.	1. Native Christian	7	1,209	662	547	Christian	All.
		Total LII 1	**7**	**1,209**	**662**	**547**		
	LIII.—Miscellaneous.	1. Not returned	...	631	404	227	Hindu No religion	630 1
		2. Others	...	591	449	142	Hindu	All.
		Total LIII 2	...	**1,222**	**853**	**369**		
		Grand Total	**3,122**	**542,358**	**288,325**	**254,033**		

TABLE XVII.—Part A.—Occupations.

TABLE XVII.—Part A.—

Class.	Order.	Sub-order and Group.	Occupations.	TOTAL POPULA					
				Total.				Mal	
				Total.	0—4	5—14	15 and over	Total.	0—4
1	2	3	4	5	6	7	8	9	10
Class A.	I.—Administration.	1.—Service of the Imperial and Provincial Governments	2. Officers	41	4	9	28	18	2
			3. Office Superintendents and clerical establishments, Police and Excise Inspectors, Sub-Registrars, etc.	807	83	161	563	602	58
			4. Messengers, Constables, Bailiffs, Warders, menials, etc.	3,679	430	674	2,575	2,396	231
			Total Sub-order 1	4,527	517	844	3,166	3,016	291
		2.—Service of Local and Municipal bodies.	5. Inspecting and Supervising Officials	23	2	3	18	12	1
			6. Clerical Establishments	37	4	12	21	28	2
			7. Menials	516	85	116	315	342	48
			Total Sub-order 2	576	91	131	354	382	51
		3.—Village Service	9. Accountants	579	100	154	325	385	68
			11. Watchmen and other menials	1,249	167	290	792	768	93
			Total Sub-order 3	1,828	267	444	1,117	1,153	161
			Total Order I.—Administration	6,931	875	1,419	4,637	4,551	503
	II.—Defence.	4.—Army	12. Officers	184	30	37	117	113	15
			13. Non-commissioned officers and privates	4,989	631	599	3,759	3,568	327
			14. Followers	520	63	105	352	312	38
			15. Administrative Establishments	41	4	11	26	33	3
			Total Sub-order 4	5,734	728	752	4,254	4,026	383
			Total Order II.—Defence	5,734	728	752	4,254	4,026	383
	III.—Foreign and Feudatory State Service.	6.—Administrative Services.	19. Chiefs, Consuls and Officers	34	2	5	27	31	1
			20. Clerical Establishments	74	7	20	47	58	4
			21. Menials, etc.	2,000	222	431	1,347	1,173	125
			Total Sub-order 6	2,108	231	456	1,421	1,262	130
		7.—Army and Marine	22. Officers	3	1	...	2	2	1
			23. Privates and seamen, etc.	107	4	11	92	90	3
			Total Sub-order 7	110	5	11	94	92	4
			Total Order III.—Foreign and Feudatory State Service.	2,218	236	467	1,515	1,354	134
Class B.	IV.—Live-Stock.	8.—Stock breeding and dealing— (a). Horses and horned cattle.	24. Horse breeders and dealers	8	..	...	8	5	...
			25. Cattle breeders and dealers and commissariat farm establishment.	861	147	234	480	322	57
		(b). Other draught, etc., animals.	26. Herdsmen	4,474	520	1,482	2,472	2,764	245
			29. Camel breeders and dealers	33	2	4	27	30	2
			30. Ass and mule breeders and dealers	3	1	...	2	1	...
		(c). Small stock	31. Sheep and goat breeders and dealers	1,005	145	345	515	849	124
			32. Pig breeders and dealers	22	3	6	13	15	1
			Total Sub-order 8	6,406	818	2,071	3,517	3,986	429
		9.—Subsidiary Services to Stock— (a). Training and doctoring live-stock.	33. Veterinary Surgeons and Assistants	2	...	...	2	2	...
			34. Farriers and gelders	89	15	15	59	47	8
			35. Horse breakers and trainers	66	10	12	44	26	3
			Total Sub-order 9	157	25	27	105	75	11
			Total Order IV.—Live-Stock	6,563	843	2,096	3,622	4,061	440
	V.—Agriculture.	10.—Interest in land	37. Land occupant, not cultivating	9,204	1,358	2,287	5,559	4,926	651
			38. Land occupant, cultivating	98,250	17,447	26,450	54,353	54,390	8,698
			40. Tenants, not cultivating	25,628	4,164	7,236	14,228	12,055	1,987
			41. Tenants and sharers, cultivating	106,731	15,371	28,837	62,523	58,388	8,098
			Total Sub-order 10	239,813	38,340	64,810	136,663	129,759	19,434
		11.—Agricultural Labourers.	42. Farm servants	626	75	161	390	332	35
			43. Field labourers and crop watchers	21,552	866	5,580	15,106	7,707	355
			Total Sub-order 11	22,178	941	5,741	15,496	8,039	390
		12.—Growers of Special Products and Trees.	50. Fruit growers	85	17	21	47	85	17
			52. Gardeners and seedsmen, etc.	392	47	75	270	304	35
			55. Forest rangers, guards, peons	83	7	16	60	54	3
			Total Sub-order 12	560	71	112	377	443	55
			Total Order V.—Agriculture	262,551	39,352	70,663	152,536	138,241	19,878

Occupations.

TION.

[Males] 5—14	15 and over.	Females. Total.	0—4	5—14	15 and over.	Occupations.	Sub-order and Group.	Order.	Class.
11	12	13	14	15	16				
2	14	23	2	7	14	2. Officers	1.—Service of the Imperial and Provincial Governments.	I.—Administration.	Class A.
115	429	205	25	46	134	3. Office Superintendents and clerical establishments, Police and Excise Inspectors, Sub-Registrars, etc.			
394	1,771	1,283	199	280	804	4. Messengers, Constables, Bailiffs, Warders, menials, etc.			
511	2,214	1,511	226	333	952	Total Sub-order 1			
...	11	11	1	3	7	5. Inspecting and Supervising Officials	2.—Service of Local and Municipal bodies.		
8	18	9	2	4	3	6. Clerical Establishments			
83	211	174	37	33	104	7. Menials			
91	240	194	40	40	114	Total Sub-order 2			
116	201	194	32	38	124	9. Accountants	3.—Village Service		
161	514	481	74	129	278	11. Watchmen and other menials			
277	715	675	106	167	402	Total Sub-order 3			
879	**3,169**	**2.380**	**372**	**540**	**1,468**	**Total Order I.—Administration**			
18	80	71	15	19	37	12. Officers	4.—Army.	II.—Defence.	
328	2,913	1,421	304	271	846	13. Non-commissioned officers and privates			
57	217	208	25	48	135	14. Followers			
7	23	8	1	4	3	15. Administrative Establishments			
410	3,233	1,708	345	342	1,021	Total Sub-order 4			
410	**3,233**	**1,708**	**345**	**342**	**1.021**	**Total order II.—Defence**			
5	25	3	1	...	2	19. Chiefs, Consuls and Officers	6.—Administrative Services.	III.—Foreign and Feudatory State Service.	
18	36	16	3	2	11	20. Clerical Establishments			
269	779	827	97	162	568	21. Menials			
292	840	846	101	164	581	Total Sub-order 6			
...	1	1	...	...	1	22. Officers	7.—Army and Marine		
8	79	17	1	3	13	23. Privates and seamen, etc.			
8	80	18	1	3	14	Total Sub-order 7			
30	**920**	**864**	**102**	**167**	**595**	**Total Order III.—Foreign and Feudatory State Service.**			
...	5	3	-	...	3	24. Horse breeders and dealers	8.—Stock breeding and dealing— (a). Horses and horned cattle.	IV.—Live-Stock.	
102	163	539	90	132	317	25. Cattle breeders and dealers and commissariat farm establishment.			
971	1,548	1,720	275	511	924	26. Herdsmen			
4	24	3	...	...	3	29. Camel breeders and dealers	(b). Other draught, etc., animals.		
...	1	2	1	...	1	30. Ass and mule breeders and dealers			
299	426	156	21	46	89	31. Sheep and goat breeders and dealers	(c). Small stock		
4	10	7	2	2	3	32. Pig breeders and dealers			
1,380	2,177	2,420	389	691	1,340	Total Sub-order 8			
...	2	...	...	...	...	33. Veterinary Surgeons and Assistants	9.—Subsidiary Services to Stock— (a). Training and doctoring live-stock.		
7	32	42	7	8	27	34. Farriers and gelders			
8	15	40	7	4	29	35. Horse breakers and trainers			
15	49	82	14	12	56	Total Sub-order 9			
1,395	**2.226**	**2.502**	**403**	**703**	**1.396**	**Total Order IV.—Live-Stock**			
1,258	3,017	4,278	707	1,029	2,542	37. Land occupant, not cultivating	10.—Interest in Land	V.—Agriculture.	Class B.
4,110	31,582	43,860	8,740	12.340	22,771	38. Land occupant, cultivating			
3,737	6,331	13.573	2,177	3,499	7,897	40. Tenants, not cultivating			
16,183	31,107	48,343	7,273	12,654	28,416	41. Tenants and sharers, cultivating			
35,288	75,037	110,054	18,906	29,522	61,626	Total Sub-order 10			
88	209	204	40	73	181	42. Farm servants	11.—Agricultural Labourers.		
2,895	4,457	13,845	511	2,685	10,649	43. Field labourers and crop watchers			
2,983	4,666	14,139	551	2,758	10,830	Total Sub-order 11			
21	47	...	...	...	...	50. Fruit growers	12.—Growers of Special Products and Trees.		
53	216	88	12	22	54	52. Gardeners and seedsmen, etc.			
8	43	29	4	8	17	55. Forest rangers, guards, peons			
82	306	117	16	30	71	Total Sub-order 12			
38,353	**80,009**	**124,310**	**19,473**	**32,310**	**72,527**	**Total Order V.—Agriculture**			

TABLE XVII.—Part A.—

Class.	Order.	Sub-order and Group.	Occupations.	TOWN. Total. Total.	0—4	5—14	15 and over.	Males. Total.	0—4	5—14	15 and over.	Females. Total.	0—4	5—14	15 and over.
				17	18	19	20	21	22	23	24	25	26	27	28
CLASS A.	I.—ADMINISTRATION.	1.—Service of the Imperial and Provincial Governments.	2. Officers	41	4	9	28	18	2	2	14	23	2	7	14
			3. Office Superintendents and clerical establishments, Police and Excise Inspectors, Sub-Registrars, etc.	724	73	148	473	553	51	109	393	181	22	39	120
			4. Messengers, Constables, Bailiffs, Warders, menials, etc.	2,213	260	399	1,554	1,413	138	228	1,047	800	122	171	507
			Total Sub-order 1	2,988	337	556	2,095	1,984	191	339	1,454	1,004	146	217	641
		2.—Service of Local and Municipal Bodies.	5. Inspecting and Supervising Officials	23	2	3	18	12	1	...	11	11	1	3	7
			6. Clerical Establishments	34	4	12	18	25	2	8	15	9	2	4	3
			7. Menials	513	85	114	314	342	48	83	211	171	37	31	103
			Total Sub-order 2	570	91	129	350	379	51	91	237	191	40	38	113
		3.—Village Service	9. Accountants	186	21	45	120	100	8	30	62	86	13	15	58
			11. Watchmen and other menials	71	11	17	43	32	5	8	19	39	6	9	24
			Total Sub-order 3	257	32	62	163	132	13	38	81	125	19	24	82
			Total Order I.—Administration	**3,815**	**460**	**747**	**2.608**	**2,495**	**255**	**468**	**1.772**	**1,320**	**205**	**279**	**836**
	II.—DEFENCE.	4.—Army	12. Officers	231	20	28	83	86	11	15	60	45	9	13	23
			13. Non-commissioned officers and privates.	3.374	407	408	2,559	2,400	210	227	1,963	974	197	181	596
			14. Followers	412	50	81	275	243	33	41	169	160	23	40	106
			15. Administrative Establishments	41	4	11	26	33	3	7	23	8	1	4	3
			Total sub-order 4	3.958	487	528	2,943	2,762	257	290	2,215	1,196	230	238	728
			Total Order II.—Defence	**3,958**	**487**	**528**	**2,918**	**2,762**	**257**	**290**	**2,215**	**1,196**	**230**	**238**	**728**
	III.—FOREIGN AND FEUDATORY STATE SERVICE.	6.—Administrative Services.	19. Chiefs, Consuls and Officers	28	...	4	24	28	...	4	24	...	...	...	...
			20. Clerical Establishments	26	3	10	13	17	...	9	8	9	3	1	5
			21. Menials, etc.	126	9	26	91	110	7	23	80	16	2	3	11
			Total Sub-order 6	180	12	40	128	155	7	36	112	25	5	4	16
		7.—Army and Marine	22. Officers	3	1	...	2	2	1	...	1	1	...	...	1
			23. Privates and seamen, etc.	26	...	...	26	26	...	...	26	...	...	...	...
			Total Sub-order 7	29	1	...	28	28	1	...	27	1	...	...	1
			Total Order III.—Foreign and Feudatory State Service.	**209**	**13**	**40**	**156**	**183**	**8**	**36**	**139**	**26**	**5**	**4**	**17**
CLASS B.	IV.—LIVE-STOCK.	8.—Stock breeding and dealing— (a). Horses and horned cattle.	24. Horse breeders and dealers	6	...	...	6	3	...	...	3	3	...	...	3
			25. Cattle breeders and dealers and commissariat farm establishment.	266	37	61	168	35	6	5	24	231	31	56	144
			26. Herdsmen	624	81	164	368	364	42	103	219	250	39	62	149
		(b). Other draught etc., animals.	29. Camel breeders and dealers	16	...	2	14	16	...	2	14	...	...	...	...
			30. Ass and mule breeders and dealers	3	1	...	2	1	...	...	1	2	1	...	1
		(c). Small stock	31. Sheep and goat breeders and dealers.	344	58	90	196	233	40	68	125	111	18	22	71
			32. Pig breeders and dealers	22	3	6	13	15	1	4	10	7	2	2	3
			Total Sub-order 8	1,271	180	324	767	667	89	182	396	604	91	142	371
		9.—Subsidiary Services to Stock— (a). Training and doctoring live-stock.	33. Veterinary Surgeons and Assistants	2	...	...	2	2	...	...	2	...	...	...	...
			34. Farriers and gelders	87	15	15	57	45	8	7	30	42	7	8	27
			35. Horse breakers and trainers	41	7	7	27	16	3	6	7	25	4	1	20
			Total Sub-order 9	130	22	22	86	63	11	13	39	67	11	9	47
			Total Order IV.—Live-Stock	**1,401**	**202**	**346**	**853**	**730**	**100**	**195**	**435**	**671**	**102**	**151**	**418**
	V.—AGRICULTURE.	10.—Interest in land	37. Land occupant, not cultivating	1,243	117	264	862	587	36	124	427	656	81	140	435
			38. Land occupant, cultivating	2,547	362	581	1,604	1,354	170	209	8·6	1,193	183	282	728
			40. Tenants, not cultivating	864	107	180	568	534	61	119	354	330	46	70	214
			41. Tenants and sharers, cultivating	994	135	224	635	471	56	89	326	523	79	135	309
			Total Sub-order 10	5,648	721	1,258	3,669	2,946	332	631	1,983	2,702	389	627	1,686
		11.—Agricultural Labourers.	42. Farm servants	35	5	8	22	35	5	8	22	...	...	...	...
			43. Field labourers and crop watchers	198	34	34	130	151	21	24	105	47	13	10	24
			Total Sub-order 11	233	39	42	152	186	26	32	128	47	13	1	24
		12.—Growers of Special Products and Trees	50. Fruit growers	85	17	21	47	85	17	21	47	...	...	...	...
			52. Gardeners and seedsmen, etc.	348	42	67	239	277	32	48	197	71	10	19	42
			55. Forest rangers, guards, peons	45	5	12	28	27	3	7	17	18	2	5	11
			Total Sub-order 12	478	64	100	314	389	52	76	261	89	12	24	53
			Total Order V.—Agriculture	**6,359**	**824**	**1,400**	**4,136**	**3,521**	**410**	**739**	**2,372**	**2.838**	**414**	**661**	**1,763**

Occupations—*contd.*

COUNTRY.												Occupations.	Sub-order and Group.	Order.	Class.
Total.				Males.				Females.							
Total.	0—4	5—14	15 and over.	Total.	0—4	5—14	15 and over.	Total.	0—4	5—14	15 and over.				
29	30	31	32	33	34	35	36	37	38	39	40				
...	...	...	...	...	...	...	...	...	...	...	...	2. Officers	1.—Service of the Imperial and Provincial Governments.	I.—Administration.	Class A.
73	10	13	50	40	7	6	35	24	3	7	14	3. Office Superintendents and clerical establishments, Police and Excise Inspectors, Sub-Registrars, etc.			
1,466	170	275	1,021	983	93	166	724	483	77	109	297	4. Messengers, Constables, Bailiffs, Warders, menials, etc.			
1,539	180	288	1,071	1,032	100	172	760	507	80	116	311	Total Sub-order 1			
...	...	...	...	...	...	...	...	...	...	...	...	5. Inspecting and Supervising Officials	2.—Service of Local and Municipal Bodies.		
3	...	...	3	3	...	..	3	...	...	...	...	6. Clerical Establishments			
3	...	2	1	...	...	...	...	3	...	2	1	7. Menials			
6	...	2	4	3	...	...	3	3	...	2	1	Total Sub-order 2			
303	79	109	205	285	60	86	139	108	19	23	66	9. Accountants	3.—Village Service		
1,178	156	273	749	736	88	153	495	442	68	120	254	11. Watchmen and other menials			
1,571	235	382	954	1,021	148	239	634	550	87	143	320	Total Sub-order 3			
3,116	415	672	2,029	2,056	248	411	1,397	1,060	167	261	632	**Total Order I.—Administration**			
53	10	9	34	27	4	3	20	26	6	6	14	12. Officers	4.—Army	II.—Defence.	
1,615	224	191	1,200	1,168	117	101	950	447	107	90	250	13. Non-commissioned officers and privates			
108	7	24	77	69	5	16	48	39	2	8	29	14. Followers			
...	...	...	...	...	...	...	...	...	...	...	...	15. Administrative Establishments			
1,776	241	224	1,311	1,264	126	120	1,018	512	115	104	293	Total Sub-order 4			
1,776	241	224	1,311	1,264	126	120	1,018	512	115	104	293	**Total Order II.— Defence**			
6	2	1	3	3	1	1	1	3	1	...	2	19 Chiefs, Consuls and Officers	6.—Administrative Services.	III.—Foreign and Feudatory States.	
48	4	10	24	41	4	9	28	7	...	1	6	20. Clerical Establishments			
1,874	213	405	1,256	1,063	118	246	699	811	95	159	557	21. Menials, etc.			
1,928	219	416	1,293	1,107	123	256	728	821	96	160	565	Total Sub-order 6			
...	...	...	...	...	...	...	...	...	...	...	...	22. Officers	7.—Army and Marine		
81	4	11	66	64	3	8	53	17	1	3	13	23. Privates and seamen, etc.			
81	4	11	66	64	3	8	53	17	1	3	13	Total Sub-order 7			
2,009	223	427	1,359	1,171	126	264	781	838	97	163	578	**Total Order III.—Foreign and Feudatory State Service.**			
2	...	...	2	2	...	...	2	...	...	...	...	24. Horse breeders and dealers	8.—Stock breeding and dealing—(a). Horses and horned cattle. (b). Other draught, etc., animals. (c). Small stock	IV.—Live-Stock.	Class B.
595	110	173	312	287	51	97	139	308	59	76	173	25. Cattle breeders and dealers and commissariat farm establishment.			
2,860	439	1,317	2,104	2,400	203	868	1,329	1,460	236	449	775	26. Herdsmen			
17	2	2	13	14	2	2	10	3	...	...	3	29. Camel breeders and dealers			
...	...	...	...	...	...	...	...	...	...	...	...	30. Ass and mule breeders and dealers			
661	87	255	319	616	84	231	301	45	3	24	18	31. Sheep and goat breeders and dealers.			
...	...	...	...	...	...	..	...	...	...	...	...	32. Pig breeders and dealers			
5,135	638	1,747	2,750	3,319	340	1,198	1,781	1,816	298	549	969	Total Sub-order 8			
...	...	...	...	...	...	...	...	...	...	...	...	33. Veterinary Surgeons and Assistants	9.—Subsidiary Services to Stock—(a). Training and doctoring live-stock.		
2	...	...	2	2	...	...	2	...	...	...	...	34. Farriers and gelders			
25	3	5	17	10	...	2	8	15	3	3	9	35. Horse breakers and trainers			
27	3	5	19	12	...	2	10	15	3	3	9	Total Sub-order 9			
5,162	641	1.752	2,769	3,331	340	1.200	1,791	1.831	301	552	978	**Total Order IV.—Live-Stock**			
7,961	1,241	2,023	4,697	4,339	615	1,134	2,590	3,622	626	889	2,107	37. Land occupant, not cultivating	10.—Interest in land	V.—Agriculture.	
95,703	17,085	25,869	52,749	53,036	8,519	13,811	30,706	42,667	8,566	12,058	22,043	38. Land occupant, cultivating			
24,764	4,057	7,047	13,650	11,521	1,926	3,618	5,977	13,243	2,131	3,429	7,683	40. Tenants, not cultivating			
105,737	15,236	28,613	61,888	57,917	8,042	16,094	33,781	47,820	7,194	12,529	28,107	41. Tenants and sharers, cultivating			
234,165	37,619	63,552	132,994	126,813	19,102	34,657	73,054	107,352	18,517	28,895	59,940	Total Sub-order 10			
591	70	153	368	297	30	80	187	294	40	73	181	42. Farm servants	11.—Agricultural Labourers.		
21,354	832	5,546	14,976	7,556	334	2,871	4,351	13,798	498	2,675	10,625	43. Field labourers and crop watchers			
21,945	902	5,699	15,344	7,853	364	2,951	4,538	14,092	538	2,748	10,806	Total Sub-order 11			
...	...	...	...	...	...	...	...	...	...	...	...	50. Fruit growers	12.—Growers of Special Products and Trees		
44	5	8	31	27	3	5	19	17	2	3	12	52. Gardeners and seedsmen, etc.			
38	2	4	32	27	...	1	26	11	2	3	6	55. Forest rangers, guards, peons			
82	7	12	63	54	3	6	45	28	4	6	18	Total Sub-order 12			
256,192	38,528	69,263	148,401	134,720	19,469	37,614	77,637	121,472	19,059	31,649	70,764	**Total Order V.—Agriculture**			

TABLE XVII.—Part A.—

Class.	Order.	Sub-order and Group.	Occupations.	TOTAL. Total. Total.	TOTAL. Total. 0—4	TOTAL. Total. 5—14	TOTAL. Total. 15 and over.	TOTAL. Ma[les]. Total.	TOTAL. Ma[les]. 0—4
1	2	3	4	5	6	7	8	9	10
CLASS C.	VI.—PERSONAL AND HOUSEHOLD SERVICES.	14.—Personal and Domestic Services.	59. Barbers	5,536	698	1,202	3,642	3,139	340
			60. Bar-pickers	1	...	.	1	1	...
			62. Castemark appliers	3	...	...	3	2	...
			63. Washermen	2,134	332	579	1,223	1,110	162
			64. Water-carriers	3,374	400	600	2,374	1,314	175
			65. Cooks	1,848	207	389	1,252	1,316	121
			66. In-door servants	7,916	948	1,478	5,490	3,694	379
			67. Grooms, coachmen and dog-boys, etc.	1,614	197	298	1,119	925	89
			68. Door-keepers, etc.	6,861	828	1,379	4,654	4,698	533
			Total Sub-order 14	29,387	3,604	5,925	19,858	16,099	1,799
		15.—Non-domestic Establishment.	69. Hotel, lodging and refreshment room-keepers	6	1	...	5	3	...
			Total Sub-order 15	6	1	...	5	3	...
		16.—Sanitation	73. Sanitary inspectors, local and municipal	6	...	1	5	4	...
			74. Sweepers	5,137	847	1,327	2,963	2,570	410
			Total Sub-order 16	5,143	847	1,328	2,968	2,574	410
			Total Order VI. Personal and Household Services	34,536	4,452	7,253	22,831	18,676	2,209
CLASS D.—PREPARATION AND SUPPLY OF MATERIAL SUBSTANCES.	VII.—FOOD AND DRINK.	17.—Animal Food	76. Milk and butter seller	976	156	257	563	416	54
			77. Ghee preparers and sellers	150	21	25	104	76	8
			79. Butchers	1,140	179	306	655	576	82
			80. Eggs dealer	36	4	7	25	31	3
			81. Fishermen	35	2	8	25	31	1
			Total Sub-order 17	2,337	362	603	1,372	1,130	148
		18.—Vegetable Food	83. Grain dealers	643	66	119	458	226	22
			84. Grain parchers	325	53	74	198	171	27
			85. Flour preparers and sellers	433	60	109	264	3	1
			86. Flour mill service	891	115	177	599	293	73
			87. Bakers	67	5	13	49	51	2
			88. Bran sellers	3	...	1	2	3	...
			89. Vegetable sellers	862	95	164	603	284	45
			90. Fruit sellers	341	50	80	211	169	24
			92. Sweetmeat makers and sellers	1,831	205	320	1,306	1,076	106
			Total Sub-order 18	5,396	649	1,057	3,690	2,276	300
		19.—Drink, Condiments and Narcotics.	94. Ice manufacturers and sellers	1	...	...	1	...	...
			95. Sodawater, lemonade manufacturers and sellers	61	8	17	36	61	8
			97. Country spirit distillers and sellers	389	63	88	238	238	41
			101. Tea sellers	2	...	...	2	...	...
			103. Sugar sellers	35	6	8	21	35	6
			104. Jaggery sellers	201	29	50	122	73	7
			105. Salt sellers	10	...	...	10	7	...
			106. Ajwain seller	2	...	...	2	2	...
			109. Grocers and general condiment dealers	3,700	444	846	2,410	2,105	231
			111. Betel-leaf sellers	240	24	49	167	151	15
			112. Tobacco sellers	381	53	109	219	188	21
			114. Opium manufacturers and sellers	68	7	7	54	56	5
			Total Sub-order 19	5,090	634	1,174	3,282	2,916	234
			Total Order VII.—Food and Drink	12,823	1,645	2,834	8,344	6,322	782
	VIII. LIGHT, FIRING AND FORAGE.	20.—Lighting	116. Oil pressers and sellers	2,885	382	687	1,816	1,473	190
			120. Torch makers and sellers	3	...	...	3	3	...
			121. Kerosine oil dealers	3	...	1	2	3	...
			122. Matches sellers	1	...	...	1	1	...
			123. Lamp sellers	1	...	...	1	1	...
			Total Sub-order 20	2,893	382	688	1,823	1,481	190
		21.—Fuel and Forage	125. Firewood and grass gatherers and sellers	2,854	375	789	1,690	1,415	188
			128. Coal dealers	1	...	...	1	1	...
			130. Cowdung fuel preparers and sellers	41	8	8	25	2	1
			Total Sub-order 21	2,896	383	797	1,716	1,418	189
			Total Order VIII.—Light, Firing and Forage	5,789	765	1,485	3,539	2,899	379
	IX.—BUILDINGS.	22.—Building Materials.	132. Brick and tile burners and sellers	11	...	3	8	3	...
			133. Lime, chunam burners and sellers	242	32	65	145	127	16
			134. Stone dealers	22	1	4	17	18	...
			135. Thatch dealers and thatchers	190	28	52	110	156	20
			Total Sub-order 22	465	61	124	280	304	36

Occupations—*contd.*

POPULATION.									
LES.		FEMALES.							
5—14	15 and over.	TOTAL.	0—4	5—14	15 and over.	OCCUPATIONS.	Sub-order and Group.	Order.	Class.
11	12	13	14	15	16				
671	2,128	2,397	352	531	1,514	50. Barbers	14.—PERSONAL AND DOMESTIC SERVICES.	VI.—PERSONAL AND HOUSEHOLD SERVICES.	CLASS C.
...	1	...	...	...	...	60. Ear-pickers			
...	2	1	...	...	1	62. Castemark appliers			
304	644	1,124	170	275	679	63. Washermen			
268	871	2,060	225	332	1,503	64. Water-carriers			
257	938	532	86	132	314	65. Cooks			
677	2,638	4,222	569	801	2,852	66. In-door servants			
153	683	689	108	145	435	67. Grooms, coachmen and dog-boys, etc.			
907	3,158	2,263	295	472	1,496	68. Door-keepers, etc.			
3,237	11,063	13,268	1,805	2,688	8,795	TOTAL SUB-ORDER 14			
...	3	3	1	...	2	69. Hotel lodging and refreshment room-keepers	15.—NON-DOMESTIC ESTABLISHMENT.		
...	3	3	1	...	2	TOTAL SUB-ORDER 15			
2	3	2	...	...	2	73. Sanitary inspectors, local and municipal	16.—SANITATION		
693	1,467	2,567	437	634	1,496	74. Sweepers			
694	1,470	2,569	437	634	1,498	TOTAL SUB-ORDER 16			
3,931	12,536	15,860	2,243	3,322	10,295	**Total Order VI.—Personal and Household Services.**			
119	243	560	102	138	320	76. Milk and butter seller	17.—ANIMAL FOOD	VII.—FOOD AND DRINK.	CLASS D.—PREPARATION AND SUPPLY OF MATERIAL SUBSTANCES.
20	48	74	13	5	56	77. Ghee preparers and sellers			
156	338	564	97	150	317	79. Butchers			
6	22	5	1	1	3	80. Eggs dealer			
8	22	4	1	...	3	81. Fishermen			
309	673	1,207	214	294	699	TOTAL SUB-ORDER 17			
40	164	417	44	79	294	83. Grain dealers	18.—VEGETABLE FOOD		
44	100	154	26	30	98	84. Grain parchers			
...	2	430	59	109	262	85. Flour preparers and sellers			
97	123	598	42	80	476	86. Flour mill service			
9	40	16	3	4	9	87. Bakers			
1	2	...	...	...	...	88. Bran sellers			
80	159	578	50	84	444	89. Vegetable sellers			
40	105	172	26	40	106	90. Fruit sellers			
193	777	755	99	127	529	92. Sweetmeat makers and sellers			
504	1,472	3,120	349	553	2,218	TOTAL SUB-ORDER 18			
...	...	1	...	...	1	94. Ice manufacturers and sellers	19.—DRINK, CONDIMENTS AND NARCOTICS.		
17	36	...	...	...	...	95. Sodawater, lemonade manufacturers and sellers			
52	145	151	22	36	93	97. Country spirit distillers and sellers			
...	...	2	...	...	2	101. Tea sellers			
8	21	...	...	...	...	103. Sugar sellers			
19	47	128	22	31	75	104. Jaggery sellers			
...	7	3	...	...	3	105. Salt sellers			
...	2	...	...	...	...	106. Ajwain seller			
475	1,399	1,595	213	371	1,011	109. Grocers and general condiment dealers			
25	111	89	9	24	56	111. Bettle-leaf sellers			
59	127	193	32	59	102	112. Tobacco sellers			
5	46	12	2	2	8	114. Opium manufacturers and sellers			
651	1,931	2,174	300	523	1,351	TOTAL SUB-ORDER 19			
1,464	4,076	6,501	863	1,370	4,[illegible]68	**Total Order VII.—Food and Drink**			
344	939	1,412	192	343	877	116. Oil pressers and sellers	20. LIGHTING	VIII.—LIGHT, FIRING AND FORAGE.	
...	3	...	...	...	...	120. Torch makers and sellers			
1	2	...	...	...	...	121. Kerosine oil dealers			
...	1	...	...	...	...	122. Matches sellers			
...	1	...	...	...	...	123. Lamp sellers			
345	946	1,412	192	343	877	TOTAL SUB-ORDER 20			
420	807	1,439	187	369	883	125. Firewood and grass gatherers and sellers	21.—FUEL AND FORAGE		
...	1	...	...	...	...	128. Coal dealers			
...	1	39	7	8	24	130. Cowdung fuel preparers and sellers			
420	809	1,478	194	377	907	TOTAL SUB-ORDER 21			
785	1,755	2,890	386	720	1,784	**Total Order VIII.—Light, Firing and Forage**			
1	2	8	...	2	6	132. Brick and tile burners and sellers	22.—BUILDING MATERIALS.	IX.—BUILDINGS.	
28	83	115	16	37	62	133. Lime, chunam burners and sellers			
2	16	4	1	2	1	134. Stone dealers			
42	94	34	8	10	16	135. Thatch dealers and thatchers			
72	195	161	25	51	85	TOTAL SUB-ORDER 22			

Table XVII A.—Occupations.—Ajmere.

TABLE XVII.—Part A.—

Class.	Order.	Sub-order and Group.	Occupations.	TOWN. Total. Total.	Total. 0—4	Total. 5—14	Total. 15 and over.	Males. Total.	Males. 0—4	Males. 5—14	Males. 15 and over.	Females. Total.	Females. 0—4	Females. 5—14	Females. 15 and over.
				17	18	19	20	21	22	23	24	25	26	27	28
CLASS C.	VI.—PERSONAL AND HOUSEHOLD SERVICES.	14.—Personal and Domestic Services.	59. Barbers	1,496	170	269	1,057	917	87	166	664	579	83	103	393
			60. Ear-pickers	1	...	...	1	1	...	...	1	...	...	...	...
			62. Castemark appliers	3	...	...	3	2	...	..	2	1	...	...	1
			63. Washermen	1,176	178	324	674	576	77	166	333	600	101	158	341
			64. Water-carriers	3,162	369	556	2,237	1,227	164	251	812	1,935	205	305	1,425
			65. Cooks	1,737	193	374	1,170	1,261	114	244	903	476	79	130	267
			66. In-door servants	4,562	558	819	3,185	1,929	189	364	1,376	2,633	369	455	1,809
			67. Grooms, coachmen and dog-boys, etc.	1,390	172	256	962	790	74	131	585	600	98	125	377
			68. Door-keepers, etc.	3,525	433	652	2,440	2,430	297	433	1,700	1,095	136	219	740
			Total Sub-order 14	17,052	2,073	3,250	11,729	9,133	1,002	1,755	6,376	7,919	1,071	1,495	5,353
		15.—Non-domestic Establishment.	69. Hotel, lodging and refreshment room-keepers.	2	...	...	2	1	...	...	1	1	...	...	1
			Total Sub-order 15	2	...	...	2	1	...	...	1	1	...	...	1
		16.—Sanitation	73. Sanitary inspectors, local and municipal.	6	...	1	5	4	...	1	3	2	...	...	2
			74. Sweepers	2,512	395	568	1,549	1,296	201	287	808	1,216	194	281	741
			Total Sub-order 16	2,518	395	569	1,554	1,300	201	288	811	1,218	194	282	743
			Total Order VI.—Personal and Household Services.	**19,572**	**2,468**	**3,819**	**13,285**	**10,434**	**1,203**	**2,043**	**7,188**	**9,138**	**1,265**	**1,776**	**6,097**
CLASS D.—PREPARATION AND SUPPLY OF MATERIAL SUBSTANCES.	VII.—FOOD AND DRINK.	17.—Animal Food	76. Milk and butter seller	605	100	144	361	240	32	59	149	365	68	85	212
			77. Ghee preparers and sellers	100	10	16	74	53	5	13	35	47	5	3	38
			79. Butchers	744	114	185	445	347	52	86	209	397	62	99	236
			80 Eggs dealer	36	4	7	25	31	3	6	22	5	1	1	3
			81. Fishermen	8	1	1	6	4	...	1	3	4	1	...	3
			Total Sub-order 17	1,493	229	353	911	675	92	165	418	818	137	188	493
		18.—Vegetable Food	83 Grain dealers	578	57	104	417	196	17	33	146	382	40	71	271
			84. Grain parchers	159	23	34	102	81	11	22	48	78	12	12	54
			85. Flour preparers and sellers	98	15	18	65	3	1	...	2	95	14	18	63
			86. Flour mill service	615	98	138	379	277	68	89	120	338	30	49	259
			87. Bakers	67	5	13	49	51	2	9	40	16	3	4	9
			88. Bran sellers	3	...	1	2	3	...	1	2	...	...	...	...
			89. Vegetable sellers	769	86	144	539	264	43	74	147	505	43	70	392
			90. Fruit sellers	307	46	67	194	150	21	33	96	157	25	34	98
			92. Sweetmeat makers and sellers	1,399	149	234	1,016	820	72	138	610	579	77	96	406
			Total Sub-order 18	3,995	479	753	2,763	1,845	235	399	1,211	2,150	244	354	1,552
		19.—Drink, Condiments and Narcotics.	94. Ice manufacturers and sellers	1	...	...	1	...	...	...	...	1	...	...	1
			95. Sodawater, lemonade manufacturers and sellers.	61	8	17	36	61	8	17	36	...	...	...	...
			97. Country spirit distillers and sellers	19	1	4	14	13	...	3	10	6	1	1	4
			101. Tea sellers	2	...	...	2	...	...	...	...	2	...	...	2
			103. Sugar sellers	35	6	8	21	35	6	8	21	...	...	...	...
			104. Jaggery sellers	184	26	46	112	64	5	17	42	120	21	29	70
			105. Salt sellers	9	...	...	9	7	...	...	7	2	...	...	2
			106. Ajwain seller	2	...	...	2	2	...	...	2	...	...	...	...
			109. Grocers and general condiment dealers.	684	81	136	467	517	60	104	353	167	21	32	114
			111. Betele-leaf sellers	199	17	37	145	131	12	20	99	68	5	17	46
			112. Tobacco sellers	330	48	96	186	164	18	44	102	166	30	52	84
			114. Opium manufacturers and sellers	67	7	7	53	55	5	5	45	12	2	2	8
			Total Sub-order 19	1,593	194	351	1,048	1,049	114	218	717	544	80	133	331
			Total Order VII.—Food and Drink	**7,081**	**902**	**1,457**	**4,722**	**3,569**	**441**	**782**	**2,346**	**3,512**	**461**	**675**	**2,376**
	VIII.—LIGHT, FIRING AND FORAGE.	20.—Lighting	116. Oil pressers and sellers	1,046	137	256	653	414	54	111	249	632	83	145	404
			120 Torch makers and sellers	3	...	...	3	3	...	...	3	...	...	...	...
			121. Kerosine oil dealers	3	...	1	2	3	...	1	2	...	...	...	...
			122. Matches sellers	1	...	...	1	1	...	...	1	...	...	...	...
			123. Lamp sellers	1	...	...	1	1	...	...	1	...	...	...	...
			Total Sub-order 20	1,054	137	257	660	422	54	112	256	632	83	145	404
		21.—Fuel and forage	125. Firewood and grass gatherers and sellers.	934	141	224	569	461	73	122	266	473	68	102	303
			128. Coal dealers	1	...	...	1	1	...	...	1	...	...	...	...
			130. Cowdung fuel preparers and sellers.	4	..	...	4	...	...	...	...	4	...	...	4
			Total Sub-order 21	939	141	224	574	462	73	122	267	477	68	102	307
			Total Order VIII.—Light, Firing and Forage.	**1,993**	**278**	**481**	**1,234**	**884**	**127**	**234**	**523**	**1,109**	**151**	**247**	**711**
	IX.—BUILDINGS.	22.—Building Materials.	132. Brick and tile burners and sellers	11	...	3	8	3	...	1	2	8	...	2	6
			133. Lime, chuam burners and sellers	168	22	44	102	91	12	20	59	77	10	24	43
			134. Stone dealers	15	...	2	13	15	...	2	13	...	...	...	...
			135 Thatch dealers and thatchers	179	27	46	106	150	19	40	91	29	8	6	15
			Total Sub-order 22	373	49	95	229	259	31	62	165	114	18	32	64

Occupations—*contd.*

COUNTRY.												Occupations.	Sub-order and Group.	Order.	Class.
Total.				Males.				Females.							
Total.	0—4	5—14	15 and over.	Total.	0—4	5—14	15 and over.	Total.	0—4	5—14	15 and over.				
29	30	31	32	33	34	35	36	37	38	39	40				
4,040	522	933	2,585	2,222	253	505	1,464	1,818	269	428	1,121	59. Barbers	14.—Personal and Domestic Services.	VI.—Personal and Household Services.	Class C.
...	...	...	...	...	...	...	...	...	...	...	...	60. Ear-pickers			
...	...	...	...	...	...	...	...	...	...	...	...	62. Castemark appliers			
1,058	154	255	649	534	85	138	311	524	69	117	338	63. Washermen			
212	31	44	137	87	11	17	59	125	20	27	78	64. Water-carriers			
111	14	15	82	55	7	13	35	56	7	2	47	65. Cooks			
3,354	390	659	2,305	1,765	190	313	1,262	1,589	200	346	1,043	66. In-door servants			
224	25	42	157	135	15	22	98	89	10	20	59	67. Grooms, coachmen and dog-boys, etc.			
2,336	395	727	2,214	2,168	236	474	1,458	1,168	159	253	756	68. Door-keepers, etc.			
12,335	1,531	2,675	8,129	6,966	797	1,482	4,687	5,369	734	1,193	3,442	Total Sub-order 14			
4	1	...	3	2	...	...	2	2	1	...	1	69. Hotel, lodging and refreshment room-keepers.	15.—Non-domestic Establishment.		
4	1	...	3	2	...	...	2	2	1	...	1	Total Sub-order 15			
...	...	...	...	...	...	...	...	...	...	...	...	73. Sanitary inspectors, local and municipal.	16.—Sanitation		
2,625	452	759	1,414	1,274	209	406	659	1,351	243	353	755	74. Sweepers			
2,625	452	759	1,414	1,274	209	406	659	1,351	243	353	755	Total Sub-order 16			
14,964	1,984	3,434	9,546	8,242	1,006	1,888	5,348	6,722	978	1,546	4,198	**Total Order VI.—Personal and Household Service.**			
371	56	113	202	176	22	60	94	195	34	53	108	76. Milk and butter seller	17.—Animal Food	VII.—Food and Drink.	Class D.—Preparation and Supply of Material Substances.
50	11	9	30	23	3	7	13	27	8	2	17	77. Ghee preparers and sellers			
396	65	121	210	229	30	70	129	167	35	51	81	79. Butchers			
...	...	...	...	...	...	...	...	...	...	...	...	80. Eggs dealer			
27	1	7	19	27	1	7	19	...	...	...	...	81. Fishermen			
844	133	250	461	455	56	144	255	389	77	106	206	Total Sub-order 17			
65	9	15	41	30	5	7	18	35	4	8	23	83. Grain dealers	18.—Vegetable Food		
166	30	40	96	90	16	22	52	76	14	18	44	84. Grain parchers			
335	45	91	199	...	...	...	...	335	45	91	199	85. Flour preparers and sellers			
276	17	39	220	16	5	8	3	260	12	31	217	86. Flour mill service			
...	...	...	...	...	...	...	...	...	...	...	...	87. Bakers			
...	...	...	...	...	...	...	...	...	...	...	...	88. Bran sellers			
93	9	20	64	20	2	6	12	73	7	14	52	89. Vegetable sellers			
34	4	13	17	19	3	7	9	15	1	6	8	90. Fruit sellers			
432	56	86	290	256	34	55	167	176	22	31	123	92. Sweetmeat makers and sellers			
1,401	170	304	927	431	65	105	261	970	105	299	666	Total Sub-order 18			
...	...	...	...	...	...	...	...	...	...	...	...	94. Ice manufacturers and sellers	19.—Drink, Condiments and Narcotics.		
...	...	...	...	...	...	...	...	...	...	...	...	95. Sodawater, lemonade manufacturers and sellers.			
370	62	84	224	225	41	49	135	145	21	35	89	97. Country spirit distillers and sellers			
...	...	...	...	...	...	...	...	...	...	...	...	101. Tea sellers			
...	...	...	...	...	...	...	...	...	...	...	...	103. Sugar sellers			
17	3	4	10	9	2	2	5	8	1	2	5	104. Jaggery sellers			
1	...	...	1	...	...	...	...	1	...	...	1	105. Salt sellers			
...	...	...	...	...	...	...	...	...	...	...	...	106. Ajwain seller			
3,016	363	710	1,943	1,588	171	371	1,046	1,428	192	339	897	109. Grocers and general condiment dealers.			
41	7	12	22	20	3	5	12	21	4	7	10	111. Betel-leaf sellers			
51	5	13	33	24	3	6	15	27	2	7	18	112. Tobacco sellers			
1	...	...	1	1	...	...	1	...	...	...	...	114. Opium manufacturers and sellers			
3,497	440	823	2,234	1,867	220	433	1,214	1,630	220	390	1,020	Total Sub-order 19			
5,742	743	1,377	3,622	2,753	341	682	1,730	2,989	402	605	1,892	**Total Order VII.—Food and Drink**			
1,839	245	431	1,163	1,059	136	233	690	780	109	198	473	116. Oil pressers and sellers	20.—Lighting	VIII.—Light, Firing and Forage.	
...	...	...	...	...	...	...	...	...	...	...	...	120. Torch makers and sellers			
...	...	...	...	...	...	...	...	...	...	...	...	121. Kerosine oil dealers			
...	...	...	...	...	...	...	...	...	...	...	...	122. Matches sellers			
...	...	...	...	...	...	...	...	...	...	...	...	123. Lamp sellers			
1,839	245	431	1,163	1,059	136	233	690	780	109	198	473	Total Sub-order 20			
1,920	234	565	1,121	954	115	298	541	966	119	267	580	125. Firewood and grass gatherers and sellers.	21.—Fuel and Forage		
...	...	...	...	...	...	...	...	...	...	...	...	128. Coal dealers			
37	8	8	21	2	1	...	1	35	7	8	20	130. Cowdung fuel preparers and sellers			
1,957	242	573	1,142	956	116	298	542	1,001	126	275	600	Total Sub-order 21			
3,796	487	1,004	2,305	2,015	252	531	1,232	1,781	235	473	1,073	**Total Order VIII.—Light, Firing and Forage.**			
...	...	...	...	...	...	...	...	...	...	...	...	132. Brick and tile burners and sellers	22.—Building Materials.	IX.—Buildings.	
74	10	21	43	36	4	8	24	38	6	13	19	133. Lime, chunam burners and sellers			
7	1	2	4	3	...	...	3	4	1	2	1	134. Stone dealers			
11	1	6	4	6	1	2	3	5	...	4	1	135. Thatch dealers and thatchers			
92	12	29	51	45	5	10	30	47	7	19	21	Total Sub-order 22			

TABLE XVII.—Part A.—

Class.	Order.	Sub order and Group.	Occupations.	TOTAL Total. Total.	 0—4	 5—14	 15 and over.	 Ma Total.	 0—4
1	2	3	4	5	6	7	8	9	10
CLASS D.—PREPARATION AND SUPPLY OF MATERIAL SUBSTANCES—contd.	IX.—BUILDINGS—contd.	23.—Artificers in Building.	137. Stone and marble workers	329	50	78	201	285	26
			138. Masons	3,318	513	757	2,048	1,791	261
			139. Builders and joiners	2	...	...	2	2	...
			140. Plasterers and house painters	5	2	1	2	5	2
			141. Mud wall and roof builders	73	9	20	44	50	5
			Total Sub-order 23	3,727	574	856	2,297	2,033	294
			Total Order IX.—Buildings	**4,192**	**635**	**980**	**2,577**	**2,337**	**330**
	X.—VEHICLES AND VESSELS.	24.—Railway Plant	144. Railway mechanics (fitters, painters, boiler makers, rivetters, etc.)	6,074	871	1,010	4,193	4,156	509
			145. Railway permanent-way, foremen, plate-layers, inspectors, etc.	230	27	37	166	148	17
			Total Sub-order 24	6,304	898	1,047	4,359	4,304	526
		25.—Carts, Carriages, etc.	146. Cart makers	4	...	2	2	4	...
			Total Sub-order 25	4	...	2	2	4	...
			Total Order X.—Vehicles and Vessels	**6,308**	**898**	**1,049**	**4,361**	**4,308**	**526**
	XI.—SUPPLEMENTARY REQUIREMENTS.	27.—Paper, etc.	153. Paper sellers	16	1	5	10	5	...
			Total Sub-order 27	16	1	5	10	5	...
		28.—Books and Prints, etc.	157. Press proprietors and printers and lithographers.	530	66	101	363	358	42
			158. Book-binders	64	7	16	41	40	3
			159. Book-sellers	74	7	16	51	44	2
			Total Sub-order 28	668	80	133	455	442	47
		29.—Watches, Clocks and Scientific Instruments.	163. Watch and clock makers and sellers	51	6	12	33	23	5
			Total Sub-order 29	51	6	12	33	23	5
		30.—Carving, Engraving etc.	170. Ivory carvers	7	2	2	3	6	2
			172. Turners	200	37	41	122	206	22
			Total Sub-order 30	207	39	43	125	212	24
		31.—Toys, Curiousities, etc.	177. Toys, kites makers and sellers	23	1	1	21	10	...
			178. Hukka stem makers and sellers	12	1	5	6	6	1
			Total Sub-order 31	35	2	6	27	16	1
		33.—Necklaces, Bracelets, Beads, Sacred Threads.	185. Bangle makers and sellers in lac	1,651	199	354	1,098	808	104
			187. Narailee bangle makers and sellers	7	1	2	4	7	1
			189. Bangle makers and sellers in glass	7	1	1	5	7	1
			193. Rosary and necklace makers and sellers	80	11	11	60	38	4
			194. Flower garland makers and sellers	33	3	10	20	11	...
			195. Artificial flower and caste-mark spangle makers and sellers.	1	...	...	1	1	...
			196. Sacred thread makers and sellers	2	...	...	2	1	...
			Total Sub-order 33	1,783	215	378	1,190	871	110
		34.—Furniture	198. Furniture makers	7	...	1	6	3	...
			199. Frame makers	2	...	1	1	2	...
			Total Sub-order 34	9	...	2	7	5	...
		35.—Harness	201. Saddlery and harness makers and sellers	6	1	1	4	3	...
			202. Saddle cloth makers, embroiderers and sellers	38	4	12	22	2	...
			Total Sub-order 35	44	5	13	26	5	...
		36.—Tools and Machinery.	204. Knife and tool makers and sellers	2	...	...	2	1	...
			205. Knife and tool grinders	7	...	...	7	4	...
			207. Mecnanic	18	6	7	5	11	3
			Total Sub-order 36	27	6	7	14	16	3
		37.—Arms and Ammunition.	209. Gun menders and sellers	23	4	7	12	9	2
			211. Gun powder makers and sellers	83	14	23	46	19	2
			212. Fire-work makers and sellers	30	2	5	23	23	1
			213. Sword and scabbard makers and sellers	34	2	14	18	22	2
			214. Shield makers and sellers	5	...	1	4	5	...
			Total Sub-order 37	175	22	50	103	78	7
			Total Order XI.—Supplementary Requirements.	**3,015**	**6**	**64**	**1,990**	**1,573**	**197**

Occupations—*contd.*

POPULATION.									
...LES.		FEMALES.				Occupations.	Sub-order and Group.	Order.	Class.
5—14	15 and over.	Total.	0—4	5—14	15 and over.				
11	12	13	14	15	16				
47	112	144	24	31	89	137. Stone and marble workers	23.—Artificers in Building.	IX.—Buildings—*contd.*	Class D.—Preparation and Supply of Material Substances—*contd.*
395	1,135	1,527	252	362	913	138. Masons			
...	2	...	...	...	...	139. Builders and joiners			
1	2	...	...	...	...	140. Plasterers and house painters			
15	30	23	4	5	14	141. Mud wall and roof builders			
458	1,281	1,694	280	398	1,016	Total Sub-order 23			
531	1,476	1,855	305	449	1,101	**Total Order IX.—Buildings**			
651	2,996	1,918	362	359	1,197	144. Railway mechanics (fitters, painters, boiler makers, rivetters, etc.)	24.—Railway Plant	X.—Vehicles and Vessels.	
21	110	82	10	16	56	145. Railway permanent-way, foremen, plate-layers, inspectors, etc.			
672	3,106	2,000	372	375	1,253	Total Sub-order 24			
2	2	...	...	...	...	146. Cart makers	25.—Carts, Carriages, etc.		
2	2	...	...	...	...	Total Sub-order 25			
674	3,108	2,000	372	375	1,253	**Total Order X.—Vehicles and Vessels**			
2	3	11	1	3	7	153. Paper sellers	27.—Paper, etc.	XI.—Supplementary Requirements.	
2	3	11	1	3	7	Total Sub-order 27			
58	258	172	24	43	105	157. Press proprietors and printers and lithographers.	28.—Books and Prints, etc		
10	27	24	4	6	14	158. Book-binders			
11	31	30	5	5	20	159. Book-sellers			
79	316	226	33	54	139	Total Sub-order 28			
7	11	28	1	5	22	163. Watch and clock makers and sellers	29.—Watches, Clocks and Scientific Instruments.		
7	11	28	1	5	22	Total Sub-order 29			
2	2	1	...	...	1	170. Ivory carvers	30.—Carving, Engraving, etc.		
24	60	94	15	17	62	172. Turners			
26	62	95	15	17	63	Total Sub-order 30			
1	9	13	1	...	12	177. Toys, kites makers and sellers	31.—Toys, Curiosities, etc.		
3	2	6	...	2	4	178. Hukka stem makers and sellers			
4	11	19	1	2	16	Total Sub-order 31			
172	532	843	95	182	566	185. Bangle makers and sellers in lac	33.—Necklaces, Bracelets, Beads, Sacred Threads.		
2	4	...	...	...	...	187. Narailee bangle makers and sellers			
1	5	...	...	...	...	189 Bangle makers and sellers in glass			
3	29	46	7	8	31	193. Rosary and necklace makers and sellers			
7	4	22	3	3	16	194. Flower garland makers and sellers			
...	1	...	..	...	...	195. Artificial flower and caste-mark spangle makers and sellers.			
...	1	1	...	...	1	196. Sacred thread makers and sellers			
185	576	912	105	193	614	Total Sub-order 33			
1	2	4	...	...	4	198. Furniture makers	34.—Furniture		
1	1	...	...	...	...	199. Frame makers			
2	3	4	...	...	4	Total Sub-order 34			
1	2	3	1	...	2	201. Saddlery and harness makers and sellers	35.—Harness		
2	...	36	4	10	22	202. Saddle cloth makers, embroiderers and sellers			
3	2	39	5	10	24	Total Sub-order 35			
...	1	1	...	...	1	204. Knife and tool makers and sellers	36.—Tools and Machinery.		
...	4	3	...	..	3	205. Knife and tool grinders			
6	2	7	3	1	3	207. Mechanic			
6	7	11	3	1	7	Total Sub-order 36			
2	5	14	2	5	7	209. Gun menders and selleres	37.—Arms and Ammunition.		
8	9	64	12	15	37	211. Gun powder makers and sellers			
5	17	7	1	...	6	212. Fire-work makers and sellers			
9	11	12	...	5	7	213. Sword and scabbard makers and sellers			
1	4	...	...	...	...	214. Shield makers and sellers			
25	46	97	15	25	57	Total Sub-order 37			
399	1,037	1,442	179	310	953	**Total Order XI.—Supplementary Requirements.**			

TABLE XVII.—Part A.—

Class.	Order.	Sub-order and Group.	Occupations.	TOWN. Total. Total.	Total. 0—4	Total. 5—14	Total. 15 and over.	Males. Total.	Males. 0—4	Males. 5—14	Males. 15 and over.	Females. Total.	Females. 0—4	Females. 5—14	Females. 15 and over.
				17	18	19	20	21	22	23	24	25	26	27	28
CLASS D.—PREPARATION AND SUPPLY OF MATERIAL SUBSTANCES—contd.	IX.—BUILDINGS—contd.	23.—Artificers in Building.	137. Stone and marble workers	26	3	5	18	23	3	5	15	3	...	...	3
			138. Masons	2,495	405	602	1,488	1,233	200	301	732	1,262	205	301	756
			139. Builders and joiners	2	...	...	2	2	...	...	2	...	...	...	...
			140. Plasterers and house painters	1	...	...	1	1	...	...	1	...	...	...	...
			141. Mud wall and roof builders	1	...	...	1	...	...	...	...	1	...	...	1
			Total Sub-order 23	2,525	408	607	1,510	1,259	203	306	750	1,266	205	301	760
			Total Order IX.—Buildings	2,898	457	702	1,739	1,518	234	369	915	1,380	223	333	824
	X.—VEHICLES AND VESSELS.	24.—Railway Plant.	144. Railway mechanics (fitters, painters, boiler makers, rivetters, etc.	6,016	870	1,004	4,142	4,098	508	645	2,945	1,918	362	359	1,197
			145. Railway permanent-way, foremen, plate-layers, inspectors, etc.	215	27	32	156	137	17	17	103	78	10	15	53
			Total Sub-order 24	6,231	897	1,036	4,298	4,235	525	662	3,048	1,996	372	374	1,250
		25.—Carts, Carriages, etc.	146. Cart makers	4	...	2	2	4	...	2	2	...	...	...	...
			Total Sub-order 25	4	...	2	2	4	...	2	2	...	...	...	...
			Total Order X.—Vehicles and Vessels.	6,235	897	1,038	4,300	4,239	525	664	3,050	1,996	372	374	1,250
	XI.—SUPPLEMENTARY REQUIREMENTS.	27.—Paper, etc.	153. Paper sellers	16	1	5	10	5	...	2	3	11	1	3	7
			Total Sub-order 27	16	1	5	10	5	...	2	3	11	1	3	7
		28.—Books and Prints, etc.	157. Press proprietors and printers and lithographers.	485	58	82	345	334	38	46	250	151	20	36	95
			158. Book-binders	64	7	16	41	40	3	10	27	24	4	6	14
			159. Book-sellers	74	7	16	51	44	2	11	31	30	5	5	20
			Total Sub-order 28	623	72	114	437	418	43	67	308	205	29	47	129
		29.—Watches, Clocks and Scientific Instruments.	163. Watch and clock makers and sellers.	44	6	10	28	17	5	5	7	27	1	5	21
			Total Sub-order 29	44	6	10	28	17	5	5	7	27	1	5	21
		30.—Carving, Engraving, etc.	170 Ivory carvers	4	2	1	1	4	2	1	1	...	...	...	...
			172. Turners	199	37	41	121	105	22	24	59	94	15	17	62
			Total Sub-order 30	203	39	42	122	109	24	25	60	94	15	17	62
		31.—Toys, Curiosities, etc.	177. Toys, kites makers and sellers	23	1	1	21	10	...	1	9	13	1	...	12
			178. Hukka stem makers and sellers	12	1	5	6	6	1	3	2	6	...	2	4
			Total Sub-order 31	35	2	6	27	16	1	4	11	19	1	2	16
		33.—Necklaces, Bracelets, Beads, Sacred Threads	185. Bangle makers and sellers in lac	849	66	171	612	386	31	77	278	463	35	94	334
			187. Narallee bangle makers and sellers	2	1	...	1	2	1	...	1	...	...	...	...
			189. Bangle makers and sellers in glass	2	1	...	1	2	1	...	1	...	...	...	...
			193. Rosary and necklace makers and sellers.	76	11	11	54	33	4	3	26	43	7	8	28
			194. Flower garland makers and sellers	33	3	10	20	11	...	7	4	22	3	3	16
			195. Artificial flower and caste-mark spangle makers and sellers.	1	...	...	1	1	...	...	1	...	...	...	...
			196. Sacred thread makers and sellers	1	...	...	1	1	...	...	1	...	...	...	...
			Total Sub-order 33	964	82	192	690	436	37	87	312	528	45	105	378
		34.—Furniture	198. Furniture makers	7	...	1	6	3	...	1	2	4	...	...	4
			199. Frame makers	1	...	...	1	1	...	...	1	...	...	...	...
			Total Sub-order 34	8	...	1	7	4	...	1	3	4	...	...	4
		35.—Harness	201. Saddlery and harness makers and sellers.	2	...	...	2	1	...	...	1	1	...	...	1
			202. Saddle cloth makers, embroiderers and sellers.	38	4	12	22	2	...	2	...	36	4	10	22
			Total Sub-order 35	40	4	12	24	3	...	2	1	37	4	10	23
		36.—Tools and Machinery.	204. Knife and tool makers and sellers.	2	...	...	2	1	...	...	1	1	...	...	1
			205. Knife and tool grinders	2	...	...	2	1	...	...	1	1	...	...	1
			207. Mechanic	18	6	7	5	11	3	6	2	7	3	1	3
			Total Sub-order 36	22	6	7	9	13	3	6	4	9	3	1	5
		37.—Arms and Ammunition.	209. Gun menders and sellers	...	...	...	...	...	...	...	...	...	...	...	...
			211. Gun powder makers and sellers	48	9	11	28	7	1	1	5	41	8	10	23
			212. Fire work makers and sellers	30	2	5	23	23	1	5	17	7	1	...	6
			213. Sword and scabbard makers and sellers.	18	1	5	12	8	1	1	6	10	...	4	6
			214. Shield makers and sellers	5	...	1	4	5	...	1	4	...	...	...	...
			Total Sub-order 37	101	12	22	67	43	3	8	32	58	9	14	35
			Total Order XI.—Supplementary Requirements.	2,056	224	411	1,421	1,064	116	207	741	992	108	204	680

Occupations—*contd.*

Country: Total: Total.	Total: 0—4	Total: 5—14	Total: 15 and over.	Males: Total.	Males: 0—4	Males: 5—14	Males: 15 and over.	Females: Total.	Females: 0—4	Females: 5—14	Females: 15 and over.	Occupations.	Sub-order and Group.	Order	Class.
29	30	31	32	33	34	35	36	37	38	39	40				
303	47	73	183	162	23	42	97	141	24	31	86	137. Stone and marble workers	23.—Artificers in Building.	IX.—Buildings—*contd.*	Class D.—Preparation and Supply of Material Substances—*contd.*
823	108	155	550	558	61	94	403	265	47	61	157	138. Masons			
...	...	...	...	...	...	...	...	...	...	...	...	139. Builders and joiners			
4	2	1	1	4	2	1	1	...	...	...	...	140. Plasterers and house painters			
72	9	20	43	50	5	15	30	22	4	5	13	141. Mud wall and roof builders			
1,202	166	249	787	774	91	152	531	428	75	97	256	Total Sub-order 23			
1,294	178	278	838	819	96	162	561	475	82	116	277	**Total Order IX.—Buildings**			
58	1	6	51	58	1	6	51	...	...	...	...	144. Railway mechanics (fitters, painters, boiler makers, rivetters, etc.)	24.—Railway Plant.	X.—Vehicles and Vessels.	
15	...	5	10	11	...	4	7	4	...	1	3	145. Railway permanent-way, foremen, plate-layers, inspectors, etc.			
73	1	11	61	69	1	10	58	4	...	1	3	Total Sub-order 24			
...	...	...	...	...	...	...	...	...	...	...	...	146. Cart makers	25.—Carts, Carriages etc.		
...	...	...	...	...	...	...	...	...	...	...	...	Total Sub-order 25			
73	1	11	61	69	1	10	58	4	...	1	3	**Total Order X.—Vehicles and Vessels.**			
...	...	...	...	...	...	...	...	...	...	...	...	153. Paper sellers	27.—Papers, etc.	XI.—Supplementary Requirements.	
...	...	...	...	...	...	...	...	...	...	...	...	Total Sub-order 27			
45	8	19	18	24	4	12	8	21	4	7	10	157. Press proprietors and printers and lithographers.	28.—Books and Prints, etc.		
...	...	...	...	...	...	...	...	...	...	...	...	158. Book-binders			
...	...	...	...	...	...	...	...	...	...	...	...	159. Book-sellers			
45	8	19	18	24	4	12	8	21	4	7	10	Total Sub-order 28			
7	...	2	5	6	...	2	4	1	...	...	1	163. Watch and clock makers and sellers.	29.—Watches, Clocks and Scientific Instruments.		
7	...	2	5	6	...	2	4	1	...	...	1	Total Sub-order 29			
3	...	1	2	2	...	1	1	1	...	...	1	170. Ivory carvers	30.—Carving, Engraving, etc.		
1	...	...	1	1	...	...	1	...	...	...	...	172. Turners			
4	...	1	3	3	...	1	2	1	...	...	1	Total Sub-order 30			
...	...	...	...	...	...	...	...	...	...	...	...	177. Toys, kites makers and sellers	31.—Toys, Curiosities, etc.		
...	...	...	...	...	...	...	...	...	...	...	...	178. Hukka stem makers and sellers			
...	...	...	...	...	...	...	...	...	...	...	...	Total Sub-order 31			
802	133	183	486	422	73	95	254	380	60	88	232	185. Bangle makers and sellers in lac	33.—Necklaces, Bracelets, Beads, Sacred Threads.		
5	...	2	3	5	...	2	3	...	...	...	...	187. Narallee bangle makers and sellers			
5	...	1	4	5	...	1	4	...	...	...	...	189. Bangle makers and sellers in glass			
6	...	...	6	3	...	...	3	3	...	...	3	193. Rosary and necklace makers and sellers.			
...	...	...	...	...	...	...	...	...	...	...	...	194. Flower garland makers and sellers			
...	...	...	...	...	...	...	...	...	...	...	...	195. Artificial flower and caste-mark spangle makers and sellers.			
1	...	...	1	...	...	...	...	1	...	...	1	196. Sacred thread makers and sellers			
819	133	186	500	435	73	98	264	384	60	88	236	Total Sub-order 33			
...	...	...	...	...	...	...	...	...	...	...	...	198. Furniture makers	34.—Furniture.		
1	...	1	...	1	...	1	...	...	...	...	...	199. Frame makers			
1	...	1	...	1	...	1	...	...	...	...	...	Total Sub-order 34			
4	1	1	2	2	...	1	1	2	1	...	1	201. Saddlery and harness makers and sellers.	35.—Harness.		
...	...	...	...	...	...	...	...	...	...	...	...	202. Saddle cloth makers, embroiderers and sellers.			
4	1	1	2	2	...	1	1	2	1	...	1	Total Sub-order 35			
...	...	...	...	...	...	...	...	...	...	...	...	204. Knife and tool makers and sellers.	36.—Tools and Machinery.		
5	...	...	5	3	...	...	3	2	...	...	2	205. Knife and tool grinders			
...	...	...	...	...	...	...	...	...	...	...	...	207. Mechanic			
5	...	...	5	3	...	...	3	2	...	...	2	Total Sub-order 36			
23	4	7	12	9	2	2	5	14	2	5	7	209. Gun menders and sellers	37.—Arms and Ammunition.		
35	5	12	18	12	1	7	4	23	4	5	14	211. Gun powder makers and sellers			
...	...	...	...	...	...	...	...	...	...	...	...	212. Fire-work makers and sellers			
16	1	9	6	14	1	8	5	2	...	1	1	213. Sword and scabbard makers and sellers.			
...	...	...	...	...	...	...	...	...	...	...	...	214. Shield makers and sellers			
74	10	28	36	35	4	17	14	39	6	11	22	Total Sub-order 37			
959	152	238	569	509	81	132	296	450	71	106	273	**Total Order XI.—Supplementary Requirements.**			

TABLE XVII.—Part A —

Class.	Order.	Sub-order and Group.	OCCUPATIONS.	TOTAL POPULA[TION] — TOTAL. — TOTAL.	0—4	5—14	15 and over.	MAL[ES]. — TOTAL.	0—4
1	2	3	4	5	6	7	8	9	10
CLASS D.—PREPARATION AND SUPPLY OF MATERIAL SUBSTANCES—*contd.*	XII.—TEXTILE FABRICS AND DRESS.	38.—WOOL AND FUR	218. Shawl weavers and sellers	51	...	7	44	51	...
			220. Blanket weavers and sellers	53	8	17	28	29	6
			221. Woollen cloth manufacturers and dealers	280	51	81	148	125	24
			222. Woollen yarn spinners and sellers	20	2	3	15	9	2
			224. Wool dyers	28	4	12	12	27	4
			TOTAL SUB-ORDER 38	432	65	120	247	241	36
		39.—SILK	228. Silk weavers and dealers	1	...	...	1	1	...
			TOTAL SUB-ORDER 39	1	...	...	1	1	...
		40.—COTTON	231. Cotton cleaners and ginners	1,679	242	366	1,071	934	145
			232. Cotton carpet and rug makers and sellers	28	1	11	16	28	1
			233. Cotton spinners	3,844	307	556	2,981	484	109
			234. Cotton weavers, mill owners and managers	12,510	1,844	3,085	7,581	6,953	939
			235. Cotton factory hands (undefined)	439	56	79	304	335	41
			236. Calenderers, fullers and printers	183	22	50	111	45	7
			237. Cotton dyers	5,426	811	1,258	3,357	2,947	394
			238. Tape makers and sellers	19	1	...	18	11	1
			239. Tents manufacturers and sellers	56	8	10	38	...	...
			TOTAL SUB-ORDER 40	24,184	3,292	5,415	15,477	11,737	1,637
		41.—JUTE, FLAX, COIR, ETC.	241. Hemp rope makers and sellers	156	27	38	91	69	13
			243. Sacks makers and sellers	52	9	9	34	23	2
			TOTAL SUB-ORDER 41	208	36	47	125	92	15
		42.—DRESS	247. Tailors and darners	3,497	433	715	2,349	1,811	226
			251. Cap sellers	4	...	1	3	2	...
			252. Turban binders	7	2	2	3	7	2
			254. Embroiderers and lace and muslin makers	103	14	33	56	90	12
			257. Piece goods dealers	2,235	310	420	1,505	1,218	170
			TOTAL SUB-ORDER 42	5,846	759	1,171	3,916	3,128	410
			Total Order XII.—Textile Fabrics and Dress	**30,671**	**4,152**	**6,753**	**19,766**	**15,199**	**2,098**
	XIII.—METALS AND PRECIOUS STONES.	43.—GOLD, SILVER AND PRECIOUS STONES.	258. Gold and silver dealers	14	1	4	9	3	...
			260. Gold and silver workers	3,485	448	759	2,218	1,864	231
			262. Goldsmiths' dust washers	44	9	9	26	24	3
			265. Electroplaters	2	...	...	2	2	...
			266. Gold and silver wire drawers and braid makers	782	85	157	540	420	44
			273. Pearl and other precious stone dealers	9	...	1	8	7	...
			TOTAL SUB-ORDER 43	4,276	543	930	2,803	2,320	278
		44.—BRASS, COPPER AND BELLMETAL.	276. Brass workers and sellers	4	...	...	4	4	...
			277. Brass pot makers and sellers	570	75	138	357	357	36
			279. Copper workers and sellers	1	...	...	1	1	...
			282. General workers in brass, copper and bellmetal	9	...	2	7	9	...
			283. Brass and copper dealers	1	...	...	1	1	...
			TOTAL SUB-ORDER 44	585	75	140	370	372	36
		45.—TIN, ZINC, MERCURY AND LEAD.	284. Tin workers and sellers	5	...	1	4	3	...
			287. Lead and quicksilver workers and sellers	20	3	3	14	6	...
			288. General workers in tin, lead and zinc	69	8	14	47	24	2
			TOTAL SUB-ORDER 45	94	11	18	65	33	2
		46.—IRON AND STEEL	289. Iron sellers	58	8	10	40	50	7
			290. Blacksmiths	2,906	461	739	1,706	1,591	219
			291. Iron dealers	63	8	17	38	38	5
			293. Lock makers and sellers	1	...	...	1	1	...
			TOTAL SUB-ORDER 46	3,028	477	766	1,785	1,680	231
			Total Order XIII.—Metals and Precious Stones	**7,983**	**1,106**	**1,854**	**5,023**	**4,405**	**547**
	XIV.—GLASS, POTTERY AND STONEWARE.	47.—GLASS AND CHINA-WARE.	297. Chinaware dealers	43	6	6	31	4	4
			TOTAL SUB-ORDER 47	43	6	6	31	4	4
		48.—EARTHEN AND STONE-WARE.	298. Potters	6,443	1,007	1,576	3,860	3,425	496
			299. Grindstone and millstone makers and sellers	35	6	9	20	16	3
			TOTAL SUB-ORDER 48	6,478	1,013	1,585	3,880	3,441	499
			Total Order XIV.—Glass, Pottery and Stone-ware.	**6,521**	**1,019**	**1,591**	**3,911**	**3,445**	**503**

Occupation—*contd.*

TION.									
LES.		FEMALES.				Occupations.	Sub-order and Group.	Order.	Class.
5—14	15 and over.	Total.	0—4	5—14	15 and over.				
11	12	13	14	15	16				
7	44	...	...	...	...	218. Shawl weavers and sellers	38.—Wool and Fur	XII.—TEXTILE FABRICS AND DRESS.	CLASS D.—PREPARATION AND SUPPLY OF MATERIAL SUBSTANCES—contd.
6	17	24	2	11	11	220. Blanket weavers and sellers			
34	67	155	27	47	81	221. Woollen cloth manufacturers and dealers			
2	5	11	...	1	10	222. Woollen yarn spinners and sellers			
12	11	1	..	...	1	224. Wool dyers			
61	144	191	29	50	103	Total Sub-order 38			
...	1	...	...	...	...	228. Silk weavers and dealers	39.—Silk		
...	1	...	...	...	...	Total Sub-order 39			
208	581	745	97	158	490	231. Cotton cleaners and ginners	40.—Cotton		
11	16	...	...	...	...	232. Cotton carpet and rug makers and sellers			
155	220	3,360	198	401	2,761	233. Cotton spinners			
1,671	4,343	5,557	905	1,414	3,238	234. Cotton weavers, mill owners and managers			
62	232	104	15	17	72	235. Cotton factory hands (undefined)			
13	25	138	15	37	86	236. Calenderers, fullers and printers			
716	1,837	2,479	417	542	1,520	237. Cotton dyers			
..	10	8	...	...	8	238. Tape makers and sellers			
...	...	56	8	10	38	239. Tents manufacturers and sellers			
2,836	7,264	12,447	1,655	2,579	8,213	Total Sub-order 40			
15	41	87	14	23	50	241. Hemp rope makers and sellers	41.—Jute, Flax, Coir, etc.		
4	17	29	7	5	17	243. Sacks makers and sellers			
19	58	116	21	28	67	Total Sub-order 41			
366	1,219	1,686	207	349	1,130	247. Tailors and darners	42.—Dress		
1	1	2	...	...	2	251. Cap sellers			
2	3	...	...	...	...	252. Turban binders			
27	51	13	2	6	5	254. Embroiderers and lace and muslin makers			
233	815	1,017	140	187	690	257. Piece goods dealers			
629	2,089	2,718	349	542	1,827	Total Sub-order 42			
3,545	9,556	15,472	2,054	3,208	10,210	**Total Order XII.—Textile Fabrics and Dress**			
...	3	11	1	4	6	258. Gold and silver dealers	43.—Gold, Silver and Precious Stones.	XIII.—METALS AND PRECIOUS STONES.	
411	1,222	1,561	217	348	996	260. Gold and silver workers			
3	18	20	6	6	8	262. Goldsmiths' dust washers			
...	2	...	...	...	...	265. Electroplaters			
82	294	362	41	75	246	266. Gold and silver wire drawers and braid makers			
1	6	2	...	...	2	273. Pearl and other precious stone dealers			
497	1,545	1,956	265	433	1,258	Total Sub-order 43			
...	4	...	...	...	...	276. Brass workers and sellers	44.—Brass, Copper and Bellmetal.		
89	232	213	39	49	125	277. Brass pot makers and sellers			
...	1	...	...	...	...	279. Copper workers and sellers			
2	7	...	...	...	...	282. General workers in brass, copper and bellmetal			
...	1	...	...	...	...	283. Brass and copper dealers			
91	245	213	39	49	125	Total Sub-order 44			
...	3	2	...	1	1	284. Tin workers and sellers	45.—Tin, Zinc, Mercury and Lead.		
...	6	14	3	3	8	287. Lead and quicksilver workers and sellers			
3	19	45	6	11	28	288. General workers in tin, lead and zinc			
3	28	61	9	15	37	Total Sub-order 45			
10	33	8	1	...	7	289. Iron sellers	46.—Iron and Steel		
377	995	1,315	242	362	711	290. Blacksmiths			
13	20	25	3	4	18	291. Iron dealers			
...	1	...	...	...	...	293. Lock makers and sellers			
400	1,049	1,348	246	366	736	Total Sub-order 46			
991	2,867	3,578	559	863	2,156	**Total Order XIII.—Metals and Precious Stones**			
...	...	39	2	6	31	297. Chinaware dealers	47.—Glass and Chinaware.	XIV.—GLASS, POTTERY AND STONEWARE.	
...	...	39	2	6	31	Total Sub-order 47			
875	2,054	3,018	511	701	1,806	298. Potters	48.—Earthen and Stoneware.		
5	8	19	3	4	12	299. Grindstone and millstone makers and sellers			
880	2,062	3,037	514	705	1,818	Total Sub-order 48			
880	2,062	3,076	516	711	1,849	**Total Order XIV.—Glass, Pottery and Stoneware.**			

TABLE XVII.—Part A.—

Class.	Order.	Sub-order and Group.	Occupations.	TOWN.											
				Total				Males.				Females.			
				Total.	0—4	5—14	15 and over.	Total.	0—4	5—14	15 and over.	Total.	0—4	5—14	15 and over.
				17	18	19	20	21	22	23	24	25	26	27	28
CLASS D.—PREPARATION AND SUPPLY OF MATERIAL SUBSTANCES—contd.	XII.—TEXTILE FABRICS AND DRESS.	38.—Wool and Fur.	218. Shawl weavers and sellers	50	...	7	43	50	...	7	43	...	...	...	...
			220. Blanket weavers and sellers	8	1	1	6	8	1	1	6	...	...	...	...
			221. Woollen cloth manufacturers and dealers.	4	...	...	4	1	...	...	1	3	...	...	3
			222. Woollen yarn spinners and sellers	14	...	2	12	3	...	1	2	11	...	1	10
			224. Wool dyers	2	1	...	1	2	1	...	1	...	...	...	...
			Total Sub-order 38	78	2	10	66	64	2	9	53	14	...	1	13
		39.—Silk	228. Silk weavers and dealers	1	...	...	1	1	...	...	1	...	...	...	...
			Total Sub-order 39	1	...	...	1	1	...	...	1	...	...	...	...
		40.—Cotton	231. Cotton cleaners and ginners	648	88	119	441	379	57	77	245	269	31	42	196
			232. Cotton carpet and rug makers and sellers.	28	1	11	16	28	1	11	16	...	...	...	...
			233. Cotton spinners	1,699	123	225	1,351	45	6	25	14	1,654	117	200	1,337
			234. Cotton weavers, mill owners and managers.	2,306	260	507	1,479	1,319	138	321	860	987	122	246	619
			235. Cotton factory hands (undefined)	363	47	68	248	318	30	58	221	45	8	10	27
			236. Calenderers, fullers and printers	109	10	27	72	34	5	11	18	75	5	16	54
			237. Cotton dyers	3,012	452	697	1,863	1,635	211	404	1,020	1,377	241	293	843
			238. Tape makers and sellers	19	1	...	18	11	1	...	10	8	...	...	8
			239. Tents manufacturers and sellers	56	8	10	38	...	...	...	...	56	8	10	38
			Total Sub-order 40	8,240	990	1,724	5,526	3,769	458	907	2,404	4,471	532	817	3,122
		41.—Jute, Flax, Coir, etc.	241. Hemp rope makers and sellers	76	11	14	51	40	5	6	29	36	6	8	22
			243. Sacks makers and sellers	8	...	2	6	4	...	1	3	4	...	1	3
			Total Sub-order 41	84	11	16	57	44	5	7	32	40	6	9	25
		42.—Dress	247. Tailors and darners	1,070	234	372	1,364	999	121	195	683	971	113	177	681
			251. Cap sellers	4	...	1	3	2	...	1	1	2	...	...	2
			252. Turban binders	7	2	2	3	7	2	2	3	...	...	...	...
			254. Embroiderers and lace and muslin makers.	14	2	6	6	2	...	...	2	12	2	6	4
			257. Piece goods dealers	1,635	214	296	1,125	893	114	166	613	742	100	130	512
			Total Sub-order 42	3,630	452	677	2,501	1,903	237	364	1,302	1,727	215	313	1,199
			Total Order XII.—Textile Fabrics and Dress.	12,033	1,455	2,427	8,151	5,781	702	1,287	3,792	6,252	753	1,14	4,359
	XIII.—METALS AND PRECIOUS STONES.	43.—Gold, Silver and Precious Stones.	258. Gold and silver dealers	14	1	4	9	3	...	...	3	11	1	4	6
			260. Gold and silver workers	1,305	136	250	919	680	72	122	486	625	64	128	433
			262. Goldsmiths' dust washers	33	9	7	17	15	3	1	11	18	6	6	6
			265. Electroplaters	2	...	...	2	2	...	...	2	...	...	...	...
			266. Gold and silver wire drawers and braid makers.	782	85	157	540	420	44	82	294	362	41	75	246
			273. Pearl and other precious stone dealers.	8	...	1	7	7	...	1	6	1	...	...	1
			Total Sub-order 43	2,144	231	419	1,494	1,127	119	206	802	1,017	112	213	692
		44.—Brass, Copper and Bellmetal.	276. Brass workers and sellers	2	...	...	2	2	...	...	2	...	...	...	...
			277. Brass pot makers and sellers	333	48	71	214	212	26	46	140	121	22	25	74
			279. Copper workers and sellers	1	...	...	1	1	...	...	1	...	...	...	...
			282. General workers in brass, copper and bellmetal.	3	...	1	2	3	...	1	2	...	...	...	...
			283. Brass and copper dealers	1	...	...	1	1	...	...	1	...	...	...	...
			Total Sub-order 44	340	48	72	220	219	26	47	146	121	22	25	74
		45.—Tin, Zinc, Mercury and Lead.	284. Tin workers and sellers	5	...	1	4	3	...	...	3	2	...	1	1
			287. Lead and quicksilver workers and sellers.	16	3	3	10	2	...	...	2	14	3	3	8
			298. General workers in tin, lead and zinc.	69	8	14	47	24	2	3	19	45	6	11	28
			Total Sub-order 45	90	11	18	61	29	2	3	24	61	9	15	37
		46.—Iron and Steel.	289. Iron sellers	58	8	10	40	50	7	10	33	8	1	...	7
			290. Blacksmiths	1,126	155	227	744	606	78	112	416	520	77	115	328
			291. Iron dealers	56	8	15	33	35	5	13	17	21	3	2	16
			293. Lock makers and sellers	1	...	...	1	1	...	...	1	...	...	...	...
			Total Sub-order 46	1,241	171	252	818	692	90	135	467	549	81	117	351
			Total Order XIII.—Metals and Precious Stones.	3,815	461	761	2,593	2,067	237	391	1,439	1,748	22	370	1,154
	XIV.—GLASS, POTTERY AND STONEWARE.	47.—Glass and China ware.	297. Chinaware dealers	43	6	6	31	4	4	...	...	39	2	6	31
			Total Sub-order 47	43	6	6	31	4	4	...	...	39	2	6	31
		48.—Earthen and Stoneware.	298. Potters	778	120	161	497	391	57	78	256	387	63	83	241
			299. Grindstone and millstone makers and sellers.	4	...	...	4	2	...	...	2	2	...	...	2
			Total Sub-order 48	782	120	161	501	393	57	78	258	389	63	83	243
			Total Order XIV.—Glass, Pottery and Stoneware.	825	126	167	532	397	61	78	258	428	65	89	274

Occupations—*contd.*

COUNTRY.												Occupations.	Sub-order and Group.	Order.	Class.
Total.				Males.				Females.							
Total.	0—4	5—14	15 and over.	Total.	0—4	5—14	15 and over.	Total.	0—4	5—14	15 and over.				
29	30	31	32	33	34	35	36	37	38	39	40				
1	...	...	1	1	...	...	1	...	...	...	...	218. Shawl weavers and sellers	38.—Wool and Fur.	XII.—Textile, Fabrics and Dress.	Class D.—Preparation and Supply of Material Substances—*contd.*
45	7	16	22	21	5	5	11	24	2	11	11	220. Blanket weavers and sellers			
276	51	81	144	124	24	34	66	152	27	47	78	221. Woollen cloth manufacturers and dealers.			
6	2	1	3	6	2	1	3	...	...	...	...	222. Woollen yarn spinners and sellers			
26	3	12	11	25	3	12	10	1	...	...	1	224. Wool dyers			
354	63	110	181	177	34	52	91	177	29	58	90	Total Sub-order 38			
...	...	...	...	...	...	...	...	...	...	...	...	228. Silk weavers and dealers	39.—Silk		
...	...	...	...	...	...	...	...	...	...	...	...	Total Sub-order 39			
1,031	154	247	630	555	88	131	336	476	65	116	294	231. Cotton cleaners and ginners	40.—Cotton		
...	...	...	...	...	...	...	...	...	...	...	...	232. Cotton carpet and rug makers and sellers.			
2,145	184	331	1,630	439	103	130	206	1,706	81	201	1,424	233. Cotton spinners			
10,204	1,584	2,518	6,102	5,634	801	1,350	3,483	4,570	783	1,168	2,619	234. Cotton weavers, mill owners and managers.			
76	9	11	56	17	2	4	11	59	7	7	45	235. Cotton factory hands (undefined)			
74	12	23	39	11	2	2	7	63	10	21	32	236. Calenderers, fullers and printers			
2,424	359	561	1,494	1,312	183	312	817	1,102	176	249	677	237. Cotton dyers			
...	...	...	...	...	...	...	...	...	...	...	...	238. Tape makers and sellers			
...	...	...	...	...	...	...	...	...	...	...	...	239. Tents manufacturers and sellers			
15,944	2,302	3,691	9,951	7,968	1,179	1,929	4,860	7,976	1,123	1,762	5,091	Total Sub-order 40			
80	16	24	40	29	8	9	12	51	8	15	28	241. Hemp rope makers and sellers	41.—Jute, Flax, Coir, etc.		
44	9	7	28	19	2	3	14	25	7	4	14	243. Sacks makers and sellers			
124	25	31	68	48	10	12	26	76	15	19	42	Total Sub-order 41			
1,527	199	343	985	812	105	171	536	715	94	172	449	247. Tailors and darners	42.—Dress		
...	...	...	...	...	...	...	...	...	...	...	...	251. Cap sellers			
...	...	...	...	...	...	...	...	...	...	...	...	252. Turban binders			
89	12	27	50	88	12	27	49	1	...	...	1	254. Embroiderers and lace and muslin makers.			
600	96	124	380	325	56	67	202	275	40	57	178	257. Piece goods dealers			
2,216	307	494	1,415	1,225	173	265	787	991	134	229	628	Total Sub-order 42			
18,638	2,697	4,326	11,615	9,418	1,396	2,258	5,764	9,220	1,301	2,068	5,851	**Total Order XII.—Textile Fabrics and Dress.**			
...	...	...	...	...	...	...	...	...	...	...	...	258. Gold and silver dealers	43.—Gold, Silver and Precious Stones.	XIII.—Metals and Precious Stones.	
2,120	312	509	1,299	1,184	159	289	736	936	153	220	563	260. Gold and silver workers			
11	...	2	9	9	...	2	7	2	...	...	2	262. Gold smiths' dust washers			
...	...	...	...	...	...	...	...	...	...	...	...	265. Electroplaters			
...	...	...	...	...	...	...	...	...	...	...	...	266. Gold and silver wire drawers and braid makers.			
1	...	...	1	...	...	...	...	1	...	...	1	273. Pearl and other precious stone dealers.			
2,132	312	511	1,309	1,193	159	291	743	939	153	220	566	Total Sub-order 43			
2	...	...	2	2	...	...	2	...	...	...	...	276. Brass workers and sellers	44.—Brass, Copper and Bellmetal.		
237	27	67	143	145	10	43	92	92	17	24	51	277. Brass pot makers and sellers			
...	...	...	...	...	...	...	...	...	...	...	...	279. Copper workers and sellers			
6	...	1	5	6	...	1	5	...	...	...	...	282. General workers in brass, copper and bellmetal.			
...	...	...	...	...	...	...	...	...	...	...	...	283. Brass and copper dealers			
245	27	68	150	153	10	44	99	92	17	24	51	Total Sub-order 44			
...	...	...	...	...	...	...	...	...	...	...	...	284. Tin workers and sellers	45.—Tin, Zinc, Mercury and Lead.		
4	...	...	4	4	...	...	4	...	...	...	...	287. Lead and quicksilver workers and sellers.			
...	...	...	...	...	...	...	...	...	...	...	...	288. General workers in tin, lead and zinc.			
4	...	...	4	4	...	...	4	...	...	...	...	Total Sub-order 45			
...	...	...	...	...	...	...	...	...	...	...	...	289. Iron sellers	46.—Iron and Steel.		
1,780	306	512	962	985	141	265	579	795	165	247	383	290. Blacksmiths			
7	...	2	5	3	...	...	3	4	...	2	2	291. Iron dealers			
...	...	...	...	...	...	...	...	...	...	...	...	293. Lock makers and sellers			
1,787	306	514	967	988	141	265	582	799	165	249	385	Total Sub-order 46			
4,168	645	1,093	2,430	2,338	310	600	1,428	1,830	335	493	1,002	**Total Order XIII.—Metals and Precious Stones.**			
...	...	...	...	...	...	...	...	...	...	...	...	297. Chinaware dealers	47.—Glass and Chinaware.	XIV.—Glass, Pottery and Stoneware.	
...	...	...	...	...	...	...	...	...	...	...	...	Total Sub-order 47			
5,665	887	1,415	3,363	2,034	439	797	1,798	2,631	448	618	1,565	298. Potters	48.—Earthen and Stoneware.		
31	6	9	16	14	3	5	6	17	3	4	10	299. Grindstone and millstone makers and sellers.			
5,696	893	1,424	3,379	2,048	442	802	1,804	2,648	451	622	1,575	Total Sub-order 48			
5,6	893	1,424	3,379	3,048	442	802	1,804	2,648	451	622	1,575	**Total Order XIV.—Glass, Pottery and Stoneware.**			

Table XVII.—A.—Occupations—Ajmere.

TABLE XVII.—Part A.—

Class.	Order.	Sub-order and Group.	Occupations.	TOTAL POPULA[TION] Total. Total.	Total. 0—4	Total. 5—14	Total. 15 and over.	Mal[es] Total.	Mal[es] 0—4
1	2	3	4	5	6	7	8	9	10
CLASS D.—PREPARATION AND SUPPLY OF MATERIAL SUBSTANCES—contd.	XV.—WOOL, CANE AND LEAVES, ETC.	49.—Timber and Wood	304. Carpenters	5,120	710	1,135	3,275	2,874	359
			Total Sub-order 49	5,120	710	1,135	3,275	2,874	359
		50.—Cane Work, Matting and Leaves, etc.	306. Bamboo and rattan splitters, workers and sellers	57	7	18	32	16	2
			307. Basket weavers and winnowing pan makers and sellers.	435	63	102	270	214	27
			308. Mat makers and sellers	166	15	42	109	76	6
			309. Screen makers and sellers	61	8	14	39	47	4
			310. Leaf plate makers and sellers	81	4	16	61	39	2
			312. Leaf fan makers and sellers	9	1	3	5	9	1
			313. Comb makers and sellers	185	40	49	96	95	22
			314. Broom makers and sellers	5	1	1	3	2	...
			Total Sub-order 50	999	139	245	615	498	64
			Total Order XV.—Wool, Cane and Leaves, etc.	6,119	849	1,380	3,890	3,372	423
	XVI.—DRUGS, GUMS, DYES, ETC.	51.—Gums, Wax and similar Forest Produce.	320 Lac collectors and sellers	57	7	14	36	39	6
			Total Sub-order 51	57	7	14	36	39	6
		52.—Drugs, Dyes, Pigments, etc.	324. Chemists and druggists	17	1	5	11	13	...
			326. Saltpetre workers and sellers	8	...	2	6	8	...
			328. Soap makers and sellers	11	1	3	7	1	...
			337. Perfume preparers and sellers	220	31	42	147	88	12
			Total Sub-order 52	256	33	52	171	110	12
			Total Order XVI.—Drugs, Gums, Dyes, etc.	313	40	66	207	149	18
	XVII.—LEATHER, HORNS, BONES AND GREASE.	53.—Leather, etc.	338. Tanners, curriers and hide sellers	6,835	1,247	1,973	3,615	3,659	631
			339. Shoe makers and sellers	3,798	658	1,007	2,133	2,291	364
			340. Leather dyers	929	168	241	520	307	48
			341. Water bag and ghee pot makers and sellers	17	3	6	8	9	1
			342. Hide and bone dealers	1,714	328	448	938	1,136	204
			Total Sub-order 53	13,293	2,404	3,675	7,214	7,402	1,248
			Total Order XVII.—Leather, Horns, Bones and Grease.	13,293	2,404	3,875	7,214	,402	1,248
CLASS E.—COMMERCE, TRANSPORT AND STORAGE.	XVIII.—COMMERCE.	54.—Dealer in Money and Securities.	346. Bankers	21	2	3	16	9	1
			347. Money lenders	9,346	1,270	2,277	5,799	4,770	633
			348. Bill discounters, etc.	32	4	4	24	21	3
			350. Money changers and testers	538	83	111	344	291	46
			351. Bank clerks and accountants	20	1	4	15	10	1
			Total Sub-order 54	9,957	1,360	2,399	6,198	5,102	684
		55.—General Merchandise	352. General merchants	1,380	126	243	1,011	1,026	88
			353. Merchants, accountants and clerks, etc.	20	3	8	9	7	...
			Total Sub-order 55	1,400	129	251	1,020	1,033	88
		56.—Dealing, unspecified	355. Shop-keepers' servants	128	25	25	78	19	1
			356. Shop-keepers	16,090	1,953	3,496	10,641	8,878	972
			357. Pedlars, hawkers, etc.	57	6	12	39	37	5
			Total Sub-order 56	16,275	1,984	3,533	10,758	8,934	978
		57.—Middlemen, etc.— (a) Brokers, etc.	358. Brokers and agents	2,448	262	404	1,782	1,266	119
			359. Auctioners	2	...	...	2	1	...
		(b) Contractors and Farmers.	361. Farmers of liquor, opium, etc.	56	8	9	39	34	4
			362. Superintendents of markets	11	...	2	9	7	...
			363. Contractors	400	48	91	261	160	18
			Total Sub-order 57	2,917	328	506	2,093	1,468	141
			Total Order XVIII.—Commerce	30,549	3,791	6,689	20,069	16,53	1,891
	XIX.—TRANSPORT AND STORAGE.	58.—Railway— (a) Administration	365. Manager, general store	1	...	...	1	1	...
			366. Traffic manager, superintendents and assistants	9	2	...	7	4	2
			368. Auditors and accountants, etc.	31	5	5	21	25	4
			369. Engineers	1	...	...	1	1	...
		(b) Working staff	370. Clerical staff and railway establishments	1,797	247	384	1,166	845	204
			371. Station masters, assistants, inspectors, overseers, etc.	133	22	23	88	67	9
			372. Guards, drivers, firemen, etc.	181	27	25	119	111	16
			373. Pointsmen, shunters, porters, signallers, etc.	2,190	292	408	1,492	896	74
			Total Sub-order 58	4,345	595	855	2,895	1,911	209

Occupations—*contd.*

TION.									
ES.		FEMALES.				OCCUPATIONS.	Sub-order and Group.	Order.	Class.
5—14	15 and over.	TOTAL.	0—4	5—14	15 and over.				
11	12	13	14	15	16				
637	1,878	2,246	351	498	1,397	304. Carpenters	49.—TIMBER AND WOOD	XV.—WOOL, CANE AND LEAVES, ETC.	CLASS D.—PREPARATION AND SUPPLY OF MATERIAL SUBSTANCES—*contd.*
637	1,878	2,246	351	498	1,397	TOTAL SUB-ORDER 49			
6	8	41	5	12	24	306. Bamboo and rattan splitters, workers and sellers	50.—CANE WORK, MATTING AND LEAVES, ETC.		
50	137	221	36	52	133	307. Basket weavers and winnowing pan makers and sellers.			
19	51	90	9	23	58	308. Mat makers and sellers			
10	33	14	4	4	6	309. Screen makers and sellers			
10	27	42	2	6	34	310. Leaf plate makers and sellers			
3	5	...	...	...	...	312. Leaf fan makers and sellers			
28	45	90	18	21	51	313. Comb makers and sellers			
1	1	3	1	...	2	314. Broom makers and sellers			
127	307	501	75	118	308	TOTAL SUB-ORDER 50			
764	2,185	2,747	426	616	1,705	**Total Order XV.—Wool, Cane and Leaves, etc.**			
8	25	18	1	6	11	320. Lac collectors and sellers	51.—GUMS, WAX AND SIMILAR FOREST PRODUCE.	XVI.—DRUGS, GUMS, DYES, ETC.	
8	25	18	1	6	11	SUB-ORDER 51			
4	9	4	1	1	2	324. Chemists and druggists	52.—DRUGS, DYES, PIGMENTS, ETC.		
2	6	...	...	...	...	326. Saltpetre workers and sellers			
...	1	10	1	3	6	328. Soap makers and sellers			
19	57	132	19	23	90	337. Perfume preparers and sellers			
25	73	146	21	27	98	TOTAL SUB-ORDER 52			
33	98	164	22	33	109	**Total Order XVI.—Drugs, Gums, Dyes, etc.**			
1,043	1,985	3,176	616	930	1,630	338. Tanners, curriers and hide sellers	53.—LEATHER, ETC.	XVII.—LEATHER, HORNS, BONES AND GREASE.	
613	1,314	1,507	294	394	819	339. Shoe makers and sellers			
82	177	622	120	150	343	340. Leather dyers			
3	5	8	2	3	3	341. Water bag and ghee pot makers and sellers			
285	647	578	124	163	291	342. Hide and bone dealers			
2,026	4,128	5,891	1,156	1,649	3,086	TOTAL SUB-ORDER 53			
2,026	4,128	5,891	1,156	1,649	3,086	**Total Order XVII.—Leather, Horns, Bones and Grease.**			
2	6	12	1	1	10	346. Bankers	54.—DEALER IN MONEY AND SECURITIES.	XVIII.—COMMERCE.	CLASS E.—COMMERCE, TRANSPORT AND STORAGE.
1,201	2,936	4,576	637	1,076	2,863	347. Money-lenders			
3	16	10	1	1	8	348. Bill discounters, etc.			
61	184	247	37	50	160	350. Money changers and testors			
1	8	10	...	3	7	351. Bank clerks and accountants			
1,268	3,150	4,855	676	1,131	3,048	TOTAL SUB-ORDER 54			
170	768	354	38	73	243	352. General merchants	55.—GENERAL MERCHANDISE		
2	5	13	3	6	4	353. Merchants, accountants and clerks, etc.			
172	773	367	41	79	247	TOTAL SUB-ORDER 55			
4	14	109	24	21	64	355. Shop-keepers' servants	56.—DEALING, UNSPECIFIED		
1,900	6,006	7,212	981	1,596	4,635	356. Shop-keepers			
6	26	20	1	6	13	357. Pedlars, hawkers, etc.			
1,910	6,046	7,341	1,006	1,623	4,712	TOTAL SUB-ORDER 56			
217	930	1,182	143	187	852	358. Brokers and agents	57.—MIDDLEMEN, ETC.—(a) Brokers, etc.		
...	1	1	...	...	1	359. Auctioners			
5	25	22	4	4	14	361. Farmers of liquor, opium, etc.	(b) Contractors and farmers.		
1	6	4	...	1	3	362. Superintendents of markets			
40	102	240	30	51	159	363. Contractors			
263	1,064	1,449	177	243	1,029	TOTAL SUB-ORDER 57			
3,613	11,033	14,012	1,900	3,076	9,036	**Total Order XVIII.—Commerce**			
...	1	...	...	...	...	365. Manager, general store	58.—RAILWAY—(a) Administration	XIX.—TRANSPORT AND STORAGE.	
...	2	5	...	...	5	366. Traffic manager, superintendents and assistants			
5	16	6	1	...	5	368. Auditors and accountants, etc.			
...	1	...	...	...	...	369. Engineers			
187	554	952	143	197	612	370. Clerical staff and railway establishments	(b) Working staff		
13	45	66	13	10	43	371. Station masters, assistants, inspectors, overseers, etc.			
20	76	69	11	15	43	372. Guards, drivers, firemen, etc.			
139	643	1,336	218	269	849	373. Pointsmen, shunters, porters, signallers, etc.			
364	1,338	2,434	386	491	1,557	TOTAL SUB-ORDER 58			

Table XVII.—A.—Occupations—Ajmere.

TABLE XVII.—Part A.—

Class.	Order	Sub-order and Group.	Occupations.	Town. Total. Total.	Town. Total. 0—4	Town. Total. 5—14	Town. Total. 15 and over.	Town. Males. Total.	Town. Males. 0—4	Town. Males. 5—14	Town. Males. 15 and over.	Town. Females. Total.	Town. Females. 0—4	Town. Females. 5—14	Town. Females. 15 and over.
				17	18	19	20	21	22	23	24	25	26	27	28
Class D.—Preparation and Supply of Material Substances—concld.	XV.—Wool, Cane and Leaves, etc.	49.—Timber and Wood	304. Carpenters	1,373	159	252	962	755	83	138	534	618	76	114	428
			Total Sub-order 49	1,373	159	252	962	755	83	138	534	618	76	114	428
		50.—Cane Work, Matting and Leaves, etc.	306. Bamboo and rattan splitters, workers and sellers.	57	7	18	32	16	2	6	8	41	5	12	24
			307. Basket weavers and winnowing pan makers and sellers.	183	18	41	124	87	9	21	57	96	9	20	67
			308. Mat makers and sellers	164	15	42	107	75	6	19	50	89	9	23	57
			309. Screen makers and sellers	61	8	14	39	47	4	10	33	14	4	4	6
			310. Leaf plate makers and sellers	70	4	14	52	39	2	10	27	31	2	4	25
			312. Leaf fan makers and sellers	7	1	3	3	7	1	3	3	...	...	...	...
			313. Comb makers and sellers	26	3	8	15	15	1	5	9	11	2	3	6
			314. Broom makers and sellers	5	1	1	3	2	...	1	1	3	1	...	2
			Total Sub-order 50	573	57	141	375	288	25	75	188	285	32	66	187
			Total Order XV.—Wool, Cane and Leaves, etc.	**1,946**	**216**	**393**	**1,337**	**1,043**	**108**	**213**	**722**	**903**	**108**	**180**	**15**
	XVI.—Drugs, Gums, Dyes, etc.	51.—Gums, Wax and similar Forest Produce.	320. Lac collectors and sellers	52	7	14	31	34	6	8	20	18	1	6	11
			Total Sub-order 51	52	7	14	31	34	6	8	20	18	1	6	11
		52.—Drugs, Dyes, Pigments, etc.	324. Chemists and druggists	17	1	5	11	13	...	4	9	4	1	1	2
			326. Saltpetre workers and sellers	8	...	2	6	8	...	2	6	...	...	...	...
			328. Soap makers and sellers	11	1	3	7	1	...	...	1	10	4	3	6
			337. Perfume preparers and sellers	216	31	41	144	84	12	18	54	132	19	23	90
			Total Sub-order 52	252	33	51	168	106	12	24	70	146	21	27	98
			Total Order XVI.—Drugs, Gums, Dyes, etc.	**304**	**40**	**65**	**199**	**140**	**18**	**32**	**90**	**164**	**22**	**33**	**109**
	XVII.—Leather, Horns, Bones and Grease.	53.—Leather, etc.	338. Tanners, curriers and hide sellers	761	110	172	479	260	30	54	176	501	80	118	303
			339. Shoe makers and sellers	1,734	341	442	951	1,190	205	311	674	544	136	131	277
			340. Leather dyers	261	55	70	135	97	19	25	53	164	36	45	83
			341. Water bag and ghee pot makers and sellers.	16	3	6	7	8	1	3	4	8	2	3	3
			342. Hide and bone dealers	60	6	14	38	38	6	11	21	22	2	3	17
			Total Sub-order 53	2,832	517	704	1,611	1,593	261	404	928	1,239	256	300	683
			Total Order XVII.—Leather, Horns, Bones and Grease.	**2,832**	**517**	**704**	**1,611**	**1,593**	**261**	**404**	**928**	**1,239**	**256**	**300**	**683**
Class E.—Commerce, Transport and Storage.	XVIII.—Commerce.	54.—Dealers in Money and Securities.	346. Bankers	21	2	3	16	9	1	2	6	12	1	1	10
			347. Money-lenders	921	105	200	616	533	66	114	353	388	39	86	263
			348. Bill discounters, etc.	32	4	4	24	22	3	3	16	10	1	1	8
			350. Money changers and testors	497	76	99	322	263	41	50	172	234	35	49	150
			351. Bank clerks and accountants	19	1	4	14	9	1	1	7	10	...	3	7
			Total Sub-order 54	1,490	188	310	992	836	112	170	554	654	76	140	438
		55.—General Merchandise.	352. General merchants	1,139	111	190	838	823	76	126	621	316	35	64	217
			353. Merchants, accountants and clerks, etc.	20	3	8	9	7	...	2	5	13	3	6	4
			Total Sub-order 55	1,159	114	198	847	830	76	128	626	329	38	70	221
		56.—Dealing unspecified.	355. Shop-keepers' servants	126	25	25	76	17	1	4	12	109	24	21	64
			356. Shop-keepers	5,134	624	987	3,523	2,580	277	480	1,823	2,554	347	507	1,700
			357. Pedlars, hawkers, etc.	36	2	7	27	17	1	1	13	19	1	6	12
			Total Sub-order, 56	5,296	651	1,019	3,626	2,614	279	455	1,880	2,682	372	534	1,776
		57.—Middlemen, etc.— (a) Brokers, etc. (b) Contractors, and farmers.	358. Brokers and agents	2,243	249	357	1,637	1,130	111	184	835	1,113	138	173	802
			359. Auctioneers	2	...	...	2	1	...	...	1	1	...	...	1
			361. Farmers of liquor, opium, etc.	49	7	7	35	30	3	4	23	19	4	3	12
			362. Superintendents of markets	11	...	2	9	7	...	1	6	4	...	1	3
			363. Contractors	373	46	85	242	144	17	36	91	229	29	49	151
			Total Sub-order 57	2,678	302	451	1,925	1,312	131	225	956	1,366	171	226	969
			Total Order XVIII.—Commerce	**10,623**	**1,255**	**1,978**	**7,390**	**5,592**	**598**	**1,008**	**3,986**	**5,031**	**657**	**970**	**3,404**
	XIX.—Transport and Storage.	58.—Railway— (a) Administration.	365. Manager, general store	1	...	...	1	1	...	...	1	...	...	...	...
			366. Traffic manager, superintendents and assistants.	9	2	...	7	4	2	...	2	5	...	..	5
			368. Auditors and accountants, etc.	31	5	5	21	25	4	5	16	6	1	...	5
			369. Engineers	1	...	...	1	1	...	...	1	...	...	...	...
			370. Clerical staff and railway establishments.	1,797	247	384	1,166	845	104	187	554	952	143	197	612
		(b) Working staff	371. Station masters, assistants, inspectors, overseers, etc.	95	15	19	61	53	7	11	35	42	8	8	26
			372. Guards, drivers, firemen, etc.	178	27	35	116	109	16	20	73	69	11	15	43
			373. Pointsmen, shunters, porters, signallers, etc.	1,923	260	363	1,300	672	56	111	505	1,251	204	252	795
			Total Sub-order 58	4,035	556	806	2,673	1,710	189	334	1,187	2,325	367	472	1,486

Occupations—*contd.*

COUNTRY.												Occupations.	Sub-order and Group.	Order	Class.
Total.				Males.				Females.							
Total.	0—4	5—14	15 and over.	Total.	0—4	5—14	15 and over.	Total.	0—4	5—14	15 and over.				
29	30	31	32	33	34	35	36	37	38	39	40				
3,747	551	883	2,313	2,119	276	499	1,344	1,628	275	384	969	304. Carpenters	49.—Timber and Wood		CLASS D.—PREPARATION AND SUPPLY OF MATERIAL SUBSTANCES—contd.
3,747	551	883	2,313	2,119	276	499	1,344	1,628	275	384	969	Total Sub-order 49			
...	...	...	...	...	...	...	...	...	...	...	...	306. Bamboo and rattan splitters, workers and sellers	50.—Cane Work, Matting and Leaves, etc.	XV.—WOOL, CANE AND LEAVES, ETC.	
252	45	61	146	127	18	29	80	125	27	32	66	307. Basket weavers and winnowing pan makers and sellers.			
2	...	...	2	1	...	...	1	1	...	...	1	308. Mat makers and sellers			
...	...	...	...	...	...	...	...	...	...	...	...	309. Screen makers and sellers			
11	...	2	9	...	...	...	...	11	...	2	9	310. Leaf plate makers and sellers			
2	...	...	2	2	...	...	2	...	...	...	...	312. Leaf fan makers and sellers			
159	37	41	81	80	21	23	36	79	16	18	45	313. Comb makers and sellers			
...	...	...	...	...	...	...	...	...	...	...	...	314. Broom makers and sellers			
426	82	104	240	210	39	52	119	216	43	52	121	Total Sub-order 50			
4,173	633	987	2,553	2,329	315	551	1,463	1,844	318	436	1,090	**Total Order XV.—Wool, Cane and Leaves, etc.**			
5	...	...	5	5	...	...	5	...	...	...	...	320. Lac collectors and sellers	51. Gums, Wax and similar Forest Produce.	XVI.—DRUGS, GUMS, DYES, ETC.	
5	...	...	5	5	...	...	5	...	...	...	...	Total Sub-order 51			
...	...	...	...	...	...	...	...	...	...	...	...	324. Chemists and druggists	52.—Drugs, Dyes, Pigments, etc.		
...	...	...	...	...	...	...	...	...	...	...	...	326. Saltpetre workers and sellers			
...	...	...	...	...	...	...	...	...	...	...	...	328. Soap makers and sellers			
4	...	1	3	4	...	1	3	...	...	...	...	337. Perfume preparers and sellers			
4	...	1	3	4	...	1	3	...	...	...	...	Total Sub-order 52			
9	...	1	8	9	...	1	8	...	...	...	...	**Total Order XVI.—Drugs, Gums, Dyes, etc.**			
6,074	1,137	1,801	3,136	3,399	601	989	1,809	2,675	536	812	1,327	338. Tanners, curriers and hide sellers	53.—Leather, etc.	XVII.—LEATHER, HORNS, BONES AND GREASE.	
2,064	317	565	1,182	1,101	159	302	640	963	158	263	542	339. Shoe makers and sellers			
668	113	171	384	210	29	57	124	458	84	114	260	340. Leather dyers			
1	...	...	1	1	...	...	1	...	...	...	...	341. Water bag and ghee pot makers and sellers			
1,654	320	434	900	1,098	198	274	626	556	122	160	274	342. Hide and bone dealers			
10,461	1,887	2,971	5,603	5,809	987	1,622	3,200	4,652	900	1,349	2,403	Total Sub-order 53			
10,461	1,887	2,971	5,603	5,809	987	1,622	3,200	4,652	900	1,349	2,403	**Total Order XVII.—Leather, Horns, Bones and Grease.**			
...	...	...	...	...	...	...	...	...	...	...	...	346. Bankers	54.—Dealer in money and Securities.	XVIII.—COMMERCE.	CLASS E.—COMMERCE, TRANSPORT AND STORAGE.
8,425	1,165	2,077	5,183	4,237	567	1,087	2,583	4,188	598	990	2,600	347. Money-lenders			
...	...	...	...	...	...	...	...	...	...	...	...	348. Bill discounters, etc.			
41	7	12	22	28	5	11	13	12	2	1	10	350. Money changers and testors			
1	...	...	1	1	...	...	1	...	...	...	...	351. Bank clerks and Accountants			
8,467	1,172	2,089	5,206	4,266	572	1,098	2,596	4,201	600	991	2,610	Total Sub-order 54			
241	15	53	173	203	12	44	147	38	3	9	26	352. General merchants	55.—General Merchandise.		
...	...	...	...	...	...	...	...	...	...	...	...	353. Merchants, accountants and clerks, etc.			
241	15	53	173	203	12	44	147	38	3	9	26	Total Sub-order 55			
2	...	...	2	2	...	...	2	...	...	...	...	355. Shop-keepers' servants	56.—Dealing unspecified.		
10,956	1,329	2,509	7,118	6,298	695	1,420	4,183	4,658	634	1,089	2,935	356. Shop-keepers			
21	4	5	12	20	4	5	11	1	...	...	1	357. Pedlars, hawkers, etc.			
10,979	1,333	2,514	7,132	6,320	699	1,425	4,196	4,659	634	1,089	2,936	Total Sub-order 56			
205	13	47	145	135	8	33	95	69	5	14	50	358. Brokers and agents	57.—Middlemen, etc.—(a) Brokers, etc.		
...	...	...	...	...	...	...	...	...	...	...	...	359. Auctioneers			
7	1	2	4	4	1	1	2	3	...	1	2	361. Farmers of liquor, opium, etc.	(b) Contractors and farmers.		
...	...	...	...	...	...	...	...	...	...	...	...	362 Superintendents of markets			
27	2	6	19	16	1	4	11	11	1	2	8	363. Contractors			
239	16	55	168	156	10	38	108	83	6	17	60	Total Sub-order 57			
19,926	2,536	4,711	12,679	10,945	1,293	2,605	7,047	8,981	1,243	2,106	5,632	**Total Order XVIII.—Commerce.**			
...	...	...	...	...	...	...	...	...	...	...	...	365. Manager, general store	58.—Railway—(a) Administration.	XIX.—TRANSPORT AND STORAGE.	
...	...	...	...	...	...	...	...	...	...	...	...	366. Traffic manager, superintendents and assistants.			
...	...	...	...	...	...	...	...	...	...	...	...	368. Auditors and accountants, etc.			
...	...	...	...	...	...	...	...	...	...	...	...	369. Engineers			
...	...	...	...	...	...	...	...	...	...	...	...	370 Clerical staff and railway establishments.			
38	7	4	27	14	2	2	10	24	5	2	17	371. Station masters, assistants, inspectors, overseers, etc.	(b) Working staff		
3	...	...	3	3	...	...	3	...	...	...	...	372. Guards, drivers, firemen, etc.			
269	32	45	192	184	18	28	138	85	14	17	54	373. Pointsmen, shunters, porters, signallers, etc.			
310	39	49	222	201	20	30	151	109	19	19	71	Total Sub-order 58			

TABLE XVII.—Part A.—

Class.	Order.	Sub-order and Group.	Occupations.	TOTAL POPULA[TION] Total. Total.	Total. 0—4	Total. 5—14	Total. 15 and over.	Mal[es] Total.	Mal[es] 0—4
1	2	3	4	5	6	7	8	9	10
CLASS B.—COMMERCE, TRANSPORT AND STORAGE—*contd.*	XIX.—TRANSPORT AND STORAGE—*contd.*	59.—ROAD— (a) Cart, carriage and tramway owners and drivers.	375. Cart owners and drivers	1,876	258	371	1,247	1,098	126
			376. Livery stable-keepers, etc.	1	...	...	1	1	...
			377. Drivers, stable boys, etc.	47	6	6	35	24	1
			378. Dooly bearers	35	...	1	34	34	...
		(b) Carriers by pack animals.	379. Pack bullock owners and drivers, &c.	253	24	55	174	212	23
			380. Camel and mule drivers	947	124	207	616	589	66
			TOTAL SUB-ORDER 59	3,159	412	640	2,107	1,958	216
		60.—WATER— (b) Working staff of vessels.	385. Boatmen	2	...	...	2	1	...
			389. Divers (not for pearls)	3	...	...	3	3	...
			TOTAL SUB-ORDER 60	5	...	...	5	4	...
		61.—MESSAGES— (a) Post, etc.	390. Postmasters and clerks	34	4	6	24	26	4
			391. Postal messengers, runners, etc.	372	37	79	256	262	25
			392. Messengers	222	28	44	150	56	8
		(b) Telegraph and Telephone.	393. Telegraph officers (Government, Railway and others) and clerical and accountant's establishments.	42	5	8	29	19	1
			394. Signallers and messengers	53	4	11	38	26	1
			TOTAL SUB-ORDER 61	723	78	148	497	389	39
		62.—STORAGE AND WEIGHING.	397. Warehouse service	2	...	...	2	1	...
			398. Porters	446	58	90	298	295	29
			399. Weighmen	158	18	23	117	103	14
			400. Watchmen (not village)	674	80	120	474	360	30
			TOTAL SUB-ORDER 62	1,280	156	233	891	759	73
			Total Order XIX.—Transport and Storage	9,512	1,241	1,876	6,395	5,021	537
CLASS F.—PROFESSIONS.	XX.—LEARNED AND ARTISTIC PROFESSIONS.	63.—RELIGION— (a) Priests, ministers, etc.	401. Priests, ministers, preachers, missionary, etc.	186	34	31	121	104	17
			402. Zenana mission service	6	2	1	3	4	2
		(b) Subsidiary religious services.	404. Religious mendicants	10,541	1,399	2,273	6,869	5,023	612
			405. Church and temple service	1,300	142	302	856	888	98
			TOTAL SUB-ORDER 63	12,033	1,577	2,607	7,849	6,009	729
		64.—EDUCATION	407. Principals, professors and teachers in colleges, schools, etc.	972	108	218	646	527	45
			408. Clerks, etc., on establishments of educational institutions.	11	2	2	7	11	2
			TOTAL SUB-ORDER 64	983	110	220	653	538	47
		65.—LITERATURE	409. Authors, editors, etc.	19	3	5	11	4	...
			410. Book copyists	4	...	1	3	3	...
			411. Private secretaries and clerks	120	11	22	87	58	3
			412. Public scribes and copyists	38	4	10	24	25	3
			TOTAL SUB-ORDER 65	181	18	38	125	90	6
		66.—LAW	414. Pleaders	111	14	27	70	51	5
			416. Mukhtiars	75	10	11	54	46	6
			418. Stamp-vendors	36	4	3	29	21	2
			419. Petition-writers	274	30	65	179	141	12
			TOTAL SUB-ORDER 66	496	58	106	332	259	25
		67.—MEDICINE. (a) Practitioners	421. Practitioners by diploma	41	10	6	25	20	5
			422. Baid, hakim, etc.	233	27	50	156	136	13
			424. Oculists	16	5	2	9	12	5
			425. Vaccinators	6	...	...	6	5	...
			426. Midwifery	20	...	...	20	...	...
		(b) Subsidiary medical service.	427. Hospital assistants and apothecaries	58	13	8	37	27	4
			428. Compounders, nurses and dispensary service	115	10	22	83	67	4
			TOTAL SUB-ORDER 67	489	65	88	336	267	31
		68.—ENGINEERING AND SURVEYING. (a) Engineers, architects and surveyors.	430. Civil engineers and architects	60	5	1	54	41	2
		(b) Subsidiary staff	432. Draughtsmen, overseers, etc.	47	7	13	27	32	6
			433. Clerks, Public Works Department	48	8	7	33	39	8
			TOTAL SUB-ORDER 68	155	20	21	114	112	16
		69.—OTHER SCIENCES. (b) Minor sciences	437. Astrologers, genealogists and horoscope casters	155	21	44	90	96	11
			TOTAL SUB-ORDER 69	155	21	44	90	96	11
		70.—PICTORIAL ART AND SCULPTURE.	440. Picture makers	6	...	...	6	6	...
			442. Photographers	10	3	2	5	5	1
			TOTAL SUB-ORDER 70	16	3	2	11	11	1

occupations—*contd.*

TION.									
ES.		FEMALES.							
5—14	15 and over.	TOTAL.	0—4	5—14	15 and over.	OCCUPATIONS	Sub-order and Group.	Order.	Class.
11	12	13	14	15	16				
195	777	778	132	176	470	375. Cart owners and drivers	59.—ROAD— (a) Cart, carriage and tramway owners and drivers.	XIX.—TRANSPORT AND STORAGE—*contd.*	CLASS E.—COMMERCE, TRANSPORT AND STORAGE—*contd.*
...	1	...	...	...	...	376. Livery stable-keepers, etc.			
2	21	23	5	4	14	377. Drivers, stable boys, etc.			
1	33	1	...	...	1	378. Dooly bearers			
43	146	41	1	12	28	379. Pack bullock owners and drivers, etc.	(b) Carriers by pack animals.		
112	411	358	58	95	205	380. Camel and mule drivers			
353	1,389	1,201	196	287	718	TOTAL SUB-ORDER 59			
...	1	1	...	...	1	385. Boatmen	60.—WATER— (b) Working staff of vessels.		
...	3	...	...	...	...	389. Divers (not for pearls)			
...	4	1	...	...	1	TOTAL SUB-ORDER 60			
2	20	8	...	4	4	390. Postmasters and clerks	61.—MESSAGES— (a) Post, etc.		
57	180	110	12	22	76	391. Postal messengers, runners, &c.			
5	43	166	20	39	107	392. Messengers			
3	15	23	4	5	14	393. Telegraph officers (Government, Railway and others) and clerical and accountant's establishments.	(b) Telegraph and Telephone.		
4	21	27	3	7	17	394. Signallers and messengers			
71	279	334	39	77	218	TOTAL SUB-ORDER 61			
...	1	1	...	...	1	397. Warehouse service	62.—STORAGE AND WEIGHING.		
68	198	151	29	22	100	398. Porters			
15	74	55	4	8	43	399. Weighmen			
63	267	314	50	57	207	400. Watchmen (not village)			
146	540	521	83	87	351	TOTAL SUB-ORDER 62			
834	3,550	4,491	704	942	2,845	**Total Order XIX.—Transport and Storage**			
16	71	82	17	15	50	401. Priests, ministers, preachers, missionary, etc.	63.—RELIGION— (a) Priests, ministers, etc.	XX.—LEARNED AND ARTISTIC PROFESSIONS.	CLASS F.—PROFESSIONS.
1	1	2	...	...	2	402. Zenana mission service			
1,110	3,291	5,528	787	1,163	3,578	404. Religious mendicants	(b) Subsidiary religious services.		
225	565	412	44	77	291	405. Church and temple service			
1,352	3,928	6,024	848	1,255	3,921	TOTAL SUB-ORDER 63			
118	364	445	63	100	282	407. Principals, professors and teachers in colleges, schools, etc.	64.—EDUCATION.		
2	7	...	...	...	...	408. Clerks, etc., on establishments of educational institutions.			
120	371	445	63	100	282	TOTAL SUB-ORDER 64			
1	3	15	3	4	8	409 Authors, editors, etc.	65.—LITERATURE.		
1	2	1	...	...	1	410. Book copyists			
6	49	62	8	16	38	411. Private secretaries and clerks			
8	14	13	1	2	10	412. Public scribes and copyists			
16	68	91	12	22	57	TOTAL SUB-ORDER 65			
13	33	60	9	14	37	414. Pleaders	66.—LAW.		
8	32	29	4	3	22	416. Mukhtiars			
1	18	15	2	2	11	418. Stamp-vendors			
35	94	133	18	30	85	419. Petition-writers			
57	177	237	33	49	155	TOTAL SUB-ORDER 66			
3	12	21	5	3	13	421. Practitioners by diploma	67.—MEDICINE. (a) Practitioners		
30	93	97	14	20	63	422. Baid, hakim, etc.			
1	6	4	...	1	3	424. Oculists			
...	5	1	...	...	1	425. Vaccinators			
...	...	20	...	...	20	426. Midwifery			
4	19	31	9	4	18	427. Hospital assistants and apothecaries	(b) Subsidiary medical service.		
10	53	48	6	12	30	428. Compounders, nurses and dispensary service			
48	188	222	34	40	148	TOTAL SUB-ORDER 67			
...	39	19	3	1	15	430. Civil engineers and architects	68.—ENGINEERING AND SURVEYING. (a) Engineers, architects and surveyors.		
9	17	15	1	4	10	432. Draughtsmen, overseers, etc.	(b) Subsidiary staff.		
6	25	9	...	1	8	433. Clerks, Public Works Department			
15	81	43	4	6	33	TOTAL SUB-ORDER 68			
25	60	59	10	19	30	437. Astrologers, genealogists and horoscope casters	69.—OTHER SCIENCES. (b) Minor sciences.		
25	60	59	10	19	30	TOTAL SUB-ORDER 69			
...	6	...	...	...	...	440. Picture makers	70.—PICTORIAL ART AND SCULPTURE.		
2	2	5	2	...	3	442. Photographers			
2	8	5	2	...	3	TOTAL SUB-ORDER 70			

TABLE XVII.—Part A.—

Class.	Order.	Sub-order and Group.	Occupations.	TOWN. Total. Total.	Total. 0—4	Total. 5—14	Total. 15 and over.	Males. Total.	Males. 0—4	Males. 5—14	Males. 15 and over.	Females. Total.	Females. 0—4	Females. 5—14	Females. 15 and over.
				17	18	19	20	21	22	23	24	25	26	27	28
CLASS E.—COMMERCE, TRANSPORT AND STORAGE—contd.	XIX.—TRANSPORT AND STORAGE—contd.	59.—Road— (a) Cart, carriage and tramway owners and drivers.	375. Cart owners and drivers	1,285	176	235	874	674	76	102	496	611	100	133	378
			376. Livery stable-keepers, etc.	...	...	...	...	...	..	...	...	...	...	...	...
			377. Drivers, stable boys, etc.	32	5	4	23	12	...	...	12	20	5	4	11
			378. Dooly bearers	35	...	1	34	34	...	1	33	1	...	...	1
		(b) Carriers by pack animals.	379. Pack bullock owners and drivers, etc.	103	14	25	64	103	14	25	64	...	...	...	...
			380. Camel and mule drivers	411	55	73	283	250	27	34	189	161	28	39	94
			TOTAL SUB-ORDER 59	1,866	250	338	1,278	1,073	117	162	794	793	133	176	484
		60.—Water— (b) Working staff of vessels.	385. Boatmen	1	...	...	1	1	...	...	1	...	...	...	...
			389. Divers (not for pearls)	3	...	...	3	3	...	...	3	...	...	...	...
			TOTAL SUB-ORDER 60	4	...	...	4	4	...	...	4	...	...	...	...
		61.—Messages— (a) Post, etc.	390. Postmasters and clerks	29	2	5	22	23	2	2	19	6	...	3	3
			391. Postal messengers, runners, etc.	262	22	54	186	173	15	38	120	89	7	16	66
			392. Messengers	198	24	41	133	40	5	4	31	158	19	37	102
		(b) Telegraph and Telephone.	393. Telegraph officers (Government, Railway and others) and clerical and accountant's establishments.	42	5	8	29	19	1	3	15	23	4	5	14
			394. Signallers and messengers	53	4	11	38	26	1	4	21	27	3	7	17
			TOTAL SUB-ORDER 61	584	57	119	408	281	24	51	206	303	33	68	202
		62.—Storage and Weighing.	397. Warehouse service	2	...	...	2	1	...	...	1	1	...	...	1
			398. Porters	314	47	59	208	212	28	43	141	102	19	16	67
			399. Weighmen	126	14	18	94	85	11	13	61	41	3	5	33
			400. Watchmen (not village)	673	80	120	473	360	30	63	267	313	50	57	206
			TOTAL SUB-ORDER 62	1,115	141	197	777	658	69	119	470	457	72	78	307
			Total Order XIX—Transport and Storage.	7,604	1,004	1,460	5,140	3,726	399	666	2,661	3,878	605	794	2,479
CLASS F.—PROFESSIONS.	XX.—LEARNED AND ARTISTIC PROFESSIONS.—contd.	63.—Religion— (a) Priests, ministers, etc.	401. Priests, ministers, preachers, missionary, etc.	107	15	19	73	66	9	11	46	41	6	8	27
		(b) Subsidiary religious services.	402. Zenana mission service	6	2	1	3	4	2	1	1	2	...	...	2
			404. Religious mendicants	2,201	221	408	1,572	1,048	87	183	778	1,553	134	225	794
			405. Church and temple service	686	71	126	489	466	51	89	326	220	20	37	163
			TOTAL SUB-ORDER 63	2,000	309	554	1,137	1,584	149	284	1,151	1,416	160	270	986
		64.—Education	407. Principals, professors and teachers in colleges, schools, etc.	719	81	168	470	395	34	94	267	324	47	74	203
			408. Clerks, etc., on establishments of educational institutions.	11	2	2	7	11	2	2	7	...	...	...	...
			TOTAL SUB-ORDER 64	730	83	170	477	406	36	96	274	324	47	74	203
		65.—Literature	409. Authors, editors, etc.	3	1	...	2	...	...	...	...	3	1	...	2
			410. Book copyists	...	...	...	...	...	...	...	...	...	...	...	...
			411. Private secretaries and clerks	77	8	13	56	24	1	1	22	53	7	12	34
			412. Public scribes and copyists	38	4	10	24	25	3	8	14	13	1	2	10
			TOTAL SUB-ORDER 65	118	13	23	82	49	4	9	36	69	9	14	46
		66.—Law	414. Pleaders	111	14	27	70	51	5	13	33	60	9	14	37
			416. Mukhtiars	70	8	11	51	41	4	8	29	29	4	3	22
			418. Stamp-vendors	32	3	3	26	20	2	1	17	12	1	2	9
			419. Petition-writers	253	27	58	168	128	10	31	87	125	17	27	81
			TOTAL SUB-ORDER 66	466	52	99	315	240	21	53	166	226	31	46	149
		67.—Medicine. (a) Practitioners	421. Practitioners by diploma	37	9	6	22	17	4	3	10	20	5	3	12
			422. Baid, hakim, etc.	179	20	37	122	111	11	26	74	68	9	11	48
			424. Oculists	12	5	1	6	12	5	1	6	...	...	...	...
			425. Vaccinators	4	...	...	4	3	...	...	3	1	...	...	1
			426. Midwifery	15	...	...	15	...	...	...	...	15	...	...	15
		(b) Subsidiary Medical service.	427. Hospital assistants and apothecaries.	57	13	8	36	26	4	4	18	31	9	4	18
			428. Compounders, nurses and dispensary service.	114	10	22	82	66	4	10	52	48	6	12	30
			TOTAL SUB-ORDER 67	418	57	74	287	235	28	44	163	183	29	30	124
		68.—Engineering and Surveying. (a) Engineers, architects and surveyors.	430. Civil engineers and architects	26	3	1	22	9	...	...	9	17	3	1	13
		(b) Subsidiary staff.	432. Draughtsmen, overseers, etc.	45	7	13	25	30	6	9	15	15	1	4	10
			433. Clerks, Public Works Department	41	6	7	28	34	6	6	22	7	...	1	6
			TOTAL SUB-ORDER 68	112	16	21	75	73	12	15	46	39	4	6	29
		69.—Other Sciences. (b) Minor sciences	437. Astrologers, genealogists and horoscope casters.	56	4	12	40	50	4	11	35	6	...	1	5
			TOTAL SUB-ORDER 69	56	4	12	40	50	4	11	35	6	...	1	5
		70.—Pictorial Art and Sculpture.	440. Picture makers	6	...	...	6	6	...	...	6	...	...	...	...
			442. Photographers	4	1	1	2	2	...	1	1	2	1	...	1
			TOTAL SUB-ORDER 70	10	1	1	8	8	...	1	7	2	1	...	1

Occupations—*contd.*

COUNTRY. Total. Total.	Total. 0—4	Total. 5—14	Total. 15 and over.	Males. Total.	Males. 0—4	Males. 5—14	Males. 15 and over.	Females. Total.	Females. 0—4	Females. 5—14	Females. 15 and over.	Occupations.	Sub-order and Group.	Order.	Class.
29	30	31	32	33	34	35	36	37	38	39	40				
591	82	136	373	424	50	93	281	167	32	43	92	375. Cart owners and drivers	59.—Road— (a) Cart, carriage and tramway owners and drivers.	XIX.—Transport and Storage—contd.	Class E.—Commerce Transport and Storage—contd.
1	...	...	1	1	...	...	1	...	...	...	...	376. Livery stable-keepers, etc.			
15	1	2	12	12	1	2	9	3	...	...	3	377. Drivers, stable boys, etc.			
...	...	...	...	...	...	...	...	...	...	...	...	378. Dooly bearers			
150	10	30	110	109	9	18	82	41	1	12	28	379. Pack bullock owners and drivers, etc.	(b) Carriers by pack animals.		
536	69	134	333	339	39	78	222	197	30	56	111	380. Camel and mule drivers			
1,293	162	302	829	885	99	191	595	408	63	111	234	Total Sub-order 59			
1	...	...	1	...	...	...	...	1	...	...	1	385. Boatmen	60.—Water— (a) Working staff of vessels.		
...	...	...	...	...	...	...	...	...	...	...	...	389. Divers (not for pearls)			
1	...	...	1	...	...	...	...	1	...	...	1	Total Sub-order 60			
5	2	1	2	3	2	...	1	2	...	1	1	390. Postmasters and clerks	61.—Messages— (a) Post, etc.		
110	15	25	70	89	10	19	60	21	5	6	10	391. Postal messengers, runners, etc.			
24	4	3	17	16	3	1	12	8	1	2	5	392. Messengers			
...	...	...	...	...	...	...	...	...	...	...	...	393. Telegraph officers (Government, Railway and others) and clerical and accountant's establishments	(b) Telegraph and Telephone.		
...	...	...	...	...	...	...	...	...	...	...	...	394. Signallers and messengers			
139	21	29	89	108	15	20	73	31	6	9	16	Total Sub-order 61			
...	...	...	...	...	...	...	...	...	...	...	...	397. Warehouse service	62.—Storage and Weighing.		
132	11	31	90	83	1	25	57	49	10	6	33	398. Porters			
32	4	5	23	18	3	2	13	14	1	3	10	399. Weighmen			
1	...	...	1	...	...	...	...	1	...	...	1	400. Watchmen (not village)			
165	15	36	114	101	4	27	70	64	11	9	44	Total Sub-order 62			
1,908	237	416	1,255	1,295	138	268	889	613	99	148	366	**Total Order XIX—Transport and Storage.**			
79	19	12	48	38	8	5	25	41	11	7	23	401. Priests, ministers, preachers, missionary, etc.	63.—Religion— (a) Priests, ministers, etc.	XX.—Learned and Artistic Professions.	Class F.—Professions.
...	...	...	...	...	...	...	...	...	...	...	...	402. Zenana mission service			
8,340	1,178	1,865	5,297	3,965	525	927	2,513	4,375	653	938	2,784	404. Religious mendicants	(b) Subsidiary religious services.		
614	71	176	367	422	47	136	239	192	24	40	128	405. Church and temple service			
9,033	1,268	2,053	5,712	4,425	580	1,068	2,777	4,608	688	985	2,935	Total Sub-order 63			
253	27	50	176	132	11	24	97	121	16	26	79	407. Principals, professors and teachers, in colleges, schools, etc.	64.—Education.		
...	...	...	...	...	...	...	...	...	...	...	...	408. Clerks, etc., on establishments of educational institutions.			
253	27	50	176	132	11	24	97	121	16	26	79	Total Sub-order 64			
16	2	5	9	4	...	1	3	12	2	4	6	409. Authors, editors, etc.	65.—Literature.		
4	...	1	3	3	...	1	2	1	...	...	1	410. Book copyists			
43	3	9	31	34	2	5	27	9	1	4	4	411. Private secretaries and clerks			
...	...	...	...	...	...	...	...	...	...	...	...	412. Public scribes and copyists			
63	5	15	43	41	2	7	32	22	3	8	11	Total Sub-order 65			
...	...	...	...	...	...	...	...	...	...	...	...	414. Pleaders	66—Law.		
5	2	...	3	5	2	...	3	...	...	...	...	416. Mukhtiars			
4	1	...	3	1	...	...	1	3	1	...	2	418. Stamp-vendors			
21	3	7	11	13	2	4	7	8	1	3	4	419. Petition-writers			
30	6	7	17	19	4	4	11	11	2	3	6	Total Sub-order 66			
4	1	...	3	3	1	...	2	1	...	...	1	421. Practitioners by diploma	67.—Medicine. (a) Practitioners.		
54	7	13	34	25	2	4	19	29	5	9	15	422. Baid, hakim, etc.			
4	...	1	3	...	...	...	...	4	...	1	3	424. Oculists			
2	...	...	2	2	...	...	2	...	...	...	...	425. Vaccinators			
5	...	...	5	...	...	...	...	5	...	...	5	426. Midwifery			
1	...	...	1	1	...	...	1	...	...	...	...	427. Hospital assistants and apothecaries.	(b) Subsidiary medical service.		
1	...	...	1	1	...	...	1	...	...	...	...	428. Compounders, nurses and dispensary service.			
71	8	14	49	32	3	4	25	39	5	10	24	Total Sub-order 67			
34	2	...	32	32	2	...	30	2	...	...	2	430. Civil engineers and architects	68.—Engineering and Surveying. (a) Engineers, architects and surveyors.		
2	...	...	2	2	...	...	2	...	...	...	...	432. Draughtsmen, overseers, etc.	(b) Subsidiary staff.		
7	2	...	5	5	2	...	3	2	...	...	2	433. Clerks, Public Works Department			
43	4	...	39	39	4	...	35	4	...	...	4	Total Sub-order 68			
99	17	32	50	46	7	14	25	53	10	18	25	437. Astrologers, genealogists and horoscope casters.	69.—Other Sciences. (b) Minor sciences.		
99	17	32	50	46	7	14	25	53	10	18	25	Total Sub-order 69			
...	...	...	...	...	...	...	...	...	...	...	...	440. Picture makers	70.—Pictorial Art and Sculpture.		
6	2	1	3	3	1	1	1	3	1	...	2	442. Photographers			
6	2	1	3	3	1	1	1	3	1	...	2	Total Sub-order 70			

TABLE XVII.—Part A.—

Class.	Order	Sub-order and Group.	Occupations.	TOTAL POPULA[TION] — Total. — Total.	0–4	5–14	15 and over.	Mal[es] — Total.	0–4
1	2	3	4	5	6	7	8	9	10
CLASS F.—PROFESSIONS—contd.	XX.—LEARNED AND ARTISTIC PROFESSIONS—contd.	71.—Musing, Acting, Dancing.	443. Musicians	3	1	1	1	...	...
			444. Drummers and trumpeters	4,116	673	1,077	2,318	2,332	347
			446. Actors, singers and dancers and their accompanists.	1,090	125	215	750	494	55
			Total Sub-order 71	5,211	790	1,293	3,119	2,826	402
			Total Order XX.—Learned and Artistic Professions.	**19,719**	**2,671**	**4,419**	**12.629**	**10,208**	**1,268**
	XXI.—SPORTS AND AMUSEMENTS.	72.—Sport	447. Jockeys	2	...	1	1	2	...
			448. Birds catchers	38	6	5	27	21	3
			Total Sub-order 72	40	6	6	28	23	3
		73.—Exhibitions and Games— (b) Conjuring, fortune and other exhibitions.	453. Buffoons	10	...	1	9	7	...
			454. Story and ballad reciters	27	1	2	24	23	1
			455. Jugglers	2	...	..	2	2	...
			456. Fortune tellers	11	3	...	8	2	1
		(c) Acrobatics and athletics.	457. Wrestlers and cricketers and acrobats	42	5	7	30	23	3
		(d) Service of places of entertainment.	460. Billiard-room service	27	4	5	18	9	2
			Total Sub-order 73	119	13	15	91	66	7
			Total Order XXI.—Sports and Amusements	**150**	**19**	**21**	**119**	**89**	**10**
CLASS G.—INDEFINITE AND INDEPENDENT.	XXIII.—INDEFINITE.	74.—Unskilled Labour— (a) Special branches.	461. Well-sinkers	26	2	2	12	16	2
			463. Road and railway labourers	400	49	104	247	243	23
			464. Stone splitters, etc.	6	1	1	4	6	1
		(b) General	467. General labourers	53,132	7,252	12,756	33,123	25,685	3,552
			Total Sub-order 74	53,553	7,304	12,863	33,386	25,050	3,578
		75.—Undefined, etc.	468. Undefined	380	22	62	296	83	9
			Total Sub-order 75	380	22	62	296	83	9
			Total Order XXIII.—Indefinite	**53 933**	**7,326**	**12,925**	**33,682**	**26,033**	**3,587**
	XXIV.—INDEPENDENT OF WORK.	76.—Property and Alms— (a) Property and Allowances.	469. House-rent	426	29	98	289	285	15
			470. Private pensioners	11	..	4	7	3	...
		(b) Charity and endowment.	472. Beggars	11,253	1,346	2,486	7,421	7,077	759
			Total Sub-order 76	11,680	1,375	2,588	7,717	7,265	774
		77.—Supported at the Public Charge— (a) Pension	473. Civil pensioners	368	36	85	247	148	13
			474. Military pensioners	548	90	126	332	391	51
		(b) Prisoners	478. Prisoners	330	...	11	319	313	...
			Total Sub-order 77	1,246	126	222	898	852	64
			Total Order XXIV.—Independent of Work	**12.926**	**1,501**	**2,810**	**8,615**	**8.117**	**838**
			Grand Total	**542,358**	**76,924**	**133,708**	**331.726**	**288,325**	**38,730**

Occupations—*contd.*

TION.									
ES.		FEMALES.				OCCUPATIONS.	Sub-order and Group.	Order.	Class.
5—14	15 and over.	TOTAL.	0—4	5—14	15 and over.				
11	12	13	14	15	16				
...	...	3	1	1	1	443. Musicians	71.—MUSING, ACTING, DANCING.	XX.—LEARNED AND ARTISTIC PROFESSIONS—*contd.*	CLASS F.—PROFESSIONS—*contd.*
618	1,367	1,786	326	459	1,001	444. Drummers and trumpeters			
98	341	596	70	117	409	446. Actors, singers and dancers and their accompanists.			
716	1,708	2,385	397	577	1,411	TOTAL SUB-ORDER 71			
2,351	6,589	9,511	1,403	2,068	6,040	**Total Order XX.—Learned and Artistic Professions.**			
1	1	...	...	..	...	447. Jockeys	72.—SPORT	XXI.—SPORTS AND AMUSEMENTS.	
1	17	17	3	4	10	448. Birds catchers			
2	18	17	3	4	10	TOTAL SUB-ORDER 72			
1	6	3	...	...	3	453. Buffoons	73.—EXHIBITIONS AND GAMES— (b) Conjuring, fortune and other exhibitions.		
...	22	4	...	2	2	454. Story and ballad reciters			
...	2	...	...	.	...	455. Jugglers			
...	1	9	2	...	7	456. Fortune tellers			
3	17	19	2	4	13	457. Wrestlers and cricketers and acrobats	(c) Acrobatics and athletics.		
1	6	18	2	4	12	460 Billiard-room service	(d) Service of places of entertainment.		
5	54	53	6	10	37	TOTAL SUB-ORDER 73			
7	72	70	9	14	47	**Total Order XXI.—Sports and Amusements**			
2	12	...	...	...	...	461. Well-sinkers	74.—UNSKILLED LABOUR— (a) Special branches.	XXIII.—INDEFINITE.	CLASS G.—INDEFINITE AND INDEPENDENT.
71	149	157	26	33	98	463. Road and railway labourers			
1	4	...	...	...	...	464. Stone splitters, etc.			
6,792	15,381	27,446	3,700	6,004	17,742	467. General labourers	(b) General		
6,866	15,546	27,603	3,726	6,037	17,840	TOTAL SUB-ORDER 74			
25	49	297	13	37	247	468. Undefined	75.—UNDEFINED, ETC.		
25	49	297	13	37	247	TOTAL SUB-ORDER 75			
6,851	15,595	27,900	3,739	6,074	18,087	**Total Order XXIII.—Indefinite**			
53	117	231	14	45	172	469. House-rent	76.—PROPERTY AND ALMS— (a) Property and Allowances.	XXIV.—INDEPENDENT OF WORK.	
2	1	8	..	2	6	570. Private pensioners			
1,539	4,769	4,176	587	937	2,652	472 Beggars	(b) Charity and endowment.		
1,594	4,887	4,415	601	984	2,830	TOTAL SUB-ORDER 76			
35	100	220	23	50	147	473. Civil pensioners	77.—SUPPORTED AT THE PUBLIC CHARGE— (a) Pension		
77	263	157	30	40	69	474. Military pensioners			
10	303	27	...	1	26	478. Prisoners	(b) Prisoners		
122	666	394	62	100	232	TOTAL SUB-ORDER 77			
1,726	5,553	4,809	663	1,084	3,062	**Total Order XXIV.—Independent of Work**			
72,762	176,833	254,033	38,194	60,946	154,893	**Grand Total**			

Table XVII.—A.—Occupations.—Ajmere.

TABLE XVII.—Part A.—

Class.	Order.	Sub-order and Group.	Occupations.	TOWN. Total. Total.	Total. 0—4	Total. 5—14	Total. 15 and over.	Males. Total.	Males. 0—4	Males. 5—14	Males. 15 and over.	Females. Total.	Females. 0—4	Females. 5—14	Females. 15 and over.
				17	18	19	20	21	22	23	24	25	26	27	28
CLASS F.—PROFESSIONS—*contd.*	XX. LEARNED AND ARTISTIC PROFESSIONS—*contd.*	71.—Music, Acting, Dancing.	443. Musicians	3	1	1	1	...	...	...	...	3	1	1	1
			444. Drummers and trumpeters	151	24	29	98	79	11	14	54	72	13	15	44
			446. Actors, singers and dancers and their accompanists.	542	54	86	402	273	32	49	192	269	22	37	210
			Total Sub-order 71	696	79	116	501	352	43	63	246	344	36	53	255
			Total Order XX.—Learned and Artistic Professions.	5,606	614	1,070	3,922	2,997	297	576	2,124	2,609	317	949	1,798
	XXI.—SPORTS AND AMUSEMENTS.	72.—Sport	447. Jockeys	2	...	1	1	2	...	1	1	...	...	...	...
			448. Birds catchers	9	...	...	9	9	...	...	9	...	...	...	...
			Total Sub-order 72	11	...	1	10	11	...	1	10	...	...	...	...
		73.—Exhibitions and Games. (*b*) Conjuring, fortune and other exhibitions.	453. Buffoons	7	...	1	6	6	...	1	5	1	...	...	1
			454. Story and ballad reciters	21	1	...	20	21	1	...	20	...	...	...	...
			455. Jugglers	2	...	...	2	2	...	...	2	...	...	...	...
			456. Fortune tellers	9	2	...	7	...	...	...	...	9	2	...	7
		(*c*) Acrobatics and athletics.	457. Wrestlers and cricketers and acrobats.	21	1	2	18	8	...	...	8	13	1	2	10
		(*d*) Service of places of entertainment.	460. Billiard-room service	27	4	5	18	9	2	1	6	18	2	4	12
			Total Sub-order 73	87	8	8	71	46	3	2	41	41	5	6	30
			Total Order XXI.—Sport and Amusements.	98	8	9		57	3	3	51	41	5	8	30
CLASS—G.—INDEFINITE AND INDEPENDENT.	XXIII.—INDEFINITE.	74.—Unskilled Labour— (*a*) Special branches.	461. Well-sinkers	6	...	...	6	6	...	...	6	...	...	...	...
			463. Road and railway labourers	204	30	40	134	48	4	7	37	156	26	33	97
			464. Stone splitters, etc.	6	1	1	4	6	1	1	4	...	..	.	...
		(*b*) General	467. General labourers	12,346	1,619	2,657	8,070	6,825	843	1,542	4,440	5,521	776	1,115	3,630
			Total Sub-order 74	12,562	1,650	2,698	8,214	6,885	848	1,550	4,487	5,677	802	1,148	3,727
		75.—Undefined, etc.	468. Undefined	353	20	55	278	76	9	24	43	277	11	31	235
			Total Sub-order 75	353	20	55	278	76	9	24	43	277	11	31	235
			Total Order XXIII.—Indefinite	12,915	1,670	2,753	8,492	6,961	857	1,574	4,530	5,954	813	1,179	3,962
	XXIV.—INDEPENDENT OF WORK.	76.—Property and Alms— (*a*) Property and Allowances.	469. House-rent	370	24	84	262	145	10	41	94	225	14	43	168
			470. Private pensioners	11	...	4	7	3	...	2	1	8	...	2	6
		(*b*) Charity and endowment.	472. Beggars	3,266	308	621	2,337	2,025	152	383	1,490	1,241	156	238	847
			Total Sub-order 76	3,647	332	709	2,606	2,173	162	426	1,585	1,474	170	283	1,021
		77.—Supported at the Public Charge— (*a*) Pension	473. Civil pensioners	239	16	53	170	65	2	17	46	174	14	36	124
			474. Military pensioners	237	27	43	167	162	16	30	116	75	11	13	51
		(*b*) Prisoners	478. Prisoners	330	...	11	319	313	...	10	303	17	...	1	16
			Total Sub-order 77	806	43	107	656	540	18	57	465	266	25	50	191
			Total Order XXIV.—Independent of Work.	4,453	375	816	3,262	2,713	180	483	2,050	1,740	195	333	1,212
			Grand Total	118,631	14,953	23,572	80,106	64,466	7,397	12,742	44,327	54,165	7,556	10,830	35,779

Occupations—*contd.*

COUNTRY.																
TOTAL.				MALES.				FEMALES.				OCCUPATIONS.	Sub-order and Group.	Order.	Class.
TOTAL.	0—4	5—14	15 and over.	TOTAL.	0—4	5—14	15 and over.	TOTAL.	0—4	5—14	15 and over.				
29	30	31	32	33	34	35	36	37	38	39	40				
...	...	...	...	...	...	...	...	...	...	...	...	443. Musicians	71.—MUSING, ACTING, DANCING.	XX.—LEARNED AND ARTISTIC PROFESSIONS—contd.	CLASS F.—PROFESSIONS—contd.
3,967	649	1,018	2,270	2,253	336	604	1,313	1,714	313	444	957	444. Drummers and trumpeters			
548	71	129	348	221	23	49	149	327	48	80	199	446. Actors, singers and dancers and their accompanists.			
4,515	720	1,177	2,618	2,474	359	653	1,462	2,041	361	524	1,156	TOTAL SUB-ORDER 71			
14,113	2,057	3,349	8,707	7,211	971	1,775	4,465	6,902	1,086	1,574	4,242	**Total Order XX.—Learned and Artistic Professions.**			
...	...	...	...	...	...	...	...	...	...	...	...	447. Jockeys	72.—Spor	XXI.—SPORTS AND AMUSEMENTS.	
29	6	5	18	12	3	1	8	17	3	4	10	448. Birds catchers			
29	6	5	18	12	3	1	8	17	3	4	10	TOTAL SUB-ORDER 72			
3	...	...	3	1	...	...	1	2	...	...	2	453. Buffoons	73.—EXHIBITIONS AND GAMES. (b) Conjuring, fortune and other exhibitions.		
6	...	2	4	2	...	...	2	4	...	2	2	454. Story and ballad reciters			
...	...	...	...	...	...	...	...	...	...	...	...	455. Jugglers			
2	1	...	1	2	1	...	1	...	...	...	...	456 Fortune-tellers			
21	4	5	12	15	3	3	9	6	1	2	3	457. Wrestlers and cricketers and acrobats.	(c) Acrobatics and athletics.		
...	...	...	...	...	...	...	...	...	...	...	...	460. Billiard-room service	(d) Service of places of entertainment.		
32	5	7	20	20	4	3	13	12	1	4	7	TOTAL SUB-ORDER 73			
61	11	12	38	32	7	4	21	29	4	8	17	**Total Order XXI.—Sport and Amusements.**			
10	2	2	6	10	2	2	6	...	...	...	...	461. Well sinker	74.—UNSKILLED LABOUR. (a) Special branches.	XXIII.—INDEFINITE.	CLASS G.—INDEFINITE AND INDEPENDENT.
196	19	64	113	195	19	64	112	1	...	...	1	463. Road and Railway labourers			
...	...	...	...	...	...	...	...	...	...	...	...	464. Stone splitters, etc.			
40,785	5,633	10,099	25,053	18,860	2,709	5,210	10,941	21,925	2,924	4,889	14,112	467. General labourers	(b) General.		
40,991	5,654	10,165	25,172	19,065	2,730	5,276	11,059	21,926	2,924	4,889	14,113	TOTAL SUB-ORDER 74			
27	2	7	18	7	...	1	6	20	2	6	12	468. Undefined	75.—UNDEFINED, &C.		
27	2	7	18	7	...	1	6	20	2	6	12	TOTAL SUB-ORDER 74			
41,018	5,656	10,172	25,190	19,072	2,730	5,277	11,065	21,946	2,926	4,895	14,125	**Total Order XXIII.—Indefinite**			
46	5	14	27	40	5	12	23	6	...	2	4	469. House-rent	76.—PROPERTY AND ALMS— (a) Property and Allowances.	XXIV.—INDEPENDENT OF WORK.	
...	...	...	...	...	...	...	...	...	...	...	...	470. Private pensioners			
7,987	1,038	1,865	5,084	5,052	607	1,166	3,279	2,935	431	699	1,805	472. Beggars	(b) Charity and endowment.		
8,033	1,043	1,879	5,111	5,092	612	1,178	3,302	2,941	431	701	1,809	TOTAL SUB-ORDER 76			
129	20	32	77	83	11	18	54	46	9	14	23	473. Civil pensioners	77.—SUPPORTED AT THE PUBLIC CHARGE— (a) Pension		
311	63	83	165	229	35	47	147	82	28	36	18	474. Military pensioners			
...	...	...	...	...	...	...	...	...	...	...	...	478. Prisoners	(b) Prisoners		
440	83	115	242	312	46	65	201	128	37	50	41	TOTAL SUB-ORDER 77			
8,473	1,126	1,994	5,353	5,404	658	1,243	3,503	3,069	468	751	1,850	**Total Order XXIV.—Independent of Work.**			
423,727	61,971	110,136	251,620	223,859	31,333	60,020	132,506	199,868	30,638	50,116	119,11 4	**Grand Total**			

TABLE XVII.—Part B.—Occupations by Districts.

Class.	Order.	Sub-order and Group.	OCCUPATIONS.	AJMERE. Total.	AJMERE. Males.	AJMERE. Females.	MERWARA. Total.	MERWARA. Males.	MERWARA. Females.
1	2	3	4	5	6	7	8	9	10
CLASS A.—GOVERNMENT.	I.—ADMINISTRATION.	1.—Service of the Imperial and Provincial Governments.	2. Officers	35	14	21	6	4	2
			3. Office superintendents and clerical establishments, police and excise inspectors, sub-registrars, etc.	722	553	169	85	49	36
			4. Messengers, constables, bailiffs, warders, menials, etc.	3,129	2,005	1,124	550	391	159
			Total Sub-order 1	3,886	2,572	1,314	641	444	197
		2.—Service of Local and Municipal Bodies.	5. Inspecting and supervising officials.	20	9	11	3	3	...
			6. Clerical establishments	34	25	9	3	3	...
			7. Menials	448	296	152	68	46	22
			Total Sub-order 2	502	330	172	74	52	22
		3.—Village Service	9. Accountants	381	264	117	198	121	77
			11. Watchmen and other menials	1,164	714	450	85	54	31
			Total Sub-order 3	1,545	978	567	283	175	108
			Total Order I.—Administration	**5,933**	**3,880**	**2,053**	**998**	**671**	**327**
	II.—DEFENCE.	4.—Army	12. Officers	158	88	70	26	25	1
			13. Non-commissioned officers and privates.	4,793	3,459	1,334	196	109	87
			14. Followers	519	311	208	1	1	...
			15. Administrative establishments	41	33	8	...	...	...
			Total Sub-order 4	5,511	3,891	1,620	223	135	88
			Total Order II.—Defence	**5,511**	**3,891**	**1,620**	**223**	**135**	**88**
	III.—FOREIGN AND FEUDATORY STATE SERVICE.	6.—Administrative Service.	19. Chiefs, consuls and officers	34	31	3	...	...	...
			20. Clerical establishments	74	58	16	...	...	...
			21. Menials, etc.	1,988	1,164	824	12	9	3
			Total Sub-order 6	2,096	1,253	843	12	9	3
		7.—Army and Marine.	22. Officers	3	2	1	...	...	...
			23. Privates and seamen, etc.	107	90	17	...	...	...
			Total Sub-order 7	110	92	18	...	...	...
			Total Order III. Foreign and Feudatory State Service.	**2,206**	**1,345**	**861**	**12**	**9**	**3**
CLASS B.—PASTURE AND AGRICULTURAL.	IV.—LIVE STOCK.	8.—Stock Breeding and Dealing— (a) Horses and horned cattle.	24. Horse breeders and dealers	8	5	3	...	...	...
			25. Cattle breeders and dealers and commissariat farm establishment.	827	322	505	34	...	34
		(b) Other draught, etc., animals.	26. Herdsmen	4,057	2,474	1,583	417	290	127
			29. Camel breeders and dealers	12	12	...	21	18	3
		(c) Small stock	30. Ass and mule breeders and dealers	3	1	2	...	...	...
			31. Sheep and goat breeders and dealers	922	776	146	83	73	10
			32. Pig breeders and dealers	22	15	7	..	...	...
			Total Sub-order 8	5,851	3,605	2,246	555	381	174
		9.—Subsidiary Services to Stock— (a) Training and doctoring live stock.	33. Veterinary surgeons and assistants	2	2	...	...	...	...
			34. Farriers and gelders	83	43	40		4	2
			35. Horse breakers and trainers	64	24	40	2	2	...
			Total Sub-order 9	149	69	80	8	6	2
			Total Order IV.—Live Stock	**6,000**	**3,674**	**2,326**	**563**	**386**	**176**

TABLE XVII.—Part B.—Occupations by Districts.

Class.	Order.	Sub-order and Group.	Occupations.	Ajmere. Total.	Ajmere. Males.	Ajmere. Females.	Merwara. Total.	Merwara. Males.	Merwara. Females.
1	2	3	4	5	6	7	8	9	10
CLASS B.—PASTURE AND AGRICULTURAL —contd.	V.—AGRICULTURAL.	10.—Interest in land.	37. Land occupant, not cultivating	6,825	3,523	3,302	2,379	1,403	976
			38. Land occupant, cultivating	58,951	28,699	30,252	39,299	25,691	13,608
			40. Tenants, not cultivating	23,481	10,236	13,245	2,147	1,819	328
			41. Tenants and sharers, cultivating	92,405	53,103	39,302	14,326	5,285	9,041
			Total Sub-order 10	181,662	95,561	86,101	58,151	34,198	23,953
		11.—Agricultural Labourers.	42. Farm servants	599	305	294	27	27	...
			43 Field labourers and crop watchers	2,792	1,344	1,448	18,760	6,363	12,397
			Total Sub-order 11	3,391	1,649	1,742	18,787	6,390	12,397
		12.—Growers of special products and trees.	50. Fruit growers	85	85	...	...	...	...
			52. Gardeners and seedsmen, etc.	365	282	83	27	22	5
			55. Forest rangers, guards, peons	25	17	8	58	37	21
			Total Sub-order 12	475	384	91	85	59	26
			Total Order V.—Agriculture	**185,528**	**97,594**	**87,934**	**77,023**	**40,647**	**36,376**
CLASS C.—PERSONAL SERVICES.	VI.—PERSONAL AND HOUSEHOLD SERVICES.	14.—Personal and Domestic Services.	59. Barbers	4,650	2,617	2,033	886	522	364
			60. Ear-pickers	1	1	...	...	...	...
			62. Castemark appliers	3	2	1	...	...	...
			63. Washermen	2,026	993	1,033	208	117	91
			64. Water-carriers	3,156	1,225	1,931	218	89	129
			65. Cooks	1,760	1,247	513	88	69	19
			66. Indoor servants	7,797	3,623	4,174	119	71	48
			67. Grooms, coachmen and dog boys, etc.	1,584	906	678	30	19	11
			68. Door-keepers, etc.	5,511	3,513	1,998	1,350	1,085	265
			Total Sub-order 14	26,488	14,127	12,361	2,899	1,972	927
		15.—Non-domestic Establishment.	69. Hotel lodging and refreshment room keepers.	2	1	1	4	2	2
			Total Sub-order 15	2	1	1	4	2	2
		16.—Sanitation	73. Sanitary inspectors, local and municipal.	6	4	2	...	...	...
			74. Sweepers	4,437	2,216	2,221	700	354	346
			Total Sub-order 16	4,443	2,220	2,223	700	354	346
			Total Order VI.—Personal and Household Services.	**30,933**	**16,34**	**14,585**	**3,603**	**2,328**	**1,275**
CLASS D.—PREPARATION AND SUPPLY OF MATERIAL SUBSTANCES.	VII.—FOOD AND DRINK.	17.—Animal Food	76. Milk and butter sellers	823	360	463	153	56	97
			77. Ghee preparers and sellers	90	52	38	60	24	36
			79. Butchers	862	432	430	278	144	134
			80. Eggs dealers	36	31	5	...	...	...
			81. Fishermen	35	31	4	...	...	...
			Total Sub-order 17	1,846	906	940	491	224	267
		18.—Vegetable Food	83. Grain dealers	535	173	362	108	53	55
			84. Grain parchers	301	160	141	24	11	13
			85. Flour preparers and sellers	113	3	110	320	...	320
			86. Floor mill service	754	265	489	137	28	109
			87. Bakers	67	51	16	...	...	...
			88. Bran sellers	...	...	...	3	3	...
			89. Vegetable sellers	708	237	471	154	47	107
			90. Fruit sellers	266	138	128	75	31	44
			92. Sweetmeat makers and sellers	1,628	957	671	203	119	84
			Total Sub-order 18	4,372	1,984	2,388	1,024	292	732

TABLE XVII.—Part B.—Occupations by Districts.

Class.	Order.	Sub-order and Group.	Occupations.	Ajmere. Total.	Ajmere. Males.	Ajmere. Females.	Merwara. Total.	Merwara. Males.	Merwara. Females.
1	2	3	4	5	6	7	8	9	10
D.—Preparation and Supply of Material Substances—*contd.*	VII.—Food and Drink—*contd.*	19.—Drink, Condiments and Narcotics.	94. Ice manufacturers and sellers	1	...	1	...	...	...
			95. Soda water, lemonade manufacturers and sellers.	61	*61*	...	...	...	...
			97. Country spirit distillers and sellers	336	*208*	128	53	*30*	23
			101. Tea sellers	2	...	2	...	...	...
			103. Sugar sellers	34	*34*	...	1	*1*	...
			104. Jaggery sellers	71	*21*	50	130	*52*	78
			105. Salt sellers	1	...	1	9	*7*	2
			106. Ajwain sellers	...	...	...	2	*2*	...
			109. Grocers and general condiment dealers.	3,513	*1,991*	1,522	187	*114*	73
			111. Betel-leaf sellers	219	*146*	83	11	*5*	6
			112. Tobacco sellers	306	*155*	151	75	*33*	42
			114. Opium manufacturers and sellers	55	*45*	10	13	*11*	2
			Total Sub-order 19	4,609	*2,661*	1,948	481	*255*	226
			Total Order VII.—Food and Drink	**10,827**	**5,551**	**5,276**	**1,996**	**771**	**1,225**
	VIII.—Light, Firing and Forage.	20.—Lighting	116. Oil pressers and sellers	2,347	*1,210*	1,137	538	*263*	275
			120. Torch makers and sellers	3	*3*	...	...	...	...
			121. Kerosine oil dealers	3	*3*	...	...	...	...
			122. Matches sellers	1	*1*	...	...	...	...
			123. Lamp sellers	1	*1*	...	...	...	...
			Total Sub-order 20	2,355	1,218	1,137	538	263	275
		21.—Fuel and Forage.	125. Firewood and grass gatherers and sellers.	1,760	*808*	952	1,094	*607*	487
			128. Coal dealers	1	*1*	...	...	...	...
			130. Cowdung fuel preparers and sellers	41	*2*	39	...	...	...
			Total Sub-order 21	1,802	811	991	1,094	607	487
			Total Order VIII.—Light, Firing and Forage.	**4,157**	**2,029**	**2,128**	**1,632**	**870**	**762**
	IX.—Buildings.	22.—Building Materials.	132. Brick and tile burners and sellers	11	*3*	8	...	...	...
			133. Lime, chunam burners and sellers	217	*118*	99	25	*9*	16
			134. Stone dealers	19	*15*	4	3	*3*	...
			135. Thatch dealers and thatchers	190	*156*	34	...	...	...
			Total Sub-order 22.	437	292	145	28	12	16
		23.—Artificers in Building.	137. Stone and marble workers	300	*159*	141	29	*26*	3
			138. Masons	2,906	*1,744*	1,162	412	*47*	365
			139. Builders and joiners	2	2	...	...	...	...
			140. Plasterers and house painters	4	*4*	...	1	*1*	...
			141. Mud wall and roof builders	73	*50*	23	...	...	...
			Total Sub-order 23	3,285	1,959	1,326	442	*74*	368
			Total Order IX.—Building	**3,722**	**2,251**	**1,471**	**470**	**86**	**384**
	X.—Vehicles and Vessels.	24. Railway plant	144. Railway mechanics (fitters, painters, boil-makers, rivettors, etc.)	6,071	*4,153*	1,918	3	*3*	...
			145. Railway permanent-way foremen, platelayers, inspectors, etc.	196	*124*	72	34	*24*	10
			Total Sub-order 24	6,267	4,277	1,990	37	27	10
		25.—Carts, Carriages, etc.	146. Cart makers	4	*4*	...	...	...	...
			Total Sub-order 25	4	4	...	...	...	...
			Total Order X.—Vehicles and Vessels	**6,271**	**4,281**	**1,990**	**37**	**27**	**10**

TABLE XVII.—Part B.—Occupations by Districts.

Class.	Order.	Sub-order and Group.	Occupations.	Ajmere. Total.	Ajmere. Males.	Ajmere. Females.	Merwara. Total.	Merwara. Males.	Merwara. Females.
1	2	3	4	5	6	7	8	9	10
D.—Preparation and supply of material substances—contd.	XI.—Supplementary requirements.	27. Paper, etc.	153. Paper sellers	6	...	6	10	5	5
			Total Sub-order 27	6	...	6	10	5	5
		28.—Books and Prints, etc.	157. Press proprietors and printers and lithographers.	485	334	151	45	24	21
			158. Book-binders	64	40	24	...	...	...
			159. Book-sellers	70	40	30	4	4	...
			Total Sub-order 28	619	414	205	49	28	21
		29.—Watches, Clocks and Scientific Instruments.	163. Watch and clock makers and sellers	51	23	28	...	...	...
			Total Sub-order 29	51	23	28	...	...	...
		30.—Carving, Engraving, etc.	170. Ivory carvers	4	3	1	3	3	...
			172. Turners	146	72	74	54	34	20
			Total Sub-order 30	150	75	75	57	37	20
		31.—Toys, Curiosities, etc.	177. Toys, kites makers and sellers	23	10	13	...	...	...
			178. Hukka stem makers and sellers	12	6	6	...	...	...
			Total Sub-order 31	35	16	19	...	...	...
		33.—Necklaces, Bracelets, Beads, Sacred Threads, etc.	185. Bangle makers and sellers in lac.	1,564	757	807	87	51	36
			187. Narailee bangle makers and sellers	5	5	...	2	2	...
			189. Bangle makers and sellers in glass.	7	7	...	...	...	...
			193. Rosary and necklace makers and sellers.	72	32	40	10	4	6
			194. Flower garland makers and sellers	33	11	22	...	...	...
			195. Artificial flower and caste-mark spangle makers and sellers.	1	1	...	...	...	...
			196. Sacred thread makers and sellers	2	1	1	...	...	...
			Total Sub-order 33	1,684	814	870	99	57	42
		34.—Furniture	198. Furniture makers	4	...	4	3	3	...
			199. Frame makers	1	1	...	1	1	...
			Total Sub-order 34	5	1	4	4	4	...
		35.—Harness	201. Saddlery and harness makers and sellers.	6	3	3	...	...	...
			202. Saddle cloth makers, embroiderers and sellers.	38	2	36	...	...	...
			Total Sub-order 35	44	5	39	...	...	...
		36.—Tools and Machinery.	204. Knife and tool makers and sellers	...	...	...	2	1	1
			205. Knife and tool grinders	5	2	3	2	2	...
			207. Mechanics	18	11	7	...	...	...
			Total Sub-order 36	23	13	10	4	3	1
		37.—Arms and Ammunition.	209. Gun makers and sellers	21	7	14	2	2	...
			211. Gunpowder makers and sellers	83	19	64	...	...	...
			212. Firework makers and sellers	30	23	7	...	...	...
			213. Sword and scabbard makers and sellers.	21	18	3	13	4	9
			214. Shield makers and sellers	5	5	...	...	...	...
			Total Sub-order 37	160	72	88	15	6	9
			Total Order XI.—Supplementary Requirements.	2,777	1,433	1,344	238	140	98

TABLE XVII.—Part B.—Occupations by Districts—*contd.*

Class.	Order.	Sub-order and Group.	OCCUPATIONS.	AJMERE. Total.	AJMERE. Males.	AJMERE. Females.	MERWARA. Total.	MERWARA. Males.	MERWARA. Females.
1	2	3	4	5	6	7	8	9	10
D.—PREPARATION AND SUPPLY OF MATERIAL SUBSTANCES—*contd.*	XII.—TEXTILE FABRICS AND DRESS.	38.—Wool and Fur	218. Shawl weavers and sellers	49	49	...	2	2	...
			220. Blanket weavers and sellers	43	29	14	10	...	10
			221. Woollen cloth manufacturers and dealers.	268	119	149	12	6	6
			222. Woollen yarn spinners and sellers	17	6	11	3	3	...
			224. Wool dyers	26	25	1	2	2	...
			Total Sub-order 38	403	228	175	29	13	16
		39.—Silk	228. Silk weavers and dealers	1	1	...	...	...	...
			Total Sub-order 39	1	1	...	...	...	...
		40.—Cotton	231. Cotton cleaners and ginners	1,265	692	573	414	242	172
			232. Cotton carpet and rug makers and sellers.	28	28	...	...	...	...
			233. Cotton spinners.	2,775	477	2,298	1,069	7	1,062
			234. Cotton weavers, mill owners and managers.	10,796	6,014	4,782	1,714	939	775
			235. Cotton factory hands (undefined)	142	51	91	297	284	13
			236. Calenderers, fullers and printers	129	29	100	54	16	38
			237. Cotton dyers	4,383	2,240	2,143	1,043	707	336
			238. Tape makers and sellers	19	11	8	...	...	...
			239. Tent manufacturers and sellers	56	...	56	...	...	...
			Total Sub-order 40	19,593	9,542	10,051	4,591	2,195	2,396
		41.—Jute, Flax, Coir, etc.	241. Hemp rope makers and sellers	143	59	84	13	10	3
			243. Sacks makers and sellers	45	20	25	7	3	4
			Total Sub-order 41	188	79	109	20	13	7
		42.—Dress	247. Tailors and darners	2,943	1,528	1,415	554	283	271
			251. Cap sellers	4	2	2	...	...	...
			252. Turban binders	7	7	...	...	...	...
			254. Embroiderers and lace and muslin makers.	101	88	13	2	2	...
			257. Piece goods dealers	1,885	1,009	876	350	209	141
			Total Sub-order 42	4 940	2,634	2 306	906	494	412
			Total Order XII.—Textile Fabrics and Dress.	**25,125**	**12,484**	**12,641**	**5,546**	**2,715**	**2,881**
	XIII.—METALS AND PRECIOUS STONES.	43.—Gold, Silver and Precious Stones.	258. Gold and silver dealers	12	3	9	2	...	2
			260. Gold and silver workers	2,827	1 533	1,294	598	331	267
			262. Goldsmiths' dust washers	30	16	14	14	8	6
			265. Electroplaters	...	...	...	2	2	...
			266. Gold and silver wire drawers and braid makers.	772	410	362	10	10	...
			273. Pearl and other precious stone dealers.	8	6	2	1	1	...
			Total Sub-order 43	3,649	1,968	1,681	627	352	275
		44.—Brass, Copper and Bell-metal.	276. Brass workers and sellers	4	4	...	...	...	...
			277. Brass pot makers and sellers	318	197	121	252	160	92
			279. Copper workers and sellers	1	1	...	...	...	...
			282. General workers in brass, copper and bell-metal.	9	9	...	...	...	...
			283. Brass and copper dealers	1	1	...	...	...	...
			Total Sub-order 44	333	212	121	252	160	92
		45.—Tin, Zinc, Mercury and Lead.	284. Tin workers and sellers	3	1	2	2	2	...
			287. Lead and quicksilver workers and sellers.	20	6	14	...	...	...
			288. General workers in tin, lead, and zinc.	65	24	41	4	...	4
			Total Sub-order 45	88	31	57	6	2	4

TABLE XVII.—Part B.—Occupations by Districts—*contd.*

Class.	Order.	Sub-order and Group.	OCCUPATIONS.	AJMERE. Total.	AJMERE. Males.	AJMERE. Females.	MERWARA. Total.	MERWARA. Males.	MERWARA. Females.
1	2	3	4	5	6	7	8	9	10
CLASS D.—PREPARATION AND SUPPLY OF MATERIAL SUBSTANCES—*contd.*	XIII.—METALS AND PRECIOUS STONES—*contd.*	46.—IRON AND STEEL	289. Iron sellers	58	50	8	...	...	...
			290. Blacksmiths	2,023	1,091	932	883	500	383
			291. Iron dealers	40	35	5	23	3	20
			293. Lock makers and sellers	1	1	...	...	...	...
			TOTAL SUB-ORDER 46	2,122	1,177	945	906	503	403
			Total Order XIII.—Metals and Precious Stones.	**6,192**	**3,388**	**2,804**	**1,791**	**1,017**	**774**
	XIV.—GLASS, POTTERY AND STONEWARE.	47.—GLASS AND CHINAWARE.	297. Chinaware dealers	43	4	39	...	...	...
			TOTAL SUB-ORDER 47	43	4	39	...	...	...
		48.—EARTHEN AND STONEWARE.	298. Potters	5,251	2,737	2,514	1,192	688	504
			299. Grind stone and mill stone makers and sellers.	31	14	17	4	2	2
			TOTAL SUB-ORDER 48	5,282	2,751	2,531	1,196	690	506
			Total Order XIV.—Glass, Pottery and Stoneware.	**5,325**	**2,755**	**2,570**	**1,196**	**690**	**506**
	XV.—WOOL, CANE AND LEAVES, ETC.	49.—TIMBER AND WOOD	304. Carpenters	4,134	2,267	1,867	986	607	379
			TOTAL SUB-ORDER 49	4,134	2,267	1,867	986	607	379
		50.—CANE-WORK, MATTING AND LEAVES, ETC.	306. Bamboo and rattan splitters, workers and sellers.	57	16	41	...	...	...
			307. Basket weavers and winnowing pan makers and sellers.	364	178	186	71	36	35
			308. Mat makers and sellers	166	76	90	...	...	...
			309. Screen makers and sellers	61	47	14	...	...	...
			310. Leaf plate makers and sellers	61	27	34	20	12	8
			312. Leaf fan makers and sellers	7	7	...	2	2	...
			313. Comb makers and sellers	161	82	79	24	13	11
			314. Broom makers and sellers	...	...	...	5	2	3
			TOTAL SUB-ORDER 50	877	433	444	122	65	57
			Total Order XV.—Wool, Cane, and Leaves, etc.	**5,011**	**2,700**	**2,311**	**1,108**	**672**	**436**
	XVI.—DRUGS, GUMS, DYES, ETC.	51.—GUMS, WAX AND SIMILAR FOREST PRODUCE.	320. Lac collectors and sellers	...	...	...	57	39	18
			TOTAL SUB-ORDER 51	...	...	...	57	39	18
		52.—DRUGS, DYES, PIGMENTS, ETC.	324. Chemists and Druggists	17	13	4	...	...	...
			326. Saltpetre workers and sellers	8	8	...	...	...	...
			328. Soap makers and sellers	10	...	10	1	1	...
			337. Perfume preparers and sellers	205	77	128	15	11	4
			TOTAL SUB-ORDER 52	240	98	142	16	12	4
			Total Order XVI.—Drugs, Gums, Dyes, etc.	**240**	**98**	**142**	**73**	**51**	**22**
	XVII.—LEATHER, HORNS, BONES AND GREASE.	53.—LEATHER	338. Tanners, curriers and hide sellers	4,375	2,221	2,154	2,460	1,438	1,022
			339. Shoe makers and sellers	3,214	1,986	1,228	584	305	279
			340. Leather dyers	849	269	580	80	38	42
			341. Water bag and ghee pot makers and sellers.	7	4	3	10	5	5
			342. Hide and bone dealers	1,713	1,136	577	1	...	1
			TOTAL SUB-ORDER 53	10,158	5,616	4,542	3,135	1,786	1,349
			Total Order XVII.—Leather, Horns, Bones, etc.	**10,158**	**5,616**	**4,542**	**3,135**	**1,786**	**1,349**

TABLE XVII.—Part B.—Occupations by Districts—*contd.*

Class.	Order.	Sub-order and Group.	Occupations.	Ajmere. Total.	Ajmere. Males.	Ajmere. Females.	Merwara. Total.	Merwara. Males.	Merwara. Female.
1	2	3	4	5	6	7	8	9	10
CLASS E.—COMMERCE, TRANSPORT, AND STORAGE.	XVIII.—COMMERCE.	51.—Dealers Money and Securities.	346. Bankers	13	1	12	8	8	...
			347. Money-lenders	6,833	3,459	3,374	2,513	1,311	1,202
			348. Bill discounters, etc.	21	21	...	11	1	10
			350. Money changers and testors	475	247	228	63	44	19
			351. Bank clerks and accountants	14	5	9	6	5	1
			Total Sub-order 54	7,356	3,733	3,623	2,601	1 369	1,232
		55.—General Merchandise.	352. General merchants	710	642	68	670	384	286
			353. Merchants, accountants and clerks, etc.	15	5	10	5	2	3
			Total Sub-order 55	725	647	78	675	386	289
		56.—Dealing, unspecified.	355. Shop-keepers, servants	1	1	...	127	18	109
			356. Shop-keepers	13,268	7,426	5,842	2,822	1,452	1,370
			357. Pedlars, hawkers, etc.	54	34	20	3	3	...
			Total Sub-order 56	13,323	7,461	5 862	2,952	1,473	1,479
		57.—Middlemen, etc.— (*a*). Brokers.	358. Brokers and agents	1,568	846	722	880	420	460
			359. Auctioneers	2	1	1	...	...	..
		(*b*). Contractors and farmers.	361. Farmers of liquor, opium, etc.	42	28	14	14	6	8
			362. Superintendents of markets	11	7	4	...	...	...
			363. Contractors	376	149	227	24	11	13
			Total Sub-order 57	1,999	1,031	968	918	437	481
			Total Order XVIII.—Commerce	**23,408**	**12,872**	**10,581**	**7,146**	**3,665**	**3,481**
	XIX.—TRANSPORT AND STORAGE.	58.—Railway— (*a*) Administration	365. Manager, general store	1	1	...	...	...	...
			366. Traffic manager, superintendents and assistants.	9	4	5	...	...	...
			368. Auditors and accountants, etc.	31	25	6	...	...	...
			369. Engineers	1	1	...	...	...	...
			370. Clerical staff and railway establishments	1,791	839	952	6	6	...
		(*b*) Working Staff	371. Station-masters, assistants, inspectors, overseers, etc.	113	57	56	20	10	10
			372. Guards, drivers, firemen, etc.	177	108	69	4	4	...
			373. Pointsmen, shunters, porters, signallers, etc.	2,096	789	1,307	96	67	29
			Total Sub-order 58	4,219	1,824	2,395	126	87	39
		59. Road— (*a*) Cart, carriage and tramway owners and drivers.	375. Cart owners and drivers	1,493	823	670	383	275	108
			376. Livery stable-keepers, etc.	1	1	...	...	...	...
			377. Drivers, stable boys, etc.	47	24	23	...	...	...
			378. Dooly bearers	35	34	1	...	...	...
		(*b*) Carriers by pack animals.	379. Pack bullock owners and drivers, etc.	253	212	41	...	...	...
			380. Camel and mule drivers	563	371	192	384	218	166
			Total Sub-order 59	2,392	1,465	927	767	493	274
		60. Water— (*b*) Working staff of vessels.	385. Boatmen	2	1	1	...	...	...
			389. Divers (not for pearls)	3	3	...	...	...	...
			Total Sub-order 60	5	4	1	...	...	...
		61. Messages— (*a*) Post, etc.	390. Postmasters and clerks	27	21	6	7	5	2
			391. Postal messengers and runners, etc.	322	224	98	50	38	12
			392. Messengers	188	40	148	34	16	18
		(*b*) Telegraph and Telephone.	393. Telegraph officers (Government, railway and others) and Clerical and Accountants establishments	41	18	23	1	1	...
			394. Signallers and messengers	49	24	25	4	2	2
			Total Sub-order 61	627	327	300	96	62	34

TABLE XVII.—Part B.—Occupations by Districts—*contd.*

Class.	Order.	Sub-order and Group.	Occupations.	Ajmere. Total.	Ajmere. Males.	Ajmere. Females.	Merwara. Total.	Merwara. Males.	Merwara. Females.
1	2	3	4	5	6	7	8	9	10
Class E.—Commerce, Transport, and Storage—*contd.*	XIX.—Transport and Storage—*contd.*	62.—Storage and Weighing.	397. Warehouse service	...	...	...	2	1	1
			398. Porters	250	143	107	196	152	44
			399. Weighmen	33	20	13	125	83	42
			400. Watchmen (not villagers)	647	345	302	27	15	12
			Total Sub-order 62	930	508	422	350	251	99
			Total Order XIX.—Transport and Storage.	**8,178**	**4,128**	**4,045**	**1,339**	**893**	**446**
Class F.—Professions.	XX.—Learned and Artistic Professions.	Religion— (*a*) Priests, ministers, etc.	401. Priests, ministers, preachers, missionary, etc.	125	61	64	61	43	18
		(*b*) Subsidiary religious services.	402. Zenana mission service	6	4	2	...	...	...
			404. Religious mendicants	9,693	4,445	5,248	848	568	280
			405. Church and temple service	1,136	787	349	164	101	63
			Total Sub-order 63	10,960	5,297	5,663	1,073	712	361
		64.—Education	407. Principals, professors and teachers in colleges, schools, etc.	878	476	402	94	51	43
			408. Clerks, etc., on establishments of educational institutions.	11	11	...	...	...	...
			Total Sub-order 64	889	487	402	94	51	43
		65.—Literature	409. Authors, editors, etc.	19	4	15	...	...	...
			410. Book copyists	4	3	1	...	...	...
			411. Private secretaries and clerks	118	58	60	2	...	2
			412. Public scribes and copyists	34	24	10	4	1	3
			Total Sub-order 65	175	89	86	6	1	5
		66.—Law	414. Pleaders	96	39	57	15	12	3
			416. Mukhtiars	70	44	26	5	2	3
			418. Stamp Vendors	34	19	15	2	2	...
			419. Petition Writers	237	123	114	37	18	19
			Total Sub-order 66	437	225	212	59	34	25
		67.—Medicine— (*a*) Practitioner	421. Practitioners by diploma	40	19	21	1	1	...
			422. Baid, hakim, etc.	227	131	96	6	5	1
			424. Oculists	16	12	4	...	...	...
		(*b*) Subsidiary Medical Service.	425. Vaccinators	5	4	1	1	1	...
			426. Midwifery	7	...	7	13	...	13
			427. Hospital assistants and apothecaries	57	26	31	1	1	...
			428. Compounders, nurses and dispensary service.	100	58	42	15	9	6
			Total Sub-order 67	452	250	202	37	17	20
		68.—Engineering and Surveying— (*a*) Engineers, architects and surveyors.	430. Civil engineers and architects	24	7	17	36	34	2
		(*b*) Subsidiary staff	432. Draughtsmen, overseers, etc.	45	30	15	2	2	...
			433. Clerks, Public Works Department	38	33	5	10	6	4
			Total Sub-order 68	107	70	37	48	42	6
		69.—Other Sciences— (*b*) Minor sciences	437. Astrologers, genealogists and horoscope casters.	43	34	9	112	62	50
			Total Sub-order 69	43	34	9	112	62	50
		70.—Pictorial Art and Sculpture.	440. Picture makers	6	6	...	...	...	...
			442. Photographers	10	5	5	...	...	...
			Total Sub-order 70	16	11	5	...	...	...

TABLE XVII.—Part B.—Occupations by Districts—*contd.*

Class.	Order.	Sub-order and Group.	Occupations.	Ajmere. Total.	Ajmere. Males.	Ajmere. Females.	Merwara. Total.	Merwara. Males.	Merwara. Females.
1	2	3	4	5	6	7	8	9	10
CLASS F.—PROFESSIONS—*contd.*	XX.—LEARNED AND ARTISTIC PROFESSIONS—*contd.*	71.—Music, Acting, Dancing.	443. Musicians	3	...	3	...	...	...
			444. Drummers and trumpeters	2,189	*1,267*	922	1,929	*1,065*	864
			446. Actors, singers and dancers and their accompanists.	961	*453*	508	129	*41*	88
			Total Sub-order 71	3,153	1,720	1,433	2,058	1,106	952
			Total Order XX.—Learned and Artistic Professions.	**16,232**	**8,183**	**8,049**	**3,487**	**2,025**	**1,462**
	XXI.—SPORTS AND AMUSEMENTS.	72.—Sport	447. Jockeys	2	*2*	...	...	...	...
			448. Bird-catchers	38	*21*	17	...	...	...
			Total Sub-order 72	40	23	17	...	...	...
		73.—Exhibition and Games— (*b*) Conjuring, fortune-telling and other exhibition.	453. Buffoons	10	*7*	3	...	...	...
			454. Story and ballad reciters	27	*23*	4	...	...	...
			455. Jugglers	2	*2*	...	...	...	...
			456. Fortune-tellers	11	*2*	9	...	...	...
		(*c*) Acrobatics and athletics.	457. Wrestlers and cricketers and acrobats.	42	*23*	19	...	...	...
		(*d*) Service of places of entertainment.	460. Billiard-room service	27	*9*	18	...	...	...
			Total Sub-order 73	119	66	53	...	...	...
			Total Order XXI.—Sports and Amusements.	**159**	**89**	**70**	...	...	...
G.—INDEFINITE AND INDEPENDENT.	XXIII.—INDEFINITE.	74.—Unskilled Labour— (*a*) Special branches	461. Well-sinkers	14	*14*	...	2	*2*	...
			463. Road and railway labourers	190	*40*	150	210	*203*	7
			464. Stone splitters, etc.	6	*6*	...	...	...	...
		(*b*) Genera	467. General labourers	47,734	*22,267*	25,467	5,397	*3,418*	1,979
			Total Sub-order 74	47,944	22,327	25,617	5,609	3,623	1,986
		75.—Undefined	468. Undefined	308	*72*	236	72	*11*	61
			Total Sub-order 75	308	72	236	72	11	61
			Total Order XXIII.—Indefinite	**48,252**	**22,399**	**25,853**	**5,681**	**3,634**	**2,047**
	XXIV.—INDEPENDENT OF WORK.	76.—Property and Alms— (*a*) Property and allowances.	469. House-rent	371	*164*	207	45	*21*	24
			470. Private pensioners	10	*3*	7	1	...	1
		(*b*) Charity and endowment.	472. Beggars	9,074	*5,845*	3,229	2,179	*1,232*	947
			Total Sub-order 76	9,455	6,012	3,443	2,225	1,253	972
		77.—Supported at the public charge— (*a*) Pension	473. Civil pensioners	256	*75*	181	112	*73*	39
			474. Military pensioners	183	*158*	25	365	*233*	132
		(*b*) Prisoners	478. Prisoners	330	*313*	17	...	...	...
			Total Sub-order 77	769	546	223	477	306	171
			Total Order XXIV.—Independent of work.	**10,224**	**6,558**	**3,666**	**2,702**	**1,559**	**1,148**
			GRAND TOTAL	**422,359**	**223,547**	**198,812**	**119,999**	**64,778**	**55,221**

TABLE XVII—Part C.—Occupations combined with Agriculture for Ajmere-Merwara.

Sub-order.	Occupation, etc.	Total persons returned under each in Table XVIIA, including those combining it with Agriculture.			Persons returned as combining an occupation with agriculture. Total Persons.			Connection with the Land. Land occupant, not cultivating.			Land occupant, cultivating.			Tenants, not cultivating.			Tenants, cultivating.			Farm servants or field labourers.		
		Total.	Males.	Females.	Total.	Males.	Females.	Total.	Males.	Females.	Total.	Males.	Females.	Total.	Males.	Females.	Total.	Males.	Females.	Total.	Males.	Females.
1	2	3	4	5	6	7	8	9	10	11	12	13	14	15	16	17	18	19	20	21	22	23
1	Total Sub-order	4,457	2,969	1,488	52	39	13	25	14	11	18	16	2	3	3	...	6	6	...	...	...	...
	3. Office superintendents and clerical establishments, police and excise inspecters, sub-registrars.	778	573	205	3	3	...	1	1	...	...	...	...	2	2	...	...	...	...	...	...	...
	4. Messengers, constables, bailiffs, warders, menials, etc.	3,679	2,396	1,283	49	36	13	24	13	11	18	16	2	1	1	...	6	6	...	...	...	...
3	Total Sub-order	1,828	1,153	675	338	210	128	216	123	93	37	32	5	42	29	13	43	26	17	...	...	...
	9. Patwaris	579	385	194	114	68	46	102	59	43	6	6	...	6	3	3	...	...	...	...	...	...
	11. Watchman and other menials	1,249	768	481	224	142	82	114	64	50	31	26	5	36	26	10	43	26	17	...	...	...
4	Total Sub-order	5,173	3,681	1,492	205	107	98	71	41	30	31	28	3	103	38	65	...	...	...	...	...	...
	12. Officers	184	113	71	3	3	...	...	...	...	3	3	...	...	...	...	...	...	...	...	...	...
	13. Non-commissioned officers and privates.	4,989	3,568	1,421	202	104	98	71	41	30	28	25	3	103	38	65	...	...	...	...	...	...
6	Total Sub-order	2,108	1,262	846	31	29	2	7	7	...	5	3	2	11	11	...	8	8	...	...	...	...
	19. Chief consuls and officers	34	31	3	3	3	...	...	...	...	...	...	...	...	...	...	3	3	...	...	...	...
	20. Clerical establishments	74	58	16	9	9	...	5	5	...	1	1	...	...	...	...	3	3	...	...	...	...
	21. Menials, etc.	2,000	1,173	827	19	17	2	2	2	...	4	2	2	11	11	...	2	2	...	...	...	...
8	Total Sub-order	5,479	3,613	1,866	202	127	75	28	7	21	26	26	...	28	28	...	120	66	54	...	...	...
	26. Herdsmen	4,474	2,764	1,710	188	127	61	28	7	21	26	26	...	28	28	...	106	66	40	...	...	...
	31. Sheep breeders, etc.	1,005	849	156	14	...	14	...	...	...	...	...	...	...	...	...	14	...	14	...	...	...
12	Total Sub-order	475	358	117	12	11	1	...	...	...	1	...	1	...	...	...	11	11	...	...	...	...
	52. Gardeners and seedsmen	392	304	88	3	3	...	...	...	...	...	...	...	...	...	...	3	3	...	...	...	...
	55. Forest rangers, guards, peons	83	54	29	9	8	1	...	...	...	1	...	1	...	...	...	8	8	...	...	...	...

TABLE XVII--Part C.—Occupations combined with Agriculture for Ajmere-Merwara—*contd.*

Sub-order.	Occupation, etc.	Total persons returned under each in Table XVIIA, including those combining it with agriculture.			Persons returned as combining an occupation with agriculture. Total Persons.			Connection with the land. Land occupant, not cultivating.			Land occupant, cultivating.			Tenants, not cultivating.			Tenants, cultivating.			Farm servants or field labourers.		
		Total.	Males.	Females.	Total.	Males.	Females.	Total.	Males.	Females.	Total.	Males.	Females.	Total.	Males.	Females.	Total.	Males.	Females.	Total.	Males.	Females.
1	2	3	4	5	6	7	8	9	10	11	12	13	14	15	16	17	18	19	20	21	22	23
14	Total Sub-order	29,383	16,096	13,287	1,582	851	731	131	92	39	436	294	142	857	319	538	158	146	12	...	...	...
	59. Barbers	5, 36	3,139	2,397	741	457	284	86	51	35	182	115	67	354	184	170	119	107	12	...	...	...
	63. Washermen	2,234	1,110	1,124	464	224	240	...	...	...	126	71	55	308	123	185	30	30	...	...	...	...
	64. Water-carriers	3,374	1,314	2,060	1	1	...	1	1	...	...	...	...	...	...	...	...	...	...	...	...	...
	65. Cooks	1,84[illegible]	1,316	532	3	3	...	...	...	...	3	3	...	...	...	...	...	...	...	...	...	...
15	66. In-door servants	7,916	3,694	4,222	251	66	185	40	38	2	10	10	...	192	9	185	9	9	...	...	...	...
	67. Grooms, coachmen, etc.	1,614	925	689	77	77	...	...	...	...	77	77	...	...	...	...	...	...	...	...	...	...
	68. Door-keepers, etc.	6,861	4,598	2,263	45	23	22	4	2	2	38	18	20	3	3	...	...	...	...	...	...	...
16	Total Sub-order	5,137	2,570	2,567	29	16	13	4	4	...	25	12	13	...	...	...	...	...	...	...	...	...
	74. Sweepers	5,137	2,570	2,567	29	16	13	4	4	...	25	12	13	...	...	...	...	...	...	...	...	...
17	Total Sub-order	2,266	1,068	1,198	57	39	18	2	...	2	18	18	...	21	10	11	16	11	5	...	...	...
	76. Milk-sellers	976	416	560	17	16	1	...	...	...	16	16	...	...	...	...	1	...	1	...	...	...
	77. Ghee-preparers and sellers	150	76	74	17	11	6	2	...	2	...	...	...	...	...	...	15	11	4	...	...	...
	79. Butchers	1,140	576	564	23	12	11	...	...	...	2	2	...	21	10	11	...	...	...	...	...	...
18	Total Sub-order	2,156	1,247	909	125	125	...	...	...	...	...	...	...	123	123	...	2	2	...	...	...	...
	84. Grain parchers	325	171	154	2	2	...	...	...	...	...	...	...	...	...	...	2	2	...	...	...	...
	92. Sweetmeat makers and sellers	1,831	1,076	755	123	123	...	...	...	...	...	...	...	123	123	...	...	...	...	...	...	...
19	Total Sub-order	4,089	2,343	1,746	92	51	41	3	3	...	35	12	23	32	32	...	22	4	18	...	...	...
	97. Country spirit distillers and sellers.	389	238	151	35	17	18	3	3	...	6	6	...	4	4	...	22	4	18	...	...	...
	109. Grocers and general condiment dealers.	3,700	2,105	1,595	57	34	23	...	...	...	29	6	23	28	28	...	...	...	...	...	...	...
20	Total Sub-order	2,885	1,473	1,412	1,153	510	643	136	5	131	187	158	29	732	253	479	98	94	4	...	...	...
	116. Oil-pressers and sellers	2,885	1,473	1,412	1,153	510	643	136	5	131	187	158	29	732	253	479	98	94	4	...	...	...

Table XVII.—Part C.—Occupations by Districts.—Ajmere.

Sub-order.	Occupation, etc.	Total persons returned under each in Table XVIIA, including those combining it with agriculture. Total.	Males.	Females.	Persons returned as combining an occupation with agriculture. Total Persons. Total.	Males.	Females.	Connection with the land. Land occupant, not cultivating. Total.	Males.	Females.	Land occupant, cultivating. Total.	Males.	Females.	Tenants, not cultivating. Total.	Males.	Females.	Tenants, cultivating. Total.	Males.	Females.	Farm servants or field labourers. Total.	Males.	Females.
1	2	3	4	5	6	7	8	9	10	11	12	13	14	15	16	17	18	19	20	21	22	23
21	Total Sub-order	2,854	1,415	1,439	103	72	31	8	5	3	10	3	7	42	29	13	43	35	8	...	...	...
	125. Firewood sellers, etc.	2,854	1,415	1,439	103	72	31	8	5	3	10	3	7	42	29	13	43	35	8	...	...	...
22	Total Sub-order	264	145	119	5	5	...	...	...	...	4	4	...	...	...	...	1	1	...	...	...	...
	133. Lime burners and sellers	242	127	115	1	1	...	...	...	...	...	...	...	...	...	...	1	1	...	...	...	...
	134. Stone dealers	22	18	4	4	4	...	...	...	...	4	4	...	...	...	...	...	...	...	...	...	...
23	Total Sub-order	3,647	1,976	1,671	78	39	39	32	...	32	...	...	...	42	38	4	4	1	3	...	...	...
	137. Stone and marble workers	329	185	144	10	10	...	...	...	...	...	...	...	10	10	...	...	...	...	...	...	...
	138. Masons	3,318	1,791	1,527	68	29	39	32	...	32	...	...	...	32	28	4	4	1	3	...	...	...
28	Total Sub-order	530	358	172	13	13	...	13	13	...	...	...	...	...	...	...	...	...	...	...	...	...
	157. Press services, etc.	530	358	172	13	13	...	13	13	...	...	...	...	...	...	...	...	...	...	...	...	...
33	Total Sub-order	1,653	809	844	26	21	5	...	...	...	17	17	...	5	...	5	4	4	...	...	...	...
	185. Bangle makers and sellers in lac.	1,651	808	843	25	21	4	...	...	...	17	17	...	4	...	4	4	4	...	...	...	...
	196. Sacred-thread makers and sellers.	2	1	1	1	...	1	...	...	...	...	...	...	1	...	1	...	...	...	...	...	...
37	Total Sub-order	23	9	14	2	2	...	...	...	...	...	...	...	2	2	...	...	...	...	...	...	...
	209. Gun menders and sellers	23	9	14	2	2	...	...	...	...	...	...	...	2	2	...	...	...	...	...	...	...
38	Total Sub-order	333	154	179	24	23	1	...	...	...	...	...	...	12	12	...	12	11	1	...	...	...
	220. Blanket weavers and sellers	53	29	24	12	12	...	...	...	...	...	...	...	12	12	...	...	...	...	...	...	...
	221. Wollen cloth manufacturers and dealers.	280	125	155	12	11	1	...	...	...	...	...	...	...	...	...	12	11	1	...	...	...

TABLE XVII.—Part C.—Occupations combined with Agriculture for Ajmere-Merwara—*contd.*

Sub-order.	Occupation, etc.	Total persons returned under each in Table XVII A, including those combining it with Agriculture.			Persons returned as combining an occupation with agriculture.																	
					Total Persons.			Connection with the land.														
								Land occupant, not cultivating.			Land occupant, cultivating.			Tenants, not cultivating.			Tenants, cultivating.			Farms servants or field labourers.		
		Total.	Males.	Females.	Total.	Males.	Females.	Total.	Males.	Females.	Total.	Males.	Females.	Total.	Males.	Females.	Total.	Males.	Females.	Total.	Males.	Females.
1	2	3	4	5	6	7	8	9	10	11	12	13	14	15	16	17	18	19	20	21	22	23
40	Total Sub-order	23,459	11,318	12,141	1,100	713	387	55	30	25	164	88	76	545	345	200	336	250	86	...	...	...
	231. Cotton cleaners and ginners	1,679	934	745	176	91	85	...	...	...	5	5	...	18	18	...	153	68	85	...	...	...
	233. " spinners	3,844	484	3,360	8	7	1	...	...	...	4	3	1	4	4	...	...	...	...	...	...	...
	234. " weavers	12,510	6,953	5,557	753	521	232	35	23	12	145	71	74	395	250	145	178	177	1	...	...	...
	237. " dyers	5,426	2,947	2,479	163	94	69	20	7	13	10	9	1	128	73	55	5	5	...	...	...	...
42	Total Sub-order	5,732	3,029	2,703	225	147	78	33	19	14	80	35	45	70	52	18	42	41	1	...	...	...
	247. Tailors, etc	3,497	1,811	1,686	193	127	66	10	7	3	77	32	45	70	52	18	36	36	...	...	...	...
	257. Piece-goods dealers	2,235	1,218	1,017	32	20	12	23	12	11	3	3	...	...	...	...	6	5	1	...	...	...
43	Total Sub-order	3,425	1,864	1,561	115	78	37	12	10	2	41	32	9	10	8	2	52	28	24	...	...	...
	260. Gold and silver workers	3,425	1,864	1,561	115	78	37	12	10	2	41	32	9	10	8	2	52	28	24	...	...	...
44	Total Sub-order	570	357	213	17	7	10	...	...	...	7	7	...	10	...	10	...	...	...	...	...	...
	277. Brasspot makers and sellers	570	357	213	17	7	10	...	...	...	7	7	...	10	...	10	...	...	...	...	...	...
46	Total Sub-order	2,906	1,591	1,315	337	214	123	73	50	23	122	79	43	129	73	56	13	12	1	...	...	...
	290. Blacksmiths	2,906	1,591	1,315	337	214	123	73	50	23	122	79	43	129	73	56	13	12	1	...	...	...
47	Total Sub order	6,443	3,425	3,018	1,331	822	509	126	47	79	209	172	37	396	352	44	600	251	349	...	...	...
	298. Potters	6,443	3,425	3,018	1,331	822	509	126	47	79	209	172	37	396	352	44	600	251	349	...	...	...
49	Total Sub-order	5,120	2,874	2,246	1,297	844	453	70	23	47	333	227	106	318	311	7	576	283	293	...	...	...
	304. Carpenters	5,120	2,874	2,246	1,297	844	453	70	23	47	333	227	106	318	311	7	576	283	293	...	...	...

Table XVII.—Part C.—Occupations by Districts.—Ajmere.

Sub-order.	Occupation, etc.	Total persons returned under each in Table XVII A, including those combining it with Agriculture. Total.	Males.	Females.	Persons returned as combining an occupation with agriculture. Total Persons. Total.	Males.	Females.	Connection with the land. Land occupant, not cultivating. Total.	Males.	Females.	Land occupant, cultivating. Total.	Males.	Females.	Tenants, not cultivating. Total.	Males.	Females.	Tenants, cultivating. Total.	Males.	Females.	Farm servants or field labourers. Total.	Males.	Females.
1	2	3	4	5	6	7	8	9	10	11	12	13	14	15	16	17	18	19	20	21	22	23
50	Total Sub-order	435	214	221	26	8	18	...	...	...	5	5	...	13	...	13	8	3	5	...	...	...
	307. Basket weavers, etc.	435	214	221	26	8	18	...	...	...	5	5	...	13	...	13	8	3	5	...	...	...
53	Total Sub-order	13,276	7,393	5,883	2,808	1,505	1,303	86	27	59	536	386	150	815	575	240	1,371	517	854	...	...	...
	338. Tanners, curriers and hide sellers.	6,835	3,659	3,176	2,332	1,114	1,218	84	26	58	508	383	125	369	188	181	1,371	517	854	...	...	...
	339. Shoe makers and sellers	3,798	2,291	1,507	116	32	84	...	...	...	25	...	25	91	32	59	...	...	...	...	...	...
	340. Leather dyers	929	307	622	9	9	...	1	1	...	3	3	...	5	5	...	...	...	...	...	...	...
	342. Hide and bone dealers	1,714	1,136	578	351	350	1	1	...	1	...	...	...	350	350	...	...	...	...	...	...	...
54	Total Sub-order	9,884	5,061	4,823	1,301	638	663	903	435	468	93	34	59	251	118	133	54	51	3	...	...	...
	347. Money-lenders	9,346	4,770	4,576	1,289	630	659	901	435	466	83	26	57	251	118	133	54	51	3	...	...	...
	350. Money changers and testors	538	291	247	12	8	4	2	...	2	10	8	2	...	...	...	...	...	...	...	...	...
55	Total Sub-order	1,380	1,026	354	76	48	28	32	22	10	23	15	8	13	9	4	8	2	6	...	...	...
	352. General merchants	1,380	1,026	354	76	48	28	32	22	10	23	15	8	13	9	4	8	2	6	...	...	...
56	Total Sub-order	16,090	8,878	7,212	1,483	736	747	498	150	348	434	333	101	155	88	67	396	165	231	...	...	...
	356. Shop-keepers	16,090	8,878	7,212	1,483	736	747	498	150	348	434	333	101	155	88	67	396	165	231	...	...	...
57	Total Sub-order	2,504	1,300	1,204	13	4	9	5	2	3	2	2	...	...	...	...	6	...	6	...	...	...
	358. Brokers and agents	2,448	1,266	1,182	8	2	6	2	2	...	...	—	...	...	...	...	6	...	6	...	...	...
	301. Farmers of liquor, opium, etc.	56	34	22	5	2	3	3	...	3	2	2	...	...	...	...	...	...	...	...	...	...
58	Total Sub-order	2,192	856	1,336	15	8	7	11	4	7	...	...	...	4	4	...	...	...	...	...	...	...
	373. Railway service, etc.	2,192	856	1,336	15	8	7	11	4	7	...	...	...	4	4	...	...	...	...	...	...	...

TABLE XVII.—Part C.—Occupations combined with Agriculture for Ajmere-Merwara—*concld.*

Sub-order.	Occupation, etc.	Total persons returned under each in Table XVIIA, including those combining it with agriculture.			Persons returned as combining an occupation with agriculture. Total Persons.			Connection with the land. Land occupant, not cultivating.			Land occupant, cultivating.			Tenants, not cultivating.			Tenants, cultivating.			Farm servants or field labourers.		
		Total.	Males.	Females.	Total.	Males.	Females.	Total.	Males.	Females.	Total.	Males.	Females.	Total.	Males.	Females.	Total.	Males.	Females.	Total.	Males.	Females.
1	2	3	4	5	6	7	8	9	10	11	12	13	14	15	16	17	18	19	20	21	22	23
59	Total Sub-order	2,823	1,687	1,136	157	35	122	...	...	...	143	22	121	3	2	1	11	11	...	...	...	...
	375. Cart owners and drivers	1,876	1,098	778	30	30	...	...	...	...	18	18	...	1	1	...	11	11	...	...	...	...
	380. Camel drivers	947	589	358	127	5	122	...	...	...	125	4	121	2	1	1	...	...	...	...	...	...
61	Total Sub-order	594	318	276	28	20	8	15	13	2	4	4	...	8	2	6	1	1	...	...	...	...
	391. Postal service	372	262	110	9	7	2	3	1	2	4	4	...	2	2	...	...	...	...	...	...	...
	392. Messengers, etc.	222	56	166	19	13	6	12	12	...	...	...	...	6	...	6	1	1	...	...	...	...
63	Total Sub-order	11,841	5,901	5,940	490	321	169	173	88	85	180	117	63	111	100	11	26	16	10	...	...	...
	404. Religious mendicant	10,541	5,013	5,528	405	266	140	148	63	85	150	111	39	94	85	9	13	6	7	...	...	...
	405. Church and temple service	1,300	888	412	85	56	29	25	25	...	30	6	24	17	15	2	13	10	3	...	...	...
64	Total Sub-order	972	527	445	4	4	...	...	...	...	...	...	...	3	3	...	1	1	...	...	...	...
	407. Teachers, etc.	972	527	445	4	4	...	...	...	...	...	...	...	3	3	...	1	1	...	...	...	...
66	Total Sub-order	111	51	60	6	6	...	6	6	...	...	...	...	...	...	...	...	...	...	...	...	...
	414. Pleaders	111	51	60	6	6	...	6	6	...	...	...	...	...	...	...	...	...	...	...	...	...
67	Total Sub-order	348	203	145	5	1	4	4	...	4	1	1	...	...	...	...	...	...	...	...	...	...
	422. Hakeem	233	136	97	4	...	4	4	...	4	...	...	...	...	...	...	...	...	...	...	...	...
	428. Dispensary service	115	67	48	1	1	...	...	...	...	1	1	...	...	...	...	...	...	...	...	...	...
69	Total Sub-order	155	96	59	18	15	3	...	...	...	7	7	...	11	8	3	...	...	...	...	...	...
	437. Genealogists, etc.	155	96	59	18	15	3	...	...	...	7	7	...	11	8	3	...	...	...	...	...	...

Tabe XVII.—Part C.—Occupations by Districts.—Ajmere.

Sub-order.	Occupation, etc.	Total persons returned under each in Table XVIIA, including those combining it with Agriculture.			Persons returned as combining an occupation with agriculture.																	
					Total Persons.			Connection with the land.														
								Land occupant, not cultivating.			Land occupant, cultivating.			Tenants, not cultivating.			Tenants, cultivating.			Farm servants, field labourers, &c.		
		Total.	Males.	Females.	Total.	Males.	Females.	Total.	Males.	Females.	Total.	Males.	Females.	Total.	Males.	Females.	Total.	Males.	Females.	Total.	Males.	Females.
1	2	3	4	5	6	7	8	9	10	11	12	13	14	15	16	17	18	19	20	21	22	23
71	Total Sub-order	5,208	2,826	2,382	938	576	362	206	97	109	411	238	173	291	219	72	30	22	8	...	...	...
	444. Drummers and trumpeters	4,118	2,332	1,786	934	574	360	204	97	107	410	237	173	290	218	72	30	22	8	...	...	...
	446. Singers, etc.	1,090	494	596	4	2	2	2	...	2	1	1	...	1	1	...	...	...	...	...	...	...
74	Total Sub-order	53,531	25,928	27,603	1,010	856	154	116	114	2	571	564	7	221	130	91	102	48	54	...	...	...
	463. Road and railway labourers	400	243	157	144	144	...	...	...	...	82	82	...	62	62	...	...	...	...	...	...	...
	467. General labourers	53,131	25,685	27,446	866	712	154	116	114	2	489	482	7	159	68	91	102	48	54	...	...	...
76	Total Sub-order	11,669	7,262	4,407	544	303	241	103	86	17	75	40	35	349	177	172	17	...	17	...	...	...
	469. House-rent	416	185	231	52	36	16	33	27	6	13	9	4	6	...	6	...	...	...	...	...	...
	472. Beggers	11,253	7,077	4,176	492	267	225	70	59	11	62	31	31	343	177	166	17	...	17	...	...	...
77	Total Sub-order	916	539	377	372	273	99	103	71	32	216	163	53	40	30	10	13	9	4	...	...	...
	473. Civil pensioners	368	148	220	93	67	26	22	15	7	25	13	12	33	30	3	13	9	4	...	...	...
	474. Military pensioners	548	391	157	279	206	73	81	56	25	191	150	41	7	...	7	...	...	...	...	...	...
	Total	...	...	...	17,845	10,472	7,373	3,306	1,608	1,698	4,507	3,194	1,313	5,821	3,533	2,288	4,211	2,137	2,074	...	...	...
	Total Agriculturists from Return XViIA	...	...	...	262,551	138,241	124,310	9,204	4,926	4,278	98,250	54,390	43,860	25,628	12,055	13,573	106,371	58,388	48,343	22,738	8,482	14,256
	GRAND TOTAL	...	...	...	280,396	148,713	131,683	12,510	6,534	5,976	102,757	57,584	45,173	31,449	15,588	15,861	110,942	60,525	50,417	22,738	8,482	14,256

TABLE A.—Christians by Sect and Race.—Part I.—SECTS.

		TOTAL.			AJMERE.			MERWARA.		
		TOTAL.	Males.	Females.	TOTAL.	Males.	Females.	TOTAL.	Males.	Females.
1	2	3	4	5	6	7	8	9	10	11
CHURCH OF ENGLAND	Foreign	523	346	177	523	346	177	...	...	...
	Eurasian	321	184	137	309	177	132	12	7	5
	Native	455	264	191	368	220	148	87	44	43
	TOTAL	1,299	794	505	1,200	743	457	99	51	48
ROMAN CATHOLIC	Foreign	203	136	67	203	136	67	...	...	...
	Eurasian	244	133	111	244	133	111	...	...	...
	Native	151	83	68	150	82	68	1	1	...
	TOTAL	598	352	246	597	351	246	1	1	...
PRESBYTERIAN	Foreign	78	49	29	64	43	21	14	6	8
	Eurasian	39	20	19	32	16	16	7	4	3
	Native	548	280	268	321	151	170	227	129	98
	TOTAL	665	349	316	412	210	207	248	139	109
UNSECTARIAN	Foreign	7	6	1	7	6	1	...	...	...
	Eurasian	6	5	1	6	5	1	...	...	...
	Native	7	5	2	3	2	1	4	3	1
	TOTAL	20	16	4	16	13	3	4	3	1
BAPTIST	Foreign	...	...	...	...	...	...	...	...	...
	Eurasian	1	1	...	1	1	...	...	...	...
	Native	...	...	...	...	...	...	...	...	...
	TOTAL	1	1	...	1	1	...	...	...	...
METHODIST	Foreign	17	8	9	16	8	8	1	...	1
	Eurasian	25	13	12	24	13	11	1	...	1
	Native	25	11	14	25	11	14	...	...	...
	TOTAL	67	32	35	65	32	33	2	...	2
LUTHERAN	Foreign	7	3	4	6	2	4	1	1	...
	Eurasian	...	...	...	...	...	...	...	...	...
	Native	...	...	...	...	...	...	...	...	...
	TOTAL	7	3	4	6	2	4	1	1	...
NOT RETURNED	Foreign	...	...	...	...	...	...	...	...	...
	Eurasian	...	...	...	...	...	...	...	...	...
	Native	23	19	4	18	15	3	5	4	1
	TOTAL	23	19	4	18	15	3	5	4	1
WESLYAN	Foreign	1	1	...	1	1	...	...	...	...
	Eurasian	...	...	...	...	...	...	...	...	...
	Native	...	...	...	...	...	...	...	...	...
	TOTAL	1	1	...	1	1	...	...	...	...
CONGREGATIONALIST	Foreign	2	...	2	2	...	2	...	...	...
	Eurasian	...	...	...	...	...	...	...	...	...
	Native	...	...	...	...	...	...	...	...	...
	TOTAL	2	...	2	2	...	2	...	...	...
	Grand Total	2,683	1,567	1,116	2,328	1,368	955	360	199	161

TABLE A.—Christians—Part II.—RACES.

		TOTAL.			AJMERE.			MERWARA.		
		TOTAL.	Males.	Females.	TOTAL.	Males.	Females.	TOTAL.	Males.	Females.
1	2	3	4	5	6	7	8	9	10	11
FOREIGN .	Church of England . .	523	346	177	523	346	177	...	...	...
	Roman Catholic . .	203	136	67	203	136	67	...	...	...
	Presbyterian . . .	78	49	29	64	43	21	14	6	8
	Unsectarian . . .	7	6	1	7	6	1	...	...	...
	Weslyan	1	1	...	1	1	...	...	...	...
	Methodist . . .	17	8	9	16	8	8	1	...	1
	Lutheran . . .	7	3	4	6	2	4	1	1	...
	Congregationalist . .	2	...	2	2	...	2	...	...	...
	TOTAL .	838	549	289	822	542	280	16	7	9
EURASIAN .	Church of England . .	321	184	137	309	177	132	12	7	5
	Roman Catholic . .	244	133	111	244	133	111	...	...	...
	Presbyterian . . .	39	20	19	32	16	16	7	4	3
	Unsectarian . . .	6	5	1	6	5	1	...	...	...
	Methodist . . .	25	13	12	24	13	11	1	...	1
	Baptist	1	1	...	1	1	...	...	...	...
	TOTAL .	636	356	280	616	345	271	20	11	9
NATIVE . .	Church of England . .	455	264	191	368	220	148	87	44	43
	Roman Catholic . .	151	83	68	150	82	68	1	1	...
	Presbyterian . . .	548	280	268	321	151	170	227	129	98
	Unsectarian . . .	7	5	2	3	2	1	4	3	1
	Not returned . . .	23	19	4	18	15	3	5	4	1
	Methodist . . .	25	11	14	25	11	14	...	...	...
	TOTAL .	1,209	662	547	885	481	404	324	181	143
	GRAND TOTAL .	2,683	1,567	1,116	2,323	1,368	955	360	199	161

TABLE B.—Christians by Race and Age.

DISTRICT.	TOTAL.			NON-ASIATICS.											EURASIANS.											ARMENIANS, ETC.										
				ALL AGES.			0—14		15—34		35—49		50 AND OVER.		ALL AGES.			0—14		15—34		35—49		50 AND OVER.		ALL AGES.			0—14		15—34		35—49		50 AND OVER.	
	TOTAL.	Males.	Females.	TOTAL.	Males.	Females.	Males.	Females.	Males.	Females.	Males.	Females.	Males.	Females.	TOTAL.	Males.	Females.	Males.	Females.	Males.	Females.	Males.	Females.	Males.	Females.	TOTAL.	Males.	Females.	Males.	Females.	Males.	Females.	Males.	Females.	Males.	Females.
1	2	3	4	5	6	7	8	9	10	11	12	13	14	15	16	17	18	19	20	21	22	23	24	25	26	27	28	29	30	31	32	33	34	35	36	37
AJMERE	2,323	1,368	955	822	542	280	98	108	323	120	87	45	34	7	616	345	271	113	126	149	101	57	28	26	16	885	481	404	211	210	176	139	65	42	29	13
MERWARA	360	199	161	16	7	9	...	2	3	5	2	...	2	2	20	11	9	5	1	4	3	1	3	1	2	324	181	143	86	74	69	60	21	8	5	1
Total	2,683	1,567	1,116	838	549	289	98	110	326	125	89	45	36	9	636	356	280	118	127	153	104	58	31	27	18	1,209	662	547	297	284	245	199	86	50	34	14

TABLE C.—Language known by the Literate by Caste.

Class.	Group.	Caste.	Religion.	Total Strength. Males. Total Males.	Males. Literate. Total.	Males. Literate. Knowing English.	Females. Total Females.	Females. Literate. Total.	Females. Literate. Knowing English.
1	2	3	4	5	6	7	8	9	10
A.—AGRICULTURAL.	I.—Military and Dominant.	1. Rajput	Hindu	9,333	1,020	76	7,049	344	...
		2. Mahratta	Do.	352	108	4	123	1	...
		3. Thakur	Do.	6	...	...	...	...	...
		4. Sikh	Sikh	151	...	...	62	...	...
			Hindu	13	50	5	5	5	...
		Total I.—4		**9,855**	**1,178**	**85**	**7,289**	**350**	...
	II.—Other Agricultural.	1. Jat	Hindu	18,929	362	5	17,395	4	...
		2. Gujar	Do.	20,332	185	2	17,536	1	...
		3. Ahir	Do.	1,290	117	9	936	3	...
		4. Mer	Hindu	14,735	...	...	15,732	...	...
			Mussalman	14	271	6	18	5	...
		5. Rawat	Hindu	17,233	...	...	13,611	...	...
			Mussalman	4	317	3	71	1	...
		6. Chita	Hindu	245	...	...	125	...	...
			Mussalman	699	3	...	499	...	...
		7. Merat	Hindu	4,941	...	...	4,081	...	...
			Mussalman	7,953	124	2	4,912	...	...
		8. Naik	Hindu	1,415	11	...	1,356	...	...
		9. Thori	Do.	57	...	...	40	...	...
		10. Mina	Do.	2,731	136	...	1,917	...	...
		11. Mali	Do.	8,452	155	10	7,921	2	...
		12. Lodha	Do.	638	12	...	699	...	...
		13. Kachhi	Do.	41	9	...	20	...	...
		14. Kurmi	Do.	155	...	...	172	...	...
		15. Kalumhi	Do.	76	34	2	43	...	...
		16. Aheri	Do.	471	5	...	410	...	...
		17. Kurmi	Do.	84	13	...	39	...	...
		18. Ghosi	Do.	109	2	...	95	...	...
		19. Satia	Do.	23	...	...	38	...	...
		20. Purubia	Do.	8	...	...	6	...	...
		21. Morai	Do.	5	...	...	1	...	...
		22. Dhaker	Do.	119	1	...	91	...	...
		Total II.—22		**100,759**	**1,757**	**89**	**87,764**	**16**	...
B.—PROFESSIONAL.	IV.—Forest and Hill Tribes.	1. Bhil	Hindu	3,999	21	2	3,753	...	...
		2. Gometi	Do.	3	3	...	5	...	...
		Total IV.—2		**4,002**	**24**	**2**	**3,758**	..	...
	V.—Priests	1. Brahman	Hindu	14,342	5,008	447	12,279	174	7
		2. Shami	Do.	92	9	...	66	2	...
		3. Acharaj	Do.	332	25	...	322	...	...
		4. Jatti	Jain	13	9	...	1	1	...
		5. Pundit	Do.	3	3	...	...	...	...
		Total V.—5		**14,782**	**5,054**	**449**	**12,668**	**177**	**7**
	VI.—Devotees	1. Sadhu	Hindu	3,261	...	...	2,597	...	...
			Jain	61	593	6	66	46	...
		2 Gosain	Hindu	681	99	3	536	4	...
		3. Agori	Do.	12	5	...	6	...	...
		4. Jogi	Do.	1,487	40	3	1,287	2	1
		5. Vishnui	Do.	25	...	...	20	...	...
		6. Fakir	Mussalman	412	15	...	285	...	...
		Total VI.—6		**5,989**	**752**	**12**	**4,797**	**52**	**1**
	VII.—Temple service	1. Bhopa	Hindu	15	...	...	8	...	...
		Total VII.—1		**15**	...	...	**8**	...	...
	VIII.—Genealogists	1. Jaga	Hindu	663	40	...	476	...	...
		2. Barwa	Do.	117	40	...	140	...	...
		3. Bhat	Do.	572	114	1	549	4	...
		4. Rao	Do.	170	35	3	204	...	...
		5. Mirasi	Hindu	...	...	...	3	...	...
			Mussalman	12	...	...	10	...	...
		Total VIII.—5		**1,534**	**229**	**4**	**1,382**	**4**	...
	IX.—Writers	1. Kayastha	Hindu	1,197	672	211	971	47	2
		Total IX.—1		**1,197**	**672**	**211**	**971**	**47**	**2**

TABLE C.—Language known by the Literate by Caste—*contd.*

Class.	Group.	Caste.	Religion.	Total Strength. Males. Total Males.	Males. Literate. Total.	Males. Literate. Knowing English.	Females. Total Females.	Females. Literate. Total.	Females. Literate. Knowing English.
1	2	3	4	5	6	7	8	9	10
B.—PROFESSIONAL—*contd.*	X.—ASTROLOGERS	1. Garura	Hindu	179	36	...	139	...	...
		2. Dakot	Do.	329	99	1	294	...	...
		3. Guru	Do.	215	...	...	164	...	...
		4. Jatshi	Do.	2	...	...	...	...	...
		Total X.—4		**725**	**135**	**1**	**597**	...	...
	XI.—MUSICIANS AND BALLAD RECITERS.	1. Kámer	Hindu	42	...	...	33	...	...
		2. Kalawat	Do.	4	...	...	...	...	...
		3. Jachak	Do.	43	...	...	42	...	...
		4. Damami	Do.	3	...	...	1	...	...
		5. Dhanka	Do.	519	5	...	511	...	...
		6. Sargara	Do.	474	4	...	452	...	...
		7. Dholi	Hindu	3,353	...	...	3,066	...	...
			Mussalman	11	179	1	10	2	...
		8. Guramanga	Hindu	17	...	...	9	...	...
			Mussalman	3	...	...	2	...	...
		9. Bajansai	Hindu	2	...	...	1	...	...
		10. Dadhi	Hindu	8	...	...	9	...	...
			Mussalman	63	...	...	54	...	...
		11. Baret	Hindu	4	...	...	2	...	...
		12. Charan	Do.	276	57	...	223	8	...
		13. Nagarchi	Do.	3	...	...	4	...	...
		14. Halimanga	Do.	...	...	...	7	...	...
		15. Ramenia	Do.	5	...	...	4	...	...
		Total XI.—15		**4,830**	**245**	**1**	**4,480**	**10**	...
C.—COMMERCIAL.	XII.—DANCERS AND SINGERS.	1. Bhagat	Hindu	14	...	...	19	...	...
		2. Patar	Do.	...	...	...	15	...	...
		Total XII.—2		**14**	...	..	**34**	...	...
	XIII.—ACTORS AND MINERS.	1. Rana	Hindu	...	...	...	2	...	...
		2. Bhand	Hindu	57	...	...	54	...	...
			Mussalman	3	...	...	3	...	...
		3. Rawal	Hindu	41	...	...	51	...	...
		Total XIII.—3		**101**	...	...	**110**	...	...
	XIV.—TRADERS	1. Mahajan Mahesri	Hindu	4,092	2,292	71	3,553	16	...
		1. Agerwal	Hindu	4,462	...	...	3,803	...	...
			Jain	962	3,386	185	863	25	1
		1. Khundelwal	Hindu	340	190	11	238	1	...
		1. Mahore	Do.	24	...	...	6	...	...
		1. Bijaburgi	Do.	379	209	5	419	3	...
		1. Khutri	Do.	726	413	139	602	22	...
		1. Jeswal	Hindu	50	...	...	28	...	...
			Jain	1	30	3	1	...	...
		1. Pulliwal	Hindu	184	...	...	135	...	...
			Jain	28	114	...	21	8	...
		1. Dhunser	Hindu	28	12	2	18	...	...
		1. Niterwal	Do.	18	...	...	13	...	...
		1. Bhundari	Do.	4	...	...	4	...	...
		1. Oswal	Hindu	12	...	...	10	...	...
			Jain	10,431	6,448	44	8,921	78	...
		1. Saragi	Jain	2,852	1,848	37	2,574	25	...
		1. Mahajan	Hindu	106	...	...	68	...	...
			Jain	75	125	6	66	8	...
		Total XIV.—1		**24,774**	*15,067*	**508**	**21,848**	*186*	**1**
D.—ARTISAN AND VILLAGE MENIAL.	XVI.—CARRIERS	1. Banjara	Hindu	84	2	...	18	...	...
		2. Raibari	Do.	1,216	5	2	1,039	...	...
		Total XVI.—2		**1,300**	*7*	**2**	**1,057**	...	...
	XVII.—GOLDSMITH	1. Sonar	Hindu	2,137	476	20	1,857	8	...
		Total XVII.—1		**2,137**	*476*	**20**	**1,857**	*8*	...
	XVIII.—BARBERS	1. Nai	Hindu	3,912	147	5	3,599	2	1
		2. Barber	Do.	142	13	...	142	...	...
		Total XVIII.—2		**4,054**	*160*	**5**	**3,741**	*2*	**1**

TABLE C.—Language known by the Literate by Caste—*contd.*

Class.	Group.	Caste.	Religion.	Total Strength. Males. Total Males.	Males. Literate. Total.	Males. Literate. Knowing English.	Females. Total Females.	Females. Literate. Total.	Females. Literate. Knowing English.
1	2	3	4	5	6	7	8	9	10
D.—Artisan and Village Menial—*contd.*	XIX.—Blacksmith	1. Lohar	Hindu	1,420	...	...	1,186	...	...
			Mussalman	26	114	...	26	...	...
		2. Sikligar	Hindu	29	...	...	7	...	...
		3. Gadolia	Do.	9	...	...	8	...	...
		Total XIX.—3		**1,484**	114	...	**1,227**	...	...
	XX.—Carpenters	1. Khati	Hindu	4,279	180	11	3,796	1	...
		2. Gawaria	Do.	251	...	...	270	...	...
		3. Dustri	Do.	5	...	...	4	...	...
		Total XX.—3		**4,535**	180	**11**	**4,070**	1	...
	XXA.—Grain Parchers and Confectioners.	1. Bharbhuja	Hindu	51	6	...	56	...	...
		Total XXA.—1		**51**	6	...	**56**	...	...
	XXB.—Perfume, Drug and Betel-leaf Sellers.	1. Tamboli	Hindu	166	43	5	146	...	...
		Total XXB.—1		**166**	43	**5**	**146**	...	...
	XXI.—Brass and Coppersmith.	1. Kasera	Hindu	55	32	...	58	...	...
		2. Tathera	Do.	99	2	...	66	...	...
		3. Bharawa	Do.	6	3	...	3	...	...
		Total XXI.—3		**160**	37	...	**127**	...	...
	XXII.—Tailors	1. Durzi	Hindu	1,475	139	13	1,267	4	1
		2. Putwa	Do.	3	2	1	3	...	...
		Total XXII.—2		**1,478**	141	**14**	**1,270**	4	**1**
	XXIII.—Weavers, Calenderers and Dyers.	1. Chhipa	Hindu	1,152	199	2	1,115	...	...
		2. Nilger	Hindu	1	...	...	2	...	...
			Mussalman	1	...	...	1	...	...
		3. Koli	Hindu	2,453	72	1	2,271	1	...
		Total XXIII.—3		**3,607**	**271**	**3**	**3,389**	**1**	...
	XXIV.—Washermen.	1. Dhobi	Hindu	1,395	22	1	1,389	1	...
		Total XXIV.—1		**1,395**	**22**	**1**	**1,389**	**1**	...
	XXV.—Cotton Cleaners.	1. Pinara	Hindu	7	1	...	5	...	...
		Total XXV.—1		**7**	**1**	...	**5**	...	...
	XXVI.—Shepherd and Wool Weavers.	1. Jatia	Hindu	5	3	...	10	...	...
		2. Gadri	Do.	71	9	...	33	1	...
		Total XXVI.—2		**76**	**12**	...	**43**	**1**	...
	XXVII.—Oil-pressers.	1. Teli	Hindu	2,425	...	...	2,309	...	...
			Mussalman	18	78	2	10	1	...
		Total XXVII.—1		**2,443**	**78**	**2**	**2,319**	**1**	...
	XXVIII.—Potters	1. Kumhar	Hindu	8,588	...	...	8,127	...	...
			Mussalman	8	178	12	9	5	...
		Total XXVIII.—1		**8,596**	**178**	**12**	**8,136**	**5**	...
	XXIX.—Glass Workers.	1. Lakhera	Hindu	478	52	...	472	...	...
		2. Paniger	Do.	5	3	3	4	...	...
		Total XXIX.—2		**483**	**55**	**3**	**476**	...	...
	XXX.—Salt Workers	1. Kharol	Hindu	1,505	5	1	1,475	...	...
		2. Khari	Do.	110	...	...	95	...	...
		Total XXX.—2		**1,615**	**5**	**1**	**1,570**	...	...

TABLE C.—Language known by the Literate by Caste—*contd.*

Class.	Group.	Caste.	Religion.	TOTAL STRENGTH.					
				Males.			Females.		
				Total Males.	Literate. Total.	Literate. Knowing English.	Total Females.	Literate. Total.	Literate. Knowing English.
1	2	3	4	5	6	7	8	9	10
D.—ARTISAN AND VILLAGE MENIAL—*concld.*	XXXV.—Fishermen, Boatmen, Palki-bearers, Cook, etc.	1. Kahar	Hindu	1,748	*67*	2	1,529	*1*	...
		2. Kir	Do.	552	*20*	...	537	...	...
		3. Bari	Do.	116	*68*	...	82	...	...
		4. Daroga	Do.	5,352	*203*	2	5,339	*7*	...
		5. Bhoi	Do.	49	*4*	...	31	...	...
		6. Bhisty	Do.	2	...	...	1	...	...
		Total XXXV.—6		**7,819**	**302**	**4**	**7,519**	**8**	...
	XXXVI.—Distillers and Toddy Drawers.	1. Kalal	Hindu	891	*92*	1	796	...	...
		2. Pasi	Do.	19	...	...	7	...	...
		Total XXXVI.—2		**910**	**92**	**1**	**803**	...	...
	XXXVII.—Butchers	1. Kasai	Mussalman	23	...	...	13	...	...
		Total XXXVII.—1		**23**	...	...	**13**	...	...
	XXXVIII	1. Chupperband	Hindu	19	...	...	17	...	...
		2. Jeswara	Do.	63	...	...	12	...	...
		3. Khatik	Do.	1,799	*21*	...	1,742	...	...
		4. Chamar	Do.	8,733	*164*	4	8,643	*2*	...
		5. Dahgar	Do.	35	...	...	27	...	...
		6. Balai	Do.	16,510	*130*	[illegible]	15,399	*1*	...
		7. Mochi	Do.	650	*58*	3	589	*1*	...
		8. Raiger	Do.	10,614	*60*	2	10,439	...	...
		9. Bola	Do.	26	...	...	23	...	...
		10. Bhanbhi	Do.	37	...	...	24	...	...
		11. Mahar	Do.	207	*99*	3	161	*3*	...
		12. Mong	Do.	22	*2*	...	10	...	...
		Total XXXVIII.—12		**38,715**	**534**	**18**	**37,086**	**7**	...
	XXXIX.—Scavengers.	1. Mehtar	Hindu	3,158	...	...	2,751	...	...
			Mussalman	5	*32*	...	3	*3*	...
		2. Sarbhangi	Hindu	1	...	...	3	...	...
		3. Bargi	Do.	6	...	...	2	...	...
		Total XXXIX.—3		**3,170**	**32**	...	**2,759**	**3**	...
E.—VAGRANT, MINOR ARTISANS AND PERFORMERS, ETC.	XLI.—Earth Workers and Stone-dressers.	1. Odh	Hindu	119	*1*	...	83	...	...
		2. Beldar	Do.	36	*1*	...	38	...	...
		3. Med	Do.	3	...	...	3	...	...
		Total XLI.—3		**158**	**2**	...	**124**	...	...
	XLIII.—Mat Makers, Cane Splitters.	1. Ganchha	Hindu	27	...	...	28	...	...
		Total XLIII.—1		**27**	...	...	**28**	...	...
	XLIV.—Hunters, Fowlers, etc.	1. Sansi	Hindu	65	...	...	70	...	...
		2. Kanjar	Do.	242	*2*	...	293	...	...
		Total XLIV.—2		**307**	**2**	...	**363**	...	...
	XLV.—Miscellaneous and Disreputable Livers.	1. Janglia	Hindu	2	...	...	4	...	...
		2. Baori	Do.	86	*8*	...	75	...	...
		3. Bageria	Do.	227	*1*	...	196	...	...
		4. Kasbi	Do.	...	...	...	2	...	...
		Total XLV.—4		**315**	**9**	...	**277**	...	...
	XLVI.—Trumblers and Acrobats.	1. Nath	Hindu	290	...	...	289	...	...
		Total XLVI.—1		**290**	...	...	**289**	...	...
	XLVII.—Jugglers, Snake-charmers and Animal Exhibitors.	1. Kalbelia	Hindu	9	...	...	3	...	...
		Total XLVII.—1		**9**	...	...	**3**	...	...

TABLE C.—Language known by the Literate by Caste—*concld.*

Class.	Group.	Caste.	Religion.	Total Strength. Males. Total Males.	Males. Literate. Total.	Males. Literate. Knowing English.	Females. Total Females.	Females. Literate. Total.	Females. Literate. Knowing English.
1	2	3	4	5	6	7	8	9	10
F.—Races and Nationalities.	XLVIII.—Non-Indian Asiatic Races.	1. Sheikh	Mussalman	17,105	1,472	145	15,449	61	...
		2. Syed	Do.	3,185	618	64	2,569	24	...
		3. Pathan	Do.	7,934	722	86	6,668	31	1
		4. Mogal	Do.	937	97	9	739	2	...
		5. Mewati	Do.	8	...	...	3	...	...
		6. Musalman	Do.	2,705	126	2	1,781	8	...
		7. Bilochi	Do.	1	...	...	...	...	...
		8. Parsi	Parsi	135	94	58	63	20	3
		9. Jew	Jew	38	23	11	33	10	2
		Total XLVIII.—9		**32,048**	**3,152**	**375**	**27,305**	**156**	**6**
	L.—Non-Asiatic Races.	1. European and Foreign	Christian	549	363	340	289	196	196
		Total L.—1		**549**	**363**	**340**	**289**	**196**	**196**
	LI.—Eurasian	1. Eurasian	Christian	356	131	123	280	77	73
		Total LI.—1		**356**	**131**	**123**	**280**	**77**	**73**
	LII.—Christian Converts.	1. Native Christian	Christian	662	471	267	547	220	33
		Total LII.—1		**662**	**471**	**267**	**547**	**220**	**33**
	LIII.—Miscellaneous	1. Not returned	Hindu	403	35	...	227	2	...
			No religion	1	...	...	...	...	...
		2. Others	Hindu	449	90	12	142	5	...
		Total LIII.—2		**853**	**125**	**12**	**369**	**7**	...
		Grand Total		**288,325**	**32,114**	**2,521**	**254,033**	**1,540**	**321**

TABLE E.—Caste, etc., by Civil Condition and Age.

Class	Group.	Caste, Tribe, etc.	Religion.	AJMERE-MERWARA. Males. All Ages. Total Males.				0—9				10—14				15-39				40 and over.			
				Total Males.	Single.	Married.	Widowed.	Total.	Single.	Married.	Widowed.	Total.	Single.	Married.	Widowed.	Total.	Single.	Married.	Widowed.	Total.	Single.	Married.	Widowed.
1	2	3	4	5	6	7	8	9	10	11	12	13	14	15	16	17	18	19	20	21	22	23	24
A.—AGRICULTURAL.	I.—Military and Dominant.	1. Rajput	Hindu	9,333	4,949	3,907	477	1,899	1,882	16	1	974	904	65	5	4,299	1,817	2,361	121	2,161	346	1,465	350
		2. Mahratta	Do.	352	69	279	4	35	35	...	...	1	1	...	...	288	32	253	3	28	1	26	1
		3. Thakur	Do.	6	2	4	...	...	...	...	...	...	...	...	...	6	2	4	...	...	...	...	...
		4. Sikh	Sikh	151	63	96	5	16	16	...	...	15	12	3	...	102	35	65	2	31	...	28	3
			Hindu	13	...	...	...	...	...	...	...	...	...	...	...	...	...	...	...	...	...	...	...
		Total I.—4	...	9,855	5,083	4,286	486	1,950	1,933	16	1	990	917	68	5	4,695	1,886	2,683	126	2,220	347	1,519	354
	II.—Other Agricultural.	1. Jat	Hindu	18,929	7,871	9,913	1,145	5,352	4,836	495	21	2,211	1,323	869	19	7,616	1,553	5,728	335	3,750	159	2,821	770
		2. Gujar	Do.	20,332	9,275	9,936	1,121	5,984	5,618	361	5	2,501	1,720	759	22	7,782	1,767	5,689	326	4,065	170	3,127	768
		3. Ahir	Do.	1,290	552	645	93	319	307	11	1	97	78	18	1	582	144	401	37	292	23	215	54
		4. Mer	Hindu	14,749	8,737	5,423	589	4,380	4,368	12	...	1,791	1,746	45	...	5,478	2,457	2,889	132	3,100	166	2,477	457
			Mussalman	14	...	...	...	...	...	...	...	...	...	...	...	...	...	...	...	...	...	...	...
		5. Rawat	Hindu	17,237	10,351	6,370	516	5,222	5,193	27	2	2,278	2,199	79	...	6,234	2,790	3,330	114	3,503	169	2,934	400
			Mussalman	4	...	...	...	...	...	...	...	...	...	...	...	...	...	...	...	...	...	...	...
		6. Chita	Hindu	245	145	90	10	80	77	1	2	39	39	...	...	75	27	47	1	51	2	42	7
			Mussalman	699	278	400	21	148	144	4	...	65	63	2	...	344	65	276	3	142	6	118	18
		7. Merat	Hindu	4,941	3,032	1,788	121	1,673	1,666	6	1	674	649	25	...	1,686	699	952	35	908	18	805	85
			Mussalman	7,953	4,873	2,875	205	2,640	2,636	4	...	1,089	1,056	32	1	2,711	1,114	1,559	38	1,513	67	1,280	166
		8. Naik	Hindu	1,415	644	713	58	405	393	12	...	172	130	41	1	523	119	398	6	315	2	262	51
		9. Thori	Do.	57	33	21	3	25	24	1	...	3	2	1	...	18	7	10	1	11	...	9	2
		10. Mina	Do.	2,731	1,519	1,106	106	645	641	4	...	288	270	18	...	1,197	532	638	27	601	76	446	79
		11. Mali	Do.	8,452	3,650	4,425	377	2,328	2,265	62	1	926	723	201	2	3,336	623	2,619	94	1,862	39	1,543	280
		12. Lodha	Do.	638	323	278	37	198	197	1	...	76	73	3	...	231	51	168	12	133	2	106	25
		13. Kachhi	Do.	41	12	25	4	7	7	...	...	3	1	2	...	21	4	16	1	10	...	7	3
		14. Kurmi	Do.	155	70	78	7	34	33	1	...	11	11	...	...	76	25	48	3	34	1	29	4
		15. Kalumbi	Do.	76	25	46	5	18	15	3	...	9	5	4	...	29	4	24	1	20	1	15	4
		16. Aheri	Do.	471	207	235	29	142	132	9	1	67	45	20	2	142	28	107	7	120	2	99	19
		17. Kunbi	Do.	84	21	57	6	10	10	...	...	2	2	...	...	57	9	44	4	15	...	13	2
		18. Ghosi	Do.	109	60	43	6	35	35	...	...	15	14	1	...	38	10	28	...	21	1	14	6
		19. Satia	Do.	23	6	15	2	5	5	...	...	1	...	1	...	8	1	7	...	9	...	7	2
		20. Purbia	Do.	8	4	3	1	2	2	...	...	...	...	...	...	6	2	3	1	...	...	...	...
		21. Morai	Do.	5	2	3	...	...	...	...	...	1	1	...	...	4	1	3	...	...	...	...	...
		22. Dhakur	Do.	119	53	58	8	31	31	...	...	6	4	2	...	64	16	43	5	18	2	13	3
		Total II.—22	...	100,759	51,743	44,546	4,470	29,683	28,635	1,014	34	12,325	10,154	2,123	48	38,258	12,048	25,027	1,183	20,493	906	16,382	3,205
	IV.—Forest and Hill Tribes.	1. Bhil	Hindu	3,999	1,954	1,942	103	1,347	1,307	36	4	512	422	87	3	1,398	217	1,145	36	742	8	674	60
		2. Gometi	Do.	3	...	3	...	...	...	...	...	...	...	...	...	2	...	2	...	1	...	1	...
		Total IV.—2	...	4,002	1,954	1,945	103	1,347	1,307	36	4	512	422	87	3	1,400	217	1,147	36	743	8	675	60
	V.—Priests	1. Brahman	Hindu	14,342	6,238	7,052	1,052	3,087	3,036	47	4	1,444	1,159	280	5	6,466	1,734	4,446	286	3,345	309	2,279	757
		2. Shami	Do.	92	28	22	42	10	10	...	...	11	7	4	...	37	7	11	19	34	4	7	23
		3. Acharaj	Do.	332	144	170	18	96	93	3	...	32	22	9	1	132	26	103	3	72	3	55	14
		4. Jatti	Jain	13	9	1	3	2	2	...	...	...	...	...	...	5	4	1	...	6	3	...	3
		5. Pundit	Do.	3	...	3	...	...	...	...	...	...	...	...	...	3	...	3	...	...	...	...	...
		Total V.—5	...	14,782	6,419	7,248	1,115	3,195	3,141	50	4	1,487	1,188	293	6	6,643	1,771	4,564	308	3,457	319	2,341	797

Class	Group.	Caste, Tribe, etc.	Religion.	AJMERE-MERWARA.																			
				Females.																			
				All Ages.				0—9				10—14				15—39				40 and over.			
				Total Females.	Single.	Married.	Widowed.	Total.	Single.	Married.	Widowed.	Total.	Single.	Married.	Widowed.	Total.	Single.	Married.	Widowed.	Total.	Single.	Married.	Widowed.
				25	26	27	28	29	30	31	32	33	34	35	36	37	38	39	40	41	42	43	44
A.—AGRICULTURAL.	I.—Military and Dominant.	1. Rajput	Hindu	7,049	1,886	3,363	1,800	1,488	1,439	46	3	569	369	194	6	2,972	68	2,517	387	2,020	10	606	1,404
		2. Mahratta	Do.	123	36	83	4	35	34	1	...	6	...	6	...	74	2	72	...	8	...	4	4
		3. Thakur	Do.	...	...	...	...	...	...	...	...	...	...	...	...	...	...	...	...	...	...	...	...
		4. Sikh	Sikh	62	28	34	5	23	22	1	...	6	6	...	...	26	...	26	...	12	...	7	5
			Hindu	5	...	...	...	...	...	...	...	...	...	...	...	...	...	...	...	...	...	...	...
		Total I.—4	...	7,239	1,950	3,480	1,809	1,546	1,495	48	3	581	375	200	6	3,072	70	2,615	387	2,040	10	617	1,413
	II.—Other Agricultural.	1. Jat	Hindu	17,395	4,708	9,843	2,844	4,998	4,083	910	5	1,678	549	1,117	12	6,795	69	6,205	521	3,924	7	1,611	2,306
		2. Gujar	Do.	17,536	5,368	9,722	2,446	5,342	4,551	788	3	1,805	740	1,051	14	6,613	71	6,175	367	3,776	6	1,708	2,062
		3. Ahir	Do.	936	273	527	136	263	234	29	...	71	35	36	...	396	4	371	21	206	...	91	115
		4. Mer	Hindu	15,732	5,550	7,801	2,399	4,293	4,243	49	1	1,440	1,114	322	4	6,033	184	5,582	267	3,984	9	1,848	2,127
			Mussalman	18	...	...	...	...	...	...	...	...	...	...	...	...	...	...	...	...	...	...	...
		5. Rawat	Hindu	12,611	6,276	5,014	1,392	4,857	4,805	49	3	1,626	1,281	342	3	4,760	186	4,412	162	2,439	4	1,211	1,224
			Mussalman	71	...	...	...	...	...	...	...	...	...	...	...	...	...	...	...	...	...	...	...
		6. Chita	Hindu	125	60	51	14	48	44	2	2	15	12	3	...	36	4	30	2	26	...	16	10
			Mussalman	499	224	230	45	166	164	2	...	55	47	8	...	200	12	179	9	78	1	41	36
		7. Merat	Hindu	4,081	1,914	1,816	351	1,494	1,478	15	1	488	385	103	...	1,430	47	1,336	47	669	4	362	301
			Mussalman	4,912	2,990	1,533	389	2,296	2,278	18	...	676	601	74	1	1,349	109	1,169	71	591	2	272	317
		8. Naik	Hindu	1,356	480	671	205	415	387	28	...	147	83	64	...	499	10	454	35	295	...	125	170
		9. Thori	Do.	40	14	22	4	10	10	...	...	4	4	...	...	17	...	16	1	9	...	6	3
		10. Mina	Do.	1,917	613	1,004	300	503	486	17	...	159	105	54	...	777	20	724	33	478	2	209	267
		11. Mali	Do.	7,921	2,404	4,223	1,294	2,263	2,072	191	...	697	299	392	6	3,179	30	2,912	237	1,782	3	728	1,051
		12. Lodha	Do.	699	260	339	100	216	212	4	...	74	41	33	...	256	7	237	12	153	...	65	88
		13. Kachhi	Do.	20	3	16	1	3	3	...	...	2	...	2	...	13	...	13	...	2	...	1	1
		14. Kurmi	Do	172	45	82	45	40	38	2	...	20	7	13	...	65	...	51	14	47	...	16	31
		15. Kalumbi	Do.	43	17	20	6	16	16	...	...	2	1	1	...	15	...	13	2	10	...	6	4
		16. Aheri	Do.	410	128	223	59	117	103	13	1	48	22	26	...	165	3	150	12	80	...	34	46
		17. Kunbi	Do.	39	11	21	7	11	10	1	...	2	1	1	...	19	...	17	2	7	...	2	5
		18. Ghosi	Do.	95	42	40	13	36	36	...	...	9	6	3	...	21	...	21	...	29	...	16	13
		19. Satia	Do.	38	17	18	3	8	8	...	...	3	3	...	...	17	4	12	1	10	2	6	2
		20. Purbia	Do.	6	2	4	...	2	2	...	...	...	...	...	...	3	...	3	...	1	...	1	...
		21. Morai	Do.	1	...	1	...	...	...	...	...	...	...	...	...	1	...	1	...	...	...	...	...
		22. Dhakur	Do.	91	30	48	13	24	21	3	...	13	9	4	...	39	...	36	3	15	...	5	10
		Total II.—22	...	87,764	31,429	44,269	12,066	27,421	25,284	2,121	16	9,034	5,345	3,649	40	32,698	760	30,119	1,819	18,611	40	8,380	10,191
	IV.—Forest and Hill Tribes.	1. Bhil	Hindu	3,753	1,403	1,953	397	1,243	1,156	87	...	406	211	193	2	1,429	34	1,317	78	675	2	356	317
		2. Gometi	Do.	5	1	3	1	1	1	...	...	...	...	...	...	3	...	3	...	1	...	...	1
		Total IV.—2	...	3,758	1,404	1,956	398	1,244	1,157	87	...	406	211	193	2	1,432	34	1,320	78	676	2	356	318
	V.—Priests	1. Brahman	Hindu	12,279	3,229	6,235	2,815	2,976	2,801	169	6	1,042	420	614	8	5,153	8	4,408	737	3,108	...	1,044	2,064
		2. Shami	Do.	66	15	32	19	7	7	...	...	8	6	2	...	26	2	17	7	25	...	13	12
		3. Acharaj	Do.	322	83	184	55	82	72	10	...	27	9	17	1	143	2	132	9	70	...	25	45
		4. Jatti	Jain	1	...	...	1	...	...	...	...	...	...	...	...	...	...	...	...	1	...	...	1
		5. Pundit	Do.	...	...	...	...	...	...	...	...	...	...	...	...	...	...	...	...	...	...	...	...
		Total V.—5	...	12,668	3,327	6,451	2,890	3,065	2,880	179	6	1,077	435	633	9	5,322	12	4,557	753	3,204	...	1,082	2,122

Table E.—Caste, etc.—Ajmere.

TABLE E.—Caste, etc., by Civil Condition and Age—*contd.*

Class.	Group.	Caste, Tribe, etc.	Religion.	AJMERE MERWARA. Males. All Ages. Total Males.	All Ages. Single.	All Ages. Married.	All Ages. Widowed.	0–9 Total.	0–9 Single.	0–9 Married.	0–9 Widowed.	10–14 Total.	10–14 Single.	10–14 Married.	10–14 Widowed.	15–39 Total.	15–39 Single.	15–39 Married.	15–39 Widowed.	40 and over. Total.	40 and over. Single.	40 and over. Married.	40 and over. Widowed.
1	2	3	4	5	6	7	8	9	10	11	12	13	14	15	16	17	18	19	20	21	22	23	24
B.—PROFESSIONAL.	VI.—Devotees	1. Sadhu	Hindu	3,261	1,740	1,425	157	892	867	23	2	338	243	92	3	1,251	398	813	40	841	232	497	112
			Jain	61	..	..	...	...	...	...	...	...	...	...	...	...	...	...	...	...	...	...	...
		2. Gusain	Hindu	681	350	261	70	118	112	6	...	65	52	11	2	277	121	141	15	221	65	103	53
		3. Agori	Do.	12	7	1	4	...	...	...	...	...	...	...	...	4	2	1	1	8	5	...	3
		4. Jogi.	Do.	1,487	727	651	109	365	349	14	2	170	133	35	2	585	188	368	29	367	57	234	76
		5. Vishnui	Do.	25	6	17	2	1	1	...	...	1	1	...	...	18	3	15	...	5	1	2	2
		6. Fakir	Mussalman	412	235	167	10	128	127	1	...	42	37	5	...	162	62	96	4	80	9	65	6
		Total VI.—6	...	**5,989**	**3,065**	**2,522**	**352**	**1,504**	**1,456**	**44**	**4**	**616**	**466**	**143**	**7**	**2,297**	**774**	**1,434**	**89**	**1,522**	**369**	**901**	**252**
	VII.—Temple Servants	1. Bhopa	Hindu	15	9	4	2	5	4	...	1	1	1	...	...	2	...	2	...	7	4	2	1
		Total VII.—1	...	**15**	**9**	**4**	**2**	**5**	**4**	...	**1**	**1**	**1**	...	...	**2**	...	**2**	...	**7**	**4**	**2**	**1**
	VIII.—Genealogists	1. Jaga	Hindu	663	276	382	5	149	149	...	...	22	20	2	...	408	107	300	1	84	...	80	4
		2. Barwa	Do.	117	66	48	3	36	36	...	...	18	13	5	...	38	14	23	1	25	3	20	2
		3. Bhat	Do	572	274	272	26	148	146	2	...	65	54	10	1	227	69	152	6	132	5	108	19
		4. Rao	Do.	170	77	75	18	48	47	1	...	21	17	4	...	66	13	43	10	35	...	27	8
		5. Mirasi	Hindu	...	3	9	...	2	2	...	...	1	1	...	...	6	...	6	...	3	...	3	...
			Mussalman	12	...	...	...	...	...	...	...	...	...	...	...	...	...	...	...	...	...	...	...
		Total VIII.—5	...	**1,534**	**696**	**786**	**52**	**383**	**380**	**3**	...	**127**	**105**	**21**	**1**	**745**	**208**	**524**	**18**	**279**	**8**	**238**	**33**
	IX.—Writers	1. Kayasth	Hindu	1,197	500	617	80	227	226	1	...	151	124	27	...	552	135	399	18	267	15	190	62
		Total IX.—1	...	**1,197**	**500**	**617**	**80**	**227**	**226**	**1**	...	**151**	**124**	**27**	...	**552**	**135**	**399**	**18**	**267**	**15**	**190**	**62**
	X.—Astrologers	1. Garura	Hindu	279	79	75	25	62	60	1	...	16	12	4	...	56	7	42	7	46	...	28	18
		2. Dakot	Do.	329	163	148	18	103	100	3	...	34	30	4	...	120	29	89	2	72	4	52	16
		3. Guru	Do.	215	106	94	15	49	46	3	...	30	24	6	...	87	33	50	4	49	3	35	11
		4. Jotshi	Do.	2	...	2	...	...	...	...	...	...	...	...	...	2	...	2	...	...	...	...	...
		Total X.—4	...	**725**	**348**	**319**	**58**	**213**	**206**	**7**	...	**80**	**66**	**14**	...	**265**	**69**	**183**	**13**	**167**	**7**	**115**	**45**
	XI.—Musicians and Ballad-reciters.	1. Kamar	Hindu	42	21	17	4	25	15	...	...	4	2	2	...	12	4	8	...	12	...	7	4
		2. Kalawat	Do.	4	2	2	...	1	1	...	...	...	...	...	...	3	1	2	...	...	...	...	...
		3. Jachak	Do.	42	23	20	...	17	17	...	...	4	4	...	...	13	2	11	...	9	...	9	...
		4. Damami	Do.	3	2	1	...	1	1	...	...	...	...	...	...	2	1	1	...	...	...	...	...
		5. Dhanka	Do.	529	211	210	18	133	131	2	...	51	42	9	...	232	36	192	4	103	2	87	14
		6. Sargara	Do.	474	193	259	22	131	128	3	...	43	32	11	...	189	31	148	10	111	2	97	12
		7. Dholi	Hindu	3,353	1,695	1,518	151	982	960	20	2	364	322	39	3	1,244	378	842	24	774	35	617	122
			Mussalman	11	...	...	...	...	...	...	...	...	...	...	...	...	...	...	...	...	...	...	...
		8. Garmanga	Hindu	17	2	14	4	2	2	...	...	...	...	...	...	14	...	20	4	4	...	4	...
			Mussalman	3	...	...	...	...	...	...	...	...	...	...	...	...	...	...	...	...	...	...	...
		9. Bajansai	Hindu	2	1	1	...	...	...	...	...	1	1	...	...	1	...	1	...	...	...	...	...

Table E.—Caste, etc.—Ajmere.

AJMERE-MERWARA.

FEMALES.

Class.	Group.	Caste, Tribe, etc.	Religion.	All Ages. Total Females.	All Ages. Single.	All Ages. Married.	All Ages. Widowed.	0—9 Total.	0—9 Single.	0—9 Married.	0—9 Widowed.	10—14 Total.	10—14 Single.	10—14 Married.	10—14 Widowed.	15—39 Total.	15—39 Single.	15—39 Married.	15—39 Widowed.	40 and over. Total.	40 and over. Single.	40 and over. Married.	40 and over. Widowed.
				25	26	27	28	29	30	31	32	33	34	35	36	37	38	39	40	41	42	43	44
B.—PROFESSIONAL.	VI.—Devotees	1. Sadhu	Hindu	2,597	797	1,453	413	803	710	91	2	315	78	236	1	975	5	925	45	570	4	201	365
			Jain	66	...	...	...	...	...	...	...	...	...	...	...	...	...	...	...	...	...	...	...
		2. Gusain	Hindu	536	156	220	160	118	108	10	...	62	35	27	...	179	6	122	51	177	7	61	109
		3. Agori	Do.	6	1	4	1	...	...	...	...	1	1	...	...	2	...	2	...	3	...	2	1
		4. Jogi	Do.	1,287	392	643	252	328	305	23	...	123	62	61	...	475	21	405	49	361	4	154	203
		5. Vishnui	Do.	20	6	14	...	8	6	2	...	...	...	...	...	10	...	10	...	2	...	2	...
		6. Fakir	Mussalman	285	120	150	15	99	97	2	...	31	21	10	...	118	2	114	2	37	...	24	13
		Total VI.—6	...	4,797	1,472	2,484	841	1,356	1,226	128	2	532	197	334	1	1,759	34	1,578	147	1,150	15	444	691
	VII.—Temple Servants	1. Bhopa	Hindu	8	2	3	3	2	2	...	...	...	...	...	...	3	...	2	1	3	...	1	2
		Total VII.—1	...	8	2	3	3	2	2	...	...	...	...	...	...	3	...	2	1	3	...	1	2
	VIII.—Genealogists	1. Jaga	Hindu	476	177	261	38	159	156	3	...	34	20	14	...	223	1	214	8	60	...	30	30
		2. Barwa	Do.	140	40	66	34	25	25	...	...	17	14	3	...	64	1	55	8	34	...	8	26
		3. Bhat	Do.	549	183	283	83	155	144	11	...	46	27	18	1	223	12	196	15	125	...	58	67
		4. Rao	Do.	204	71	81	52	50	48	2	...	29	22	4	3	76	1	55	20	49	...	20	29
		5. Mirasi	Hindu	13	9	4	...	7	7	...	...	2	2	...	...	3	...	3	...	1	...	1	...
			Mussalman	...	...	...	...	...	...	...	...	...	...	...	...	...	...	...	...	...	...	...	...
		Total VIII.—5	...	1,382	480	695	207	396	380	16	...	128	85	39	4	589	15	523	51	269	...	117	152
	IX.—Writers	1. Kayasth	Hindu	971	274	532	165	247	236	11	...	87	35	51	1	443	3	387	53	194	...	83	111
		Total IX.—1	...	971	274	532	165	247	236	11	...	87	35	51	1	443	3	387	53	194	...	83	111
	X.—Astrologers	1. Garura	Hindu	139	47	58	34	39	38	1	...	11	8	3	...	39	1	35	3	50	...	19	31
		2. Dakot	Do.	294	98	159	37	88	87	1	...	20	10	10	...	123	1	120	2	63	...	28	35
		3. Guru	Do.	164	51	87	26	42	39	3	...	17	9	8	...	64	2	58	4	41	1	18	22
		4. Jotshi	Do.	...	...	...	...	...	...	...	...	...	...	...	...	...	...	...	...	...	...	...	...
		Total X.—4	...	597	196	304	97	169	164	5	...	48	27	21	...	226	4	213	9	154	1	65	88
	XI.—Musicians and Ballad-reciters.	1. Kamar	Hindu	33	12	16	5	12	11	1	...	3	...	3	...	9	...	9	...	9	1	3	5
		2. Kalawat	Do.	...	...	...	...	...	...	...	...	...	...	...	...	...	...	...	...	...	...	...	...
		3. Jachak	Do.	42	18	22	2	15	14	1	...	4	4	...	...	15	...	15	...	8	...	6	2
		4. Damami	Do.	1	...	1	...	...	...	...	...	...	...	...	...	1	...	1	...	...	...	...	...
		5. Dhanka	Do.	511	167	285	59	157	146	11	...	28	16	12	...	231	5	212	14	95	...	50	45
		6. Sargara	Do.	452	137	254	61	137	119	17	1	45	17	28	...	169	1	161	7	101	...	48	53
		7. Dholi	Hindu	3,076	1,059	1,548	469	896	845	50	1	319	198	119	3	1,149	13	1,057	79	713	3	323	387
			Mussalman	20	...	...	...	...	...	...	...	...	...	...	...	...	...	...	...	...	...	...	...
		8. Garmanga	Hindu	9	2	8	1	2	1	...	...	2	1	1	...	3	...	3	...	5	...	4	1
			Mussalman	2	...	...	...	...	...	...	...	...	...	...	...	...	...	...	...	...	...	...	...
		9. Bajansai	Hindu	1	...	1	...	...	...	...	...	...	...	...	...	...	...	...	...	1	...	1	...

TABLE E.—Caste, etc., by Civil Condition and Age—*contd.*

Class.	Group.	Caste, Tribe, etc.	Religion.	AJMERE-MERWARA. Males. All Ages. Total Males.	All Ages. Single.	All Ages. Married.	All Ages. Widowed.	0—9 Total.	0—9 Single.	0—9 Married.	0—9 Widowed.	10—14 Total.	10—14 Single.	10—14 Married.	10—14 Widowed.	15—39 Total.	15—39 Single.	15—39 Married.	15—39 Widowed.	40 and over. Total.	40 and over. Single.	40 and over. Married.	40 and over. Widowed.
1	2	3	4	5	6	7	8	9	10	11	12	13	14	15	16	17	18	19	20	21	22	23	24
B.—PROFESSIONAL—*concld.*	XI.—Musicians and Ballad-reciters—*contd.*	10. Dadhi	Hindu	8	27	41	3	13	12	1	...	9	9	...	...	30	5	25	...	29	1	25	3
			Mussalman	63	...	...	...	...	...	...	...	...	...	...	...	...	...	...	...	...	...	...	...
		11. Baret	Hindu	4	1	2	1	1	1	...	...	...	...	...	...	1	...	1	...	2	...	1	1
		12. Charan	Do.	376	123	136	17	59	59	...	...	24	19	5	...	117	39	76	2	76	6	55	15
		13. Nagarchi	Do.	3	...	3	...	...	...	...	...	...	...	...	...	1	...	1	...	2	...	2	...
		14. Halimanga	Do.	...	...	...	...	...	...	...	...	...	...	...	...	...	...	...	...	...	...	...	...
		15. Rawania	Do.	5	4	1	...	1	1	...	...	...	...	...	...	3	2	1	...	1	1	...	...
		Total XI.—15	...	**4,830**	**2,305**	**2,305**	**220**	**1,856**	**1,328**	**26**	**2**	**500**	**431**	**66**	**3**	**1,862**	**499**	**319**	**44**	**1,112**	**47**	**894**	**171**
	XII.—Dancers and Singers.	1. Bhagat	Hindu	14	6	8	...	6	6	...	...	1	...	1	...	5	...	5	...	2	...	2	...
		2. Patar	Do.	...	...	...	...	...	...	...	...	...	...	...	...	...	...	...	...	...	...	...	...
		Total XII.—2	...	**14**	**6**	**8**	...	**6**	**6**	...	...	**1**	...	**1**	...	**5**	...	**5**	...	**2**	...	**2**	...
	XIII.—Actors and Mimes.	1. Rana	Hindu	...	...	...	...	...	...	...	...	...	...	...	...	...	...	...	...	...	...	...	...
		2. Bhand	Hindu	57	38	21	1	19	19	...	...	10	10	...	...	17	7	9	1	14	2	12	...
			Mussalman	3	...	...	...	...	...	...	...	...	...	...	...	...	...	...	...	...	...	...	...
		3. Rawal	Hindu	41	26	12	3	17	16	...	1	3	3	...	...	13	6	7	...	8	1	5	2
		Total XIII.—3	...	**101**	**64**	**33**	**4**	**36**	**35**	...	**1**	**13**	**13**	...	...	**30**	**13**	**16**	**1**	**22**	**3**	**17**	**2**
C.—COMMERCIAL.	XIV.—Traders	1. Mahajan	Hindu	10,425	4,662	4,908	855	2,174	2,169	5	...	1,081	935	144	2	4,722	1,310	3,189	223	2,448	248	1,570	630
			Jain	14,349	7,341	5,996	1,012	3,294	3,279	14	1	1,584	1,449	133	2	6,199	2,144	3,831	224	3,272	469	2,018	785
		Total XIV.—1		**24,774**	**12,008**	**10,904**	**1,867**	**5,468**	**5,448**	**19**	**1**	**2,665**	**2,384**	**277**	**4**	**10,921**	**3,454**	**7,020**	**447**	**5,720**	**717**	**3,588**	**1,415**
	XVI.—Carriers	1. Banjara	Hindu	84	28	45	11	4	4	...	...	2	2	...	...	62	21	34	7	16	1	11	4
		2. Raibari	Do.	1,216	553	604	59	331	313	18	...	143	106	36	1	507	120	373	14	235	14	177	44
		Total XVI.—2		**1,300**	**581**	**649**	**70**	**335**	**317**	**18**	...	**145**	**108**	**36**	**1**	**569**	**141**	**407**	**21**	**251**	**15**	**188**	**48**
	XVII.—Goldsmith	1. Sonar	Hindu	2,137	947	1,055	135	515	507	8	...	224	182	42	...	863	220	603	40	535	38	402	95
		Total XVII.—1		**2,137**	**[1947**	**1,055**	**135**	**515**	**507**	**8**	...	**224**	**182**	**42**	...	**863**	**220**	**603**	**40**	**535**	**38**	**402**	**95**
	XVIII.—Barbers	1. Nai	Hindu	3,912	1,663	2,039	210	990	963	25	2	439	312	123	4	1,594	357	1,183	54	889	31	708	150
		2. Barbers	Do.	142	56	80	6	38	35	3	...	18	14	3	1	56	7	48	1	30	...	26	4
		Total XVIII.—2		**4,054**	**1,719**	**2,119**	**216**	**1,028**	**998**	**28**	**2**	**457**	**326**	**126**	**5**	**1,650**	**364**	**1,231**	**55**	**919**	**31**	**734**	**154**

Table E.—Caste, etc.—Ajmere.

Class.	Group.	Caste, Tribe, etc.	Religion.	AJMERE—MERWARA. Females. All Ages. Total Females.	Single.	Married.	Widowed.	0—9 Total.	Single.	Married.	Widowed.	10—14 Total.	Single.	Married.	Widowed.	15—39 Total.	Single.	Married.	Widowed.	40 and over. Total.	Single.	Married.	Widowed.
				25	26	27	28	29	30	31	32	33	34	35	36	37	38	39	40	41	42	43	44
B.—PROFESSIONAL—contd.	XI.—Musicians and Ballad-reciters—contd.	10. Dadhi	Hindu	9	20	34	9	15	15	...	...	10	5	5	...	21	...	20	1	37	...	9	8
			Musalman	54	...	...	...	...	...	...	...	...	...	...	...	...	...	...	...	...	...	...	...
		11. Baret	Hindu	2	...	2	...	...	...	...	...	...	...	...	...	1	...	1	...	1	...	1	...
		12. Charan	Do.	223	69	110	44	58	56	1	1	20	11	8	...	88	...	82	6	57	1	19	37
		13. Nagarchi	Do.	4	2	2	...	2	2	...	...	...	...	...	...	1	...	1	...	1	...	1	...
		14. Halimanga	Do.	7	3	3	1	2	2	...	...	1	1	...	...	2	...	2	...	2	...	1	1
		15. Rawania	Do.	4	...	2	2	...	...	...	...	...	...	...	...	2	...	2	...	2	...	...	2
		Total XI.—15	...	4,430	1,489	2,288	653	1,295	1,211	81	3	432	254	176	2	1,692	19	1,566	107	1,011	5	465	541
	XII.—Dancers and Singers.	1. Bhagat	Hindu	19	7	11	1	4	3	1	...	3	3	...	...	7	1	6	...	5	...	4	1
		2. Patar	Do.	15	14	1	...	3	3	...	...	1	1	...	...	9	8	1	...	2	2	...	...
		Total XII.—2	...	34	21	12	1	7	6	1	...	4	4	...	...	16	9	7	...	7	2	4	1
C.—COMMERCIAL.	XIII.—Actors and Mimes.	1. Rana	Hindu	2	...	...	2	...	...	...	...	...	...	...	...	...	...	...	...	2	...	...	2
		2. Bhand	Hindu	54	22	27	8	22	18	3	1	4	4	...	...	18	...	17	1	13	...	7	6
			Musalman	3	...	...	...	...	...	...	...	...	...	...	...	...	...	...	...	...	...	...	...
		3. Rawal	Hindu	51	18	20	13	17	17	...	...	2	1	1	...	18	...	15	3	14	...	4	10
		Total XIII.—3	...	110	40	47	23	39	35	3	1	6	5	1	...	36	...	32	4	29	...	11	18
	XIV.—Traders	1. Mahajan	Hindu	8,897	2,514	4,429	1,954	2,137	2,110	26	1	741	373	365	3	3,701	26	3,200	466	2,318	5	829	1,484
			Jain	12,446	4,022	5,686	2,738	3,144	3,106	31	7	1,216	817	394	5	5,126	87	4,189	750	2,960	12	972	1,976
		Total XIV.—1	. . .	21,343	6,536	10,115	4,692	5,281	5,216	57	8	1,957	1,190	759	8	8,827	113	7,408	1,216	5,278	17	1,801	3,460
	XVI.—Carriers	1. Banjara	Hindu	18	6	7	5	5	5	...	...	1	1	...	...	7	...	6	1	5	...	1	4
		2. Raibari	Do.	1,039	321	504	214	302	269	31	2	111	48	63	...	382	2	337	43	244	2	73	169
		Total XVI.—2	. . .	1,057	327	511	219	307	274	31	2	112	49	63	...	389	2	343	44	249	2	74	173
	XVII.—Goldsmith	1. Sonar	Hindu	1,857	497	1,003	357	446	408	36	2	165	77	87	1	746	5	678	63	500	7	202	291
		Total XVII.—1	. . .	1,857	497	1,008	357	446	408	36	2	165	77	87	1	746	5	678	63	500	7	202	291
	XVIII.—Barbers	1. Nai	Hindu	3,599	980	1,955	664	913	837	75	1	326	130	192	4	1,485	11	1,355	119	875	2	333	540
		2. Barbers	Do.	142	40	84	18	45	36	9	...	11	3	8	...	56	1	52	3	30	...	15	15
		Total XVIII.—2	. . .	3,741	1,020	2,039	682	958	873	84	1	337	133	200	4	1,541	12	1,407	122	905	2	348	555

TABLE E.—Caste, etc., by Civil Condition and Age—*contd.*

AJMERE-MERWARA. MALES.

Class.	Group.	Caste, Tribe, etc.	Religion.	All Ages. Total Males.	All Ages. Single.	All Ages. Married.	All Ages. Widowed.	0—9 Total.	0—9 Single.	0—9 Married.	0—9 Widowed.	10—14 Total.	10—14 Single.	10—14 Married.	10—14 Widowed.	15—39 Total.	15—39 Single.	15—39 Married.	15—39 Widowed.	40 and over. Total.	40 and over. Single.	40 and over. Married.	40 and over. Widowed.
1	2	3	4	5	6	7	8	9	10	11	12	13	14	15	16	17	18	19	20	21	22	23	24
D.—Artisan and Village Menial.	XIX.—Blacksmith	1. Lohar	Hindu	1,420	647	731	68	350	343	6	1	168	146	22	...	616	143	454	19	312	15	249	48
			Mussalman	26	...	...	...	...	...	...	...	...	...	...	...	...	...	...	...	...	...	...	...
		2. Sikligar	Hindu	29	12	12	5	2	2	...	...	3	3	...	...	16	7	7	2	8	...	5	3
		3. Gadolia	Do.	9	5	4	...	2	2	...	...	1	1	...	...	3	2	1	...	3	...	3	...
		Total XIX.—3		1,484	664	747	73	354	347	6	1	172	150	22	...	635	152	462	21	323	15	257	51
	XX.—Carpenters.	1. Khati	Hindu	4,279	1,708	2,340	231	1,110	1,064	45	1	476	325	145	6	1,736	290	1,380	66	957	29	770	158
		2. Gawaria	Do.	251	131	114	6	76	75	...	1	39	35	4	...	90	19	70	1	46	2	40	4
		3. Dustri	Do.	5	2	3	...	1	1	...	...	...	...	...	...	4	1	3	...	...	...	...	...
		Total XX.—3		4,535	1,841	2,457	237	1,187	1,140	45	2	515	360	149	6	1,830	310	1,453	67	1,003	31	810	162
	XXA.—Grain-parchers and Confectioners.	1. Bhanbhuja	Hindu	51	22	26	3	11	11	...	...	5	5	...	...	22	6	15	1	13	...	11	2
		Total XXA.—1		51	22	26	3	11	11	...	...	5	5	...	...	22	6	15	1	13	...	11	2
	XXB.—Perfume, Drug and Betel-leaf Sellers.	1. Tamboli	Hindu	166	68	80	18	33	33	...	...	14	10	4	...	72	23	44	5	47	2	32	13
		Total XXB.—1		166	68	80	18	33	33	...	...	14	10	4	...	72	23	44	5	47	2	32	13
	XXI.—Brass and Coppersmiths.	1. Kasera	Hindu	55	21	28	6	9	8	1	...	7	5	2	...	25	7	16	2	14	1	9	4
		2. Tathera	Do.	99	47	42	10	29	29	...	...	5	3	2	...	47	14	30	3	18	1	10	7
		3. Bharawa	Do.	6	2	3	1	...	...	...	...	1	1	...	...	2	1	1	...	3	...	2	1
		Total XXI.—3		160	70	73	17	38	37	1	...	13	9	4	...	74	22	47	5	35	2	21	12
	XXII.—Tailors	1. Darzi	Hindu	1,475	591	791	93	334	325	9	...	140	109	29	2	621	144	454	23	380	13	299	68
		2. Patwa	Do.	3	...	3	...	...	...	...	...	...	...	...	...	2	...	2	...	1	...	1	...
		Total XXII.—2		1,478	591	794	93	334	325	9	...	140	109	29	2	623	144	456	23	381	13	300	68
	XXIII.—Weavers, Calenderers and Dyers.	1. Chhipa	Hindu	1,152	452	606	94	288	268	18	2	120	83	37	...	455	82	352	21	289	19	199	71
		2. Nilgar	Hindu	1	...	2	...	...	...	...	...	...	...	...	...	2	...	2	...	...	...	...	...
			Mussalman	1	...	...	...	...	...	...	...	...	...	...	...	...	...	...	...	...	...	...	...
		3. Koli	Hindu	2,453	1,010	1,343	100	666	661	5	...	196	173	23	...	1,056	163	862	31	535	13	453	69
		Total XXIII.—3		3,607	1,462	1,951	194	954	929	23	2	316	256	60	...	1,513	245	1,216	52	824	32	652	140
	XXIV.—Washermen	1. Dhobi	Hindu	1,395	642	685	68	446	418	25	3	153	129	24	...	535	91	425	19	261	4	211	46
		Total XXIV.—1		1,395	642	685	68	446	418	25	3	153	129	24	...	535	91	425	19	261	4	211	46

Class.	Group.	Caste, Tribe, etc.	Religion.	AJMERE-MERWARA. Females. All Ages. Total Females.	All Ages. Single.	All Ages. Married.	All Ages. Widowed.	0—9 Total.	0—9 Single.	0—9 Married.	0—9 Widowed.	10—14 Total.	10—14 Single.	10—14 Married.	10—14 Widowed.	15—39 Total.	15—39 Single.	15—39 Married.	15—39 Widowed.	40 and over. Total.	40 and over. Single.	40 and over. Married.	40 and over. Widowed.
				25	26	27	28	29	30	31	32	33	34	35	36	37	38	39	40	41	42	43	44
D.—ARTISAN AND VILLAGE MENIAL.	XIX.—Blacksmith	1. Lohar	Hindu	1,186	438	621	153	368	352	16	...	140	80	59	1	446	6	414	26	278	...	132	126
			Mussalman	26	...	...	...	...	...	...	...	...	...	...	...	...	...	...	...	...	...	...	...
		2. Sikligar	Hindu	7	3	3	1	3	3	...	...	...	...	...	...	3	...	3	...	1	...	...	1
		3. Gadolia	Do.	8	3	4	1	...	...	...	...	3	3	...	...	2	...	2	...	3	...	2	1
		Total XIX.—3		1,227	444	628	155	371	355	16	...	148	83	59	1	451	6	419	26	282	...	134	128
	XX.—Carpenters	1. Khati	Hindu	3,796	1,038	2,150	608	1,022	895	123	4	372	121	245	5	1,466	19	1,342	105	937	3	440	494
		2. Gawaria	Do.	270	117	121	32	92	91	1	...	23	21	2	...	91	4	82	5	64	1	36	27
		3. Dustri	Do.	4	1	2	1	...	...	...	...	1	1	...	...	2	...	2	...	1	...	...	1
		Total XX.—3		4,070	1,156	2,273	641	1,114	986	124	4	396	143	247	5	1,559	23	1,426	110	1,002	4	476	522
	XXA.—Grain-parchers and Confectioners.	1. Bhanbhuja	Hindu	56	24	24	8	21	20	1	...	4	4	...	...	20	...	19	1	11	...	4	7
		Total XXA.—1		56	24	24	8	21	20	1	...	4	4	...	...	20	...	19	1	11	...	4	7
	XXB.—Perfume, Drug and Betel-leaf Sellers.	1. Tamboli	Hindu	146	45	73	28	39	39	...	...	12	6	6	...	65	...	58	7	30	...	9	21
		Total XXB.—1		146	45	73	28	39	39	...	...	12	6	6	...	65	...	58	7	30	...	9	21
	XXI.—Brass and Coppersmith.	1. Kasera	Hindu	58	21	28	9	17	16	1	...	9	5	4	...	19	...	18	1	13	...	5	8
		2. Tathera	Do.	66	24	34	8	18	16	2	...	6	3	3	...	28	5	22	1	14	...	7	7
		3. Bharawa	Do.	3	...	1	2	...	...	...	...	1	...	1	...	...	...	...	...	2	...	...	2
		Total XXI.—3		127	45	63	19	35	32	3	...	16	8	8	...	47	5	40	2	29	...	12	17
	XXII.—Tailors	1. Darzi	Hindu	1,267	331	719	217	299	279	19	1	109	44	62	3	518	7	473	38	341	1	165	175
		2. Patwa	Do.	3	...	2	1	...	...	...	...	...	...	...	...	2	...	2	...	1	...	...	1
		Total XXII.—2		1,270	331	721	218	299	279	19	1	109	44	62	3	520	7	475	38	342	1	165	176
	XXIII.—Weavers, Calenderers, and Dyers.	1. Chhipa	Hindu	1,115	308	622	185	302	269	33	...	108	35	68	5	440	4	401	35	265	...	120	145
		2. Nilgar	Hindu	2	1	1	1	1	1	...	...	...	...	...	...	1	...	1	...	1	...	...	1
			Mussalman	1	...	...	...	...	...	...	...	...	...	...	...	...	...	...	...	...	...	...	...
		3. Koli	Hindu	2,271	718	1,268	285	664	640	24	...	150	67	82	1	1,020	9	958	53	437	2	204	231
		Total XXIII.—3		3,389	1,027	1,891	471	967	910	57	...	258	102	150	6	1,461	13	1,360	88	703	2	324	377
	XXIV.—Washermen	1. Dhobi	Hindu	1,389	498	694	197	457	428	29	...	140	60	80	...	519	8	484	27	273	2	101	170
		Total XXIV.—1		1,389	498	694	197	457	428	29	...	140	60	80	...	519	8	484	27	273	2	101	170

TABLE E.—Caste, etc., by Civil Condition and Age—*contd.*

Class.	Group.	Caste, Tribe, etc.	Religion.	AJMERE-MERWARA.																			
				Males.																			
				All Ages.				0—9				10—14				15—39				40 and over.			
				Total Males.	Single.	Married.	Widowed.	Total.	Single.	Married.	Widowed.	Total.	Single.	Married.	Widowed.	Total.	Single.	Married.	Widowed.	Total.	Single.	Married.	Widowed.
1	2	3	4	5	6	7	8	9	10	11	12	13	14	15	16	17	18	19	20	21	22	23	24
D.—ARTISAN AND VILLAGE MENIAL—contd.	XXV.—Cotton cleaners.	1. Pinara	Hindu	7	3	4	...	1	1	...	...	2	2	...	...	3	...	3	...	1	...	1	...
		Total XXV.—1		7	3	4	...	1	1	...	...	2	2	...	...	3	...	3	...	1	...	1	...
	XXVI.—Shepherds and Wool-weavers.	1. Jatia	Hindu	5	1	4	...	1	1	...	...	1	...	1	...	2	...	2	...	1	...	1	...
		2. Gadri	Do.	71	25	41	5	13	13	...	...	5	5	...	...	38	4	31	3	15	3	10	2
		Total XXVI.—2		76	26	45	5	14	14	...	...	6	5	1	...	40	4	33	3	16	3	11	2
	XXVII.—Oil-pressers.	1. Teli	Hindu	2,425	1,004	1,326	113	669	625	37	7	273	198	74	1	941	159	746	36	560	22	469	69
			Mussalman	18	...	...	...	...	...	...	...	...	...	...	...	...	...	...	...	...	...	...	...
		Total XXVII.—1		2,443	1,094	1,326	113	669	625	37	7	273	198	74	1	941	159	746	36	560	22	469	69
	XXVIII.—Potters	1. Kumhar	Hindu	8,588	3,597	4,617	382	2,482	2,357	120	5	900	652	239	9	3,420	551	2,750	119	1,794	37	1,508	249
			Mussalman	8	...	...	...	...	...	...	...	...	...	...	...	...	...	...	...	...	...	...	...
		Total XXVIII.—1		8,596	3,597	4,617	382	2,482	2,357	120	5	900	652	239	9	3,420	551	2,750	119	1,794	37	1,508	249
	XXIX.—Glass-workers.	1. Lakbera	Hindu	478	200	259	19	133	130	3	...	41	34	7	...	195	34	156	5	109	2	93	14
		2. Paniger	Do.	5	5	...	...	1	1	...	...	...	...	...	...	4	4	...	...	...	...	...	...
		Total XXIX.—2		483	205	259	19	134	131	3	...	41	34	7	...	199	38	156	5	109	2	93	14
	XXX.—Salt-workers.	1. Kharol	Hindu	1,505	701	739	65	483	465	18	...	168	124	44	...	535	104	418	13	319	8	259	52
		2. Khari	Do.	110	55	47	8	36	36	...	...	7	7	...	...	48	11	33	4	19	1	14	4
		Total XXX.—2		1,615	756	786	73	519	501	18	...	175	131	44	...	583	115	451	17	338	9	273	56
	XXXV.—Fishermen, Boatmen, Palki-bearers, Cooks, etc.	1. Kahar	Hindu	1,748	840	825	83	459	455	4	...	178	164	14	...	749	205	518	26	360	16	289	57
		2. Kir	Do.	552	287	249	16	200	192	5	3	79	65	13	...	178	29	145	4	95	...	86	9
		3. Bari	Do.	116	50	59	7	24	24	...	...	15	14	1	...	53	11	42	...	24	1	16	7
		4. Darogah	Do.	5,352	2,652	2,432	268	1,394	1,372	19	3	657	571	84	2	2,270	652	1,453	65	1,131	57	876	198
		5. Bhoi	Do.	49	19	23	7	11	10	1	...	2	2	...	...	22	7	11	4	14	...	11	3
		6. Bhishty	Do.	2	1	1	...	1	1	...	...	...	...	...	...	1	...	1	...	...	...	...	...
		Total XXXV.—6		7,819	3,849	3,589	381	2,089	2,054	29	6	931	817	112	2	3,173	904	2,170	99	1,626	74	1,278	274
	XXXVI.—Distillers and Toddy drawers.	1. Kalal	Hindu	891	424	408	59	252	242	8	2	113	93	20	...	335	83	231	21	191	6	149	36
		2. Pasi	Do.	19	7	11	1	3	2	1	...	...	...	...	...	13	5	7	1	3	...	3	...
		Total XXXVI.—2		910	431	419	60	255	244	9	2	113	93	20	...	348	88	238	22	194	6	152	36

Class.	Group.	Caste, Tribe, etc.	Religion.	AJMERE–MERWARA. Females. All Ages. Total Females.	Single.	Married.	Widowed.	0–9 Total.	Single.	Married.	Widowed.	10–14 Total.	Single.	Married.	Widowed.	15–39 Total.	Single.	Married.	Widowed.	40 and over. Total.	Single.	Married.	Widowed.
				25	26	27	28	29	30	31	32	33	34	35	36	37	38	39	40	41	42	43	44
D.—Artisan and Village Menial—contd.	XXV.—Cotton cleaners	1. Pinjara	Hindu	5	2	2	1	2	2	...	...	...	...	...	...	1	...	1	...	2	...	1	1
		Total XXV.—1		5	2	2	1	2	2	...	...	...	...	...	...	1	...	1	...	2	...	1	1
	XXVI.—Shepherds and Wool-weavers.	1. Jatia	Hindu	10	5	3	2	4	4	...	...	1	1	...	...	2	...	2	...	3	...	1	2
		2. Gadri	Do.	33	3	27	3	3	3	...	...	1	...	1	...	22	...	22	...	7	...	4	3
		Total XXVI.—2		43	8	30	5	7	7	...	...	2	1	1	...	24	...	24	...	10	...	5	5
	XXVII.—Oil-pressers.	1. Teli	Hindu	2,309	630	1,337	352	641	541	97	3	239	81	156	2	381	8	322	51	558	...	262	296
			Mussalman	10	...	...	...	...	...	...	...	...	...	...	...	...	...	...	...	...	...	...	...
		Total XXVII.—1		2,319	630	1,337	352	641	541	97	3	239	81	156	2	381	8	322	51	558	...	262	296
	XXVIII.—Potters	1. Kumhar	Hindu	8,127	2,478	4,496	1,162	2,381	2,121	254	6	823	325	496	2	3,146	29	2,938	179	1,786	3	808	975
			Mussalman	9	...	...	...	...	...	...	...	...	...	...	...	...	...	...	...	...	...	...	...
		Total XXVIII.—1		8,136	2,478	4,496	1,162	2,381	2,121	254	6	823	325	496	2	3,146	29	2,938	179	1,786	3	808	975
	XXIX.—Glass-workers.	1. Lakhera	Hindu	472	146	259	67	130	122	8	...	43	21	22	...	180	3	170	9	117	...	59	58
		2. Panigar	Do.	4	2	...	2	1	1	...	...	1	1	...	...	...	...	...	...	2	...	...	2
		Total XXIX.—2		476	148	259	69	131	123	8	...	44	22	22	...	182	3	170	9	119	...	59	60
	XXX.—Saltworkers	1. Kharol	Hindu	1,475	505	773	197	458	413	43	2	166	83	79	4	533	9	499	25	318	...	152	166
		2. Khari	Do.	95	34	47	14	26	26	...	...	11	8	3	...	40	...	38	2	18	...	6	12
		Total XXX.—2		1,570	539	820	211	484	439	43	2	177	91	82	4	573	9	537	27	336	...	158	178
	XXXV.—Fishermen, Boatmen, Palki-bearers, Cook, etc.	1. Kahar	Hindu	1,529	577	743	209	485	476	9	...	160	97	63	...	592	4	541	47	292	...	130	162
		2. Kir	Do.	537	223	254	60	194	188	5	1	55	34	21	...	193	1	182	10	95	...	45	49
		3. Bari	Do.	82	14	52	16	15	12	3	...	5	2	3	...	40	...	36	4	23	...	10	12
		4. Darogah	Do.	5,339	1,460	2,742	1,137	2,261	1,185	71	5	454	223	229	2	2,259	44	2,023	193	1,365	8	420	937
		5. Bhoi	Do.	31	10	18	3	11	10	1	...	...	...	...	...	11	...	11	...	9	...	6	3
		6. Bhishty	Do.	1	...	1	...	...	...	...	...	...	...	...	...	1	...	1	...	...	...	...	...
		Total XXXV.—6		7,519	2,284	3,810	1,425	1,966	1,871	89	6	674	356	316	2	3,096	49	2,793	254	1,783	8	612	1,163
	XXXVI.—Distillers and toddy drawers.	Kalal	Hindu	796	263	397	136	233	216	17	...	77	38	38	1	292	6	262	24	194	3	80	111
		Pasi	Do.	7	2	3	2	1	1	...	...	1	1	...	...	1	...	1	...	4	...	2	2
		Total XXXVI.—2		803	265	400	138	234	217	17	...	78	39	38	1	293	6	263	24	198	3	82	113

TABLE E.—Caste, etc., by Civil Condition and Age—*contd.*

Class.	Group.	Caste, Tribe, etc.	Religion.	AJMERE-MERWARA. Males. All Ages. Total Males.	All Ages. Single.	All Ages. Married.	All Ages. Widowed.	0—9 Total.	0—9 Single.	0—9 Married.	0—9 Widowed.	10—14 Total.	10—14 Single.	10—14 Married.	10—14 Widowed.	15—39 Total.	15—39 Single.	15—39 Married.	15—39 Widowed.	40 and over. Total.	40 and over. Single.	40 and over. Married.	40 and over. Widowed.
1	2	3	4	5	6	7	8	9	10	11	12	13	14	15	16	17	18	19	20	21	22	23	24
D.—Artisan and village menial—*contd.*	XXXVII.—Butchers	1 Kasai	Musalman	23	16	7	...	9	9	...	...	6	6	...	...	4	1	3	...	4	...	4	...
		Total XXXVII.—1		23	16	7	...	9	9	...	...	6	6	...	...	4	1	3	...	4	...	4	...
	XXXVIII.—Leather workers.	1. Chupperband	Hindu	19	10	9	...	8	8	...	...	1	1	...	...	9	1	8	...	1	...	1	...
		2. Jeswara	Do.	63	16	45	2	8	8	...	...	1	...	1	...	44	7	36	1	10	1	8	1
		3. Khatik	Do.	1,799	725	984	90	513	479	31	3	230	154	75	1	660	89	547	24	396	3	331	62
		4. Chamar	Do.	8,733	3,991	4,425	317	2,847	2,772	70	5	882	757	120	5	2,177	452	1,631	94	1,727	10	1,504	213
		5. Dabgar	Do.	35	13	19	3	7	6	1	...	8	5	3	...	9	1	8	...	11	1	7	3
		6. Balai	Do.	16,510	7,633	8,201	676	4,929	4,761	152	6	1,966	1,580	374	12	6,052	1,225	4,658	168	3,573	66	3,017	490
		7. Mochi	Do.	650	258	364	28	194	182	11	1	68	47	21	...	258	28	222	8	130	1	110	19
		8. Raigar	Do.	10,624	5,113	4,992	509	3,455	3,409	41	5	1,260	1,071	188	1	3,736	608	3,038	90	2,163	25	1,725	413
		9. Bolai	Do.	26	14	11	1	9	9	...	...	4	4	...	...	9	1	8	...	4	...	3	1
		10. Bhanbhi	Do.	37	24	11	2	10	10	...	...	8	8	...	...	13	6	6	1	6	...	5	1
		11. Mahar	Do.	207	88	113	6	41	41	...	...	22	21	...	...	132	26	104	2	13	...	9	4
		12. Mong	Do.	22	5	17	...	2	2	...	...	...	...	...	...	20	3	17	...	...	...	...	...
		Total XXXVIII.—12		38,715	17,890	19,191	1,634	12,013	11,687	306	20	4,549	3,648	882	19	14,119	2,448	283	388	8,034	107	6,720	1,207
	XXXIX.—Scavengers	1. Mehtar	Hindu	3,158	1,531	1,480	152	960	939	19	2	302	261	39	2	1,295	308	918	69	606	23	504	79
			Musalman	5	...	...	...	...	...	...	...	...	...	...	...	...	...	...	...	...	...	...	...
		2. Sarbhangi	Hindu	1	1	...	...	1	1	...	...	...	...	...	...	...	...	...	...	...	...	...	...
		3. Bargi	Do.	6	1	5	...	1	1	...	...	1	...	1	...	3	...	3	...	1	...	1	...
		Total XXXIX.—3		3,170	1,533	1,485	152	962	941	19	2	303	261	40	2	1,298	308	921	69	607	23	505	79
E.—Vagrant, minor artisans and performers, etc.	XLI.—Earth workers and stone dressers.	1. Odh	Hindu	119	71	35	13	34	34	...	...	14	13	1	...	46	24	18	4	25	...	16	9
		2. Beldar	Do.	36	9	22	5	6	6	...	...	3	2	1	...	15	1	14	...	12	...	7	5
		3. Med	Do.	3	...	3	...	...	...	...	...	1	...	1	...	...	...	...	...	2	...	2	...
		Total XLI.—3		158	80	60	18	40	40	...	...	18	15	3	...	61	25	32	4	39	...	25	14
	XLIII.—Mat makers and cane splitters.	1. Ganchha	Hindu	27	16	11	...	10	10	...	...	4	4	...	...	12	2	10	...	1	...	1	...
		Total XLIII.—1		27	16	11	...	10	10	...	...	4	4	...	...	12	2	10	...	1	...	1	...
	XLIV.—Hunters, fowlers, etc.	1. Sansi	Hindu	65	38	26	1	21	20	1	...	5	5	...	...	27	11	16	...	12	2	9	1
		2. Kanjer	Do.	242	146	93	3	82	82	...	...	34	29	5	...	82	33	47	2	44	2	41	1
		Total XLIV.—2		307	184	119	4	103	102	1	...	39	34	5	...	109	44	73	2	56	4	50	2
	XLV.—Miscellaneous and disreputable livers	1. Janglia	Hindu	2	...	2	...	...	...	...	...	...	...	...	...	2	...	2	...	...	...	...	...
		2. Baori	Do.	86	46	39	1	28	28	...	...	12	11	...	...	26	7	19	...	21	...	20	1

Table E.—Caste, etc.—Ajmere.

AJMERE-MERWARA. — FEMALES.

Class.	Group.	Caste, Tribe, etc.	Religion.	All Ages: Total Females	All Ages: Single.	All Ages: Married.	All Ages: Widowed.	0—9: Total.	0—9: Single.	0—9: Married.	0—9: Widowed.	10—14: Total.	10—14: Single.	10—14: Married.	10—14: Widowed.	15—39: Total.	15—39: Single.	15—39: Married.	15—39: Widowed.	40 and over: Total.	40 and over: Single.	40 and over: Married.	40 and over: Widowed.
				25	26	27	28	29	30	31	32	33	34	35	36	37	38	39	40	41	42	43	44
D.—Artisan and Village Menial—contd.	XXXVII.—Butchers	1 Kasai	Musalman	13	5	7	1	5	4	1	...	...	...	...	...	4	1	3	...	4	...	3	1
		Total XXXVII.—1		**13**	**5**	**7**	**1**	**5**	**4**	**1**	...	...	...	...	...	**4**	**1**	**3**	...	**4**	...	**3**	**1**
	XXXVIII.—Leather workers.	1. Chuppeband	Hindu	17	7	7	3	6	6	...	...	1	1	...	...	7	...	7	...	3	...	...	3
		2. Jeswara	Do.	12	2	9	1	2	2	...	...	...	...	...	...	9	...	9	...	1	...	...	1
		3. Khatik	Do.	1,742	557	985	196	577	489	84	4	174	61	112	1	667	8	625	34	324	1	164	159
		4. Chamar	Do.	8,643	3,043	4,495	1,105	2,813	2,620	150	3	848	338	442	8	3,340	23	3,102	215	1,642	3	762	878
		5. Dabgar	Do.	27	9	13	5	8	8	...	...	2	1	1	...	9	...	7	2	8	...	5	3
		6. Balai	Do	15,399	5,151	8,250	1,999	4,666	4,249	409	8	1,564	775	777	12	5,897	121	5,466	309	3,272	5	1,598	1,669
		7. Mochi	Do.	589	192	325	72	191	170	21	...	52	22	30	...	331	...	282	10	114	...	52	62
		8. Raigar	Do.	10,439	4,160	5,073	1,206	3,492	3,401	86	5	1,157	707	446	4	3,848	46	3,630	172	1,948	6	911	1,035
		9. Pola	Do.	23	10	10	3	10	10	...	...	...	...	...	...	9	...	8	1	4	...	2	2
		10. Bhanbhi	Do.	24	9	13	2	7	7	...	...	2	2	...	...	11	...	11	...	4	...	2	3
		11. Mahar	Do.	161	63	73	25	54	53	1	...	15	9	6	...	72	1	61	10	20	...	4	16
		12. Mong	Do.	10	4	6	...	4	4	...	...	...	...	...	...	6	...	6	...	...	...	...	...
		Total XXXVIII.—12		**37,086**	**13,209**	**19,259**	**4,618**	**11,830**	**11,019**	**791**	**20**	**3,815**	**1,976**	**1,814**	**25**	**14,107**	**200**	**13,154**	**753**	**7,334**	**14**	**3,500**	**3,820**
	XXXIX.—Scavengers	Mehtar	Hindu	2,751	1,031	1,443	280	900	861	39	...	237	144	91	2	1,128	25	1,060	43	489	1	253	235
			Musalman	3	...	...	...	...	...	...	...	...	...	...	...	...	...	...	...	...	...	...	...
		2. Sarbhangi	Hindu	3	1	1	1	1	1	...	...	...	...	...	...	1	...	1	...	1	...	...	1
		3. Bargi	Do.	2	1	1	...	1	1	...	...	...	...	...	...	1	...	1	...	...	...	...	...
		Total XXXIX.—3		**2,759**	**1,033**	**1,445**	**281**	**902**	**863**	**39**	...	**237**	**144**	**91**	**2**	**1,130**	**25**	**1,062**	**43**	**490**	**1**	**253**	**236**
E.—Vagrant, Minor Artisans and Performers, etc.	XLI.—Earth workers and stone dressers.	1. Odh	Hindu	83	35	37	11	25	24	1	...	13	9	4	...	32	2	27	3	13	...	5	8
		2. Beldar	Do.	38	16	20	2	14	14	...	...	2	2	...	...	16	...	16	...	6	...	4	2
		3. Med	Do.	3	...	3	...	...	...	...	...	1	...	1	...	1	...	1	...	1	...	1	...
		Total XLI.—3		**124**	**51**	**60**	**13**	**39**	**38**	**1**	...	**16**	**11**	**5**	...	**49**	**2**	**44**	**3**	**20**	...	**10**	**10**
	XLIII.—Mat makers and cane splitters.	1. Gauchha	Hindu	28	11	10	7	10	10	...	...	1	1	...	...	8	...	8	...	9	...	2	7
		Total XLIII.—1		**28**	**11**	**10**	**7**	**10**	**10**	...	...	**1**	**1**	...	...	**8**	...	**8**	...	**9**	...	**2**	**7**
	XLIV.—Hunters fowlers, etc.	1. Sansi	Hindu	70	28	37	5	20	20	...	...	5	4	1	...	31	3	27	1	14	1	9	4
		2. Kanjer	Do.	293	150	104	39	102	101	1	...	34	30	4	...	93	17	69	7	64	2	30	32
		Total XLIV.—2		**363**	**178**	**141**	**44**	**122**	**121**	**1**	...	**39**	**34**	**5**	...	**124**	**20**	**96**	**8**	**78**	**3**	**39**	**36**
	XLV.—Miscellaneous and disreputable livers.	1. Janglia	Hindu	4	1	3	...	1	1	...	...	1	...	1	...	2	...	2	...	...	...	...	...
		2. Baori	Do.	75	26	42	7	15	14	1	...	14	11	3	...	32	1	30	1	14	...	8	6

TABLE E.—Caste, etc., by Civil Condition and Age—*contd.*

Class.	Group.	Caste, Tribe, etc.	Religion.	AJMERE-MERWARA. Males. All Ages				0—9				10—14				15—39				40 and over.			
				Total Males.	Single	Married.	Widowed.	Total.	Single.	Married.	Widowed	Total.	Single.	Married.	Widowed	Total.	Single.	Married.	Widowed	Total.	Single.	Married.	Widowed.
1	2	3	4	5	6	7	8	9	10	11	12	13	14	15	16	17	18	19	20	21	22	23	24
B.—Vagrant, Minor Artisans and Performers, etc.—contd.	XLV.—Miscellaneous and Disreputable Livers—contd.	3. Bagaria	Hindu	227	128	94	5	83	83	...	...	27	25	2	...	77	20	56	1	40	...	36	4
		4. Kasbi	Do.	...	...	...	...	...	...	...	...	...	...	...	...	...	...	...	...	...	...	...	...
		Total XLV.-4		315	174	135	6	111	111	...	...	38	36	2	...	105	27	77	1	61	...	56	5
	XLVI.—Tumblers and Acrobats.	1. Nath	Hindu	290	155	119	16	93	89	3	1	35	31	4	...	101	30	66	5	61	5	46	10
		Total XLVI.—1		290	155	119	16	93	89	3	1	35	31	4	...	101	30	66	5	61	5	46	10
	XLVII.—Jugglers, Snake Charmers and Animal Exhibitors.	1. Kalbelia	Hindu	9	5	4	...	2	2	...	...	1	1	...	...	5	2	3	...	1	...	1	...
		Total XLVII.—1		9	5	4	...	2	2	...	...	1	1	...	...	5	2	3	...	1	...	1	...
F.—Races and Nationalities.	XLVIII.—Non-Indian Asiatic Races.	1. Sheikh	Musalman	17,105	7,828	8,301	976	4,348	4,235	109	4	1,740	1,468	268	4	7,092	1,907	4,001	184	3,925	218	3,023	684
		2. Saiyad	Do.	3,185	1,490	1,526	169	769	759	10	...	329	300	28	1	1,274	384	846	44	813	47	642	124
		3. Pathan	Do.	7,934	3,911	3,579	444	2,056	2,028	25	3	840	748	91	1	3,261	1,023	2,105	133	1,777	112	1,358	307
		4. Mogal	Do.	937	446	438	53	235	227	8	1	95	83	12	...	388	125	251	12	218	11	167	40
		5. Mewati	Do.	8	4	2	2	2	2	...	...	2	1	1	...	1	1	...	...	3	...	1	2
		6. Musalman	Do.	2,705	1,488	1,079	138	745	738	6	1	290	270	17	3	1,071	450	584	37	599	30	472	97
		7. Bilochi	Do.	1	...	1	...	...	...	...	...	...	...	...	...	1	...	1	...	...	...	...	...
		8. Parsi	Parsi	135	60	70	5	27	27	...	...	9	8	1	...	72	24	46	2	27	1	23	3
		9. Jew	Jew	38	24	14	...	17	17	...	...	4	4	...	...	12	3	9	...	5	...	5	...
		Total XLVIII.—9		32,048	15,251	15,010	1,787	8,200	8,033	158	9	3,309	2,882	418	9	13,172	3,917	8,743	512	7,367	419	5,691	1,257
	L.—Non-Asiatic Races	1. European and Foreign	Christian	549	391	146	12	102	102	...	...	15	15	...	...	353	268	83	2	79	6	63	10
		Total L.—1		549	391	146	12	102	102	...	...	15	15	...	...	353	268	83	2	79	6	63	10
	LI.—Eurasian	1. Eurasian	Christian	356	214	123	19	90	90	...	...	27	25	1	1	182	93	86	3	57	6	36	15
		Total LI.—1		356	214	123	19	90	90	...	...	27	25	1	1	182	93	86	3	57	6	36	15
	LII.—Christian Converts.	1. Native Christian	Christian	662	394	250	18	198	198	...	...	81	80	1	...	293	111	173	9	90	5	76	9
		Total LII—1		662	394	250	18	198	198	...	...	81	80	1	...	293	111	173	9	90	5	76	9
	LIII.—Miscellaneous.	1. Not returned	Hindu	403	245	141	18	92	85	7	...	46	41	5	...	196	92	101	3	70	27	28	15
			No religion	1	...	...	...	...	...	...	...	...	...	...	...	...	...	...	...	...	...	...	...
		2. Others	Hindu	449	297	141	11	102	97	5	...	60	52	5	3	176	101	75	...	111	47	56	8
		Total LIII.—2		853	542	282	29	194	182	12	...	106	93	10	3	372	193	176	3	181	74	84	23
		GRAND TOTAL		288,325	139,518	134,146	14,661	78,898	76,690	2,094	114	32,594	2[illegible],978	5,479	137	114,954	32,115	78,948	3,891	61,879	3,735	47,625	10,519

Table E.—Caste, etc.—Ajmere.

Class.	Group.	Caste, Tribe, etc.	Religion.	AJMERE-MERWARA. Females. All Ages. Total Females.	All Ages. Single.	All Ages. Married.	All Ages. Widowed.	0—9 Total.	0—9 Single.	0—9 Married.	0—9 Widowed.	10—14 Total.	10—14 Single.	10—14 Married.	10—14 Widowed.	15—39 Total.	15—39 Single.	15—39 Married.	15—39 Widowed.	40 and over. Total.	40 and over. Single.	40 and over. Married.	40 and over. Widowed.
				25	26	27	28	29	30	31	32	33	34	35	36	37	38	39	40	41	42	43	44
E.—Vagrant, Minor Artisans and Performers, etc.—contd.	XLV.—Miscellaneous and disreputable livers—contd.	3. Bagaria	Hindu	196	79	94	23	62	59	3	...	24	16	7	1	78	4	65	3	39	...	20	19
		4. Kasbi	Do.	2	...	2	...	...	...	...	...	...	...	...	...	2	...	2	...	...	...	...	...
		Total XLV.—4		277	106	141	30	77	74	3	...	39	27	11	1	108	5	99	4	53	...	28	26
	XLVI.—Tumblers and Acrobats.	1. Nath	Hindu	289	105	128	56	89	88	1	...	22	13	9	...	104	4	94	6	74	...	24	50
		Total XLVI.—1		289	105	128	56	89	88	1	...	22	13	9	...	104	4	94	6	74	...	24	50
	XLVII.—Jugglers, snake charmers and animal exhibitors.	1. Kalbelia	Hindu	3	...	2	1	...	...	...	...	...	...	...	...	1	...	1	...	2	...	1	1
		Total XLVII.—1		3	...	2	1	...	...	...	...	...	...	...	...	1	...	1	...	2	...	1	1
F.—Races and Nationalities.	XLVIII.—Non-Indian Asiatic Races.	1. Sheikh	Musalman	15,449	5,262	7,928	2,259	4,339	4,088	245	6	2,420	805	596	19	6,206	306	5,484	416	3,484	63	1,603	1,818
		2. Saiyad	Do.	2,569	921	1,261	387	695	666	27	2	259	182	76	1	1,046	70	896	80	569	3	262	304
		3. Pathan	Do.	6,668	2,216	3,437	1,015	1,883	1,782	98	3	604	352	247	5	2,693	70	2,456	167	1,488	12	636	840
		4. Mogal	Do.	779	268	344	127	220	212	8	...	62	44	17	1	266	11	237	18	192	1	82	108
		5. Mewati	Do.	3	1	1	1	2	1	...	...	...	...	...	...	2	...	1	...	1	...	...	1
		6. Musalman	Do.	1,781	750	810	221	576	558	18	...	218	165	53	...	686	24	612	50	301	3	127	171
		7. Bilochi	Do.	...	...	...	...	...	...	...	...	...	...	...	...	...	...	...	...	...	...	...	...
		8. Parsi	Parsi	63	30	33	...	21	21	...	...	9	8	1	...	29	1	28	...	4	...	4	...
		9. Jew	Jew	33	18	14	1	13	13	...	...	5	5	...	...	13	...	13	...	2	...	1	1
		Total XLVIII.—9		27,305	9,466	13,828	4,011	7,748	7,341	398	11	2,577	1,561	990	26	10,940	482	9,727	731	6,040	82	2,715	3,243
	L.—Non-Asiatic Races	1. European and Foreign	Christian	289	147	126	16	96	96	...	...	15	15	...	...	145	36	106	3	33	...	20	13
		Total L.—1		289	147	126	16	96	96	...	...	15	15	...	...	145	36	106	3	33	...	20	13
	LI.—Eurasian	1. Eurasian	Christian	280	152	106	22	105	105	...	...	33	33	...	...	108	14	90	4	34	...	16	18
		Total LI.—1		280	152	106	22	105	105	...	...	33	33	...	...	108	14	90	4	34	...	16	18
	LII.—Christian Converts.	1. Native Christian	Christian	547	294	230	23	197	196	1	...	75	73	2	...	236	24	207	5	39	1	20	18
		Total LII.—1		547	294	230	23	197	196	1	...	75	73	2	...	236	24	207	5	39	1	20	18
	LIII.—Miscellaneous	1. Not returned	Hindu	227	57	130	40	48	39	3	...	19	14	5	...	118	4	102	12	48	...	20	28
			No religion	...	...	...	...	...	...	...	...	...	...	...	...	...	...	...	...	...	...	...	...
		2. Others	Hindu	142	37	74	31	28	25	3	...	14	8	6	...	65	4	54	7	35	...	11	24
		Total LIII.—2		369	94	204	71	70	64	6	...	33	22	11	...	183	8	156	19	83	...	31	52
		GRAND TOTAL		254,083	85,239	129,397	39,397	74,218	69,236	4,885	97	24,922	13,697	11,067	158	98,876	2,079	89,521	7,276	56,017	227	23,924	31,866

G. I. C. P. O.—No. 4 C. C. I.—28-2-03.—325.